The tyranny and
fall of Edward II
1321–1326

The tyranny and fall of Edward II 1321–1326

NATALIE FRYDE

CAMBRIDGE UNIVERSITY PRESS

CAMBRIDGE

LONDON · NEW YORK · MELBOURNE

Published by the Syndics of the Cambridge University Press
The Pitt Building, Trumpington Street, Cambridge CB2 1RP
Bentley House, 200 Euston Road, London NW1 2DB
32 East 57th Street, New York, NY 10022, USA
296 Beaconsfield Parade, Middle Park, Melbourne 3206, Australia

© Cambridge University Press 1979

First published 1979

Printed in Great Britain by The Anchor Press Ltd
and bound by Wm Brendon & Son Ltd
both of Tiptree, Essex

Library of Congress Cataloguing in Publication Data

Fryde, Natalie.
The tyranny and fall of Edward II, 1321–1326.

Bibliography: p.
Includes index.
1. Edward II, King of England, 1284–1327. 2. Great
Britain – History – Edward II, 1307–1327. 3. Great
Britain – Kings and rulers – Biography. I. Title.
DA230.F78   942.03´6´0924 [B]   78–56179

ISBN 0 521 22201 X

D188

Contents

Preface

The pleasantest part of a book to compose is indubitably the preface in which one has the opportunity to thank people for the help which they have given. Since this volume has been several years in the making, my thanks span a considerable period of time and more than one country. Latterly, it was accepted as a dissertation by the Freie Universität Berlin and I should like to thank most heartily Professor Wolfgang von Stromer, both for his help and advice and for the stimulus provided by the pages of his *Oberdeutsche Hochfinanz*, a study of finance and politics in the same period in Germany. I am most grateful, too, to the Dean, Professor Kurze, and the History Faculty, for the trouble which they have taken in accepting this work. In its early stages, when we were together researching in the Public Record Office, Dr Seymour Phillips and Dr J. Maddicott were most generous in help and advice. In reading the completed manuscript I am obliged to Dr Brian Howells, whose criticism of an early draft was most helpful, to Professor P. Wolff of Toulouse for his pertinent remarks on the chapter relating to France and, above all, to Professor R. R. Davies, who greatly improved both its English and its clarity and saved me from falling into many pit-holes in Wales and elsewhere. I wish also to thank my husband for his endless enthusiasm for this book and for his aid as critic and corrector. It was he who first introduced me to Edward II and the Despensers and those who know him will appreciate how much help he gave me to write this book.

As far as institutional thanks are concerned, I should like to record my gratitude once again to the staff of the Public Record Office for their unfailing help and courtesy and to the Librarian of the Society of Antiquaries for his ever-friendly welcome to that library. I am also indebted to the British Academy for honouring me with a research award and to the Rockefeller Centre at Bellagio for their hospitality in 1977.

Aberystwyth, 4 February 1979   Natalie Fryde

Abbreviations

Ann.Lond.	*Annales Londonienses*
Ann.Paul.	*Annales Paulini.*
Avesbury	See under *Murimuth*
Baker	*Chronicon Galfridi le Baker de Swynebroke (1303–56)*
B.B.C.S.	*Bulletin of the Board of Celtic Studies*
B.I.H.R.	*Bulletin of the Institute of Historical Research*
B.L.	British Library
Br.d.Bar.	*Brevia directa Baronibus*
Bridlington	*Gesta Edwardi de Carnarvon Auctore Canonico Bridlingtoniensi*
Brut	*Brut*, ed. F. W. Brie, vol. I. *E.E.T.S.*, orig. ser., 131 (1906)
C.Anc.C.	*Calendar of Ancient Correspondence concerning Wales*
C.Anc.Deeds	*Calendar of Ancient Deeds*
C.A.P.	*Calendar of Ancient Petitions concerning Wales*
C.Chanc.Warr.	*Calendar of Chancery Warrants*
C.Ch.R.	*Calendar of Charter Rolls*
C.Cl.R.	*Calendar of Close Rolls*
C.Fine R.	*Calendar of Fine Rolls*
C.I.M.	*Calendar of Inquisitions Miscellaneous*
C.I.P.M.	*Calendar of Inquisitions Post Mortem*
Cartae Glam,	*Cartae et alia Munimenta quae ad dominium de Glamorgan pertinent*

C.Pap.R.	*Calendar of Papal Registers relating to Great Britain and Ireland, II, Letters (1305–42)*
C.P.R.	*Calendar of Patent Rolls*
Ec.H.R.	*Economic History Review*
E.H.R.	*English Historical Review*
Foedera	*Foedera*, ed. T. Rymer, Record Commission, 2 vols. (London, 1816–18)
French Chron.Lond.	*Croniques de Londres*
Fryde 'Pessagno' (1978)	N. M. Fryde 'Antonio Pessagno of Genoa', *Studi in Memoria di Federigo Melis*, II (1978)
Guisborough	*Chronicle of Walter of Guisborough*
K.R.	King's Remembrancer's records
K.R.Exch.Acc.Various	King's Remembrancer's Exchequer Accounts Various (E. 101)
K.R.Mem.r.	King's Remembrancer's Memoranda roll (E. 159)
Lanercost	*Chronicon de Lanercost*
Leyc.Chron.	*Henrici Knighton, Leycestrensis Chronicon*
List Mem.R.	*List of Welsh Entries in the Memoranda Rolls, 1282–1343*
Lit.Cant.	*Literae Cantuarienses*
L.T.R.Mem.r.	Lord Treasurer's Remembrancer's Memoranda roll (E. 368)
Melsa	*Chronica Monasterii de Melsa*
Mem.St.Edmunds.	*Memorials of St. Edmunds Abbey*
Murimuth	*Chronica Adae Murimuth*
Parl.Writs	*Parliamentary Writs and Writs of Military Service*
P.R.O.	Public Record Office
Glam.Co.History	*The Glamorgan County History*
Rot.Parl.	*Rotuli Parliamentorum*
R.S.	*Rolls Series*
S.C.	Special Collections

Scalacronica	*Scalacronica of Thomas Gray of Heton*
S.H.R.	*Scottish Historical Review*
Trans.Cumb.West.Arch.Soc.	*Transactions of the Cumberland and Westmorland Archaeological Society*
T.R.H.S.	*Transactions of the Royal Historical Society*
Vita	*Vita Edwardi Secundi*
Welsh Hist.Rev.	*Welsh History Review*

I

Problems and sources

This book is not an attempt to provide a systematic narrative of the reign of Edward II. Its purpose is to reconsider the last years of the reign from a large body of evidence, some of it familiar but hitherto partly neglected, much of it new. The importance of this period has tended either to be underestimated or misunderstood because it is a very abnormal period in English history. It encompasses the rule of Edward II and his favourites, the Despensers, Hugh the father and Hugh the son, and provides one of the few examples in English history of a period of tyrannical rule which, for a time, met no overt political opposition in the country. It is impossible to discuss this period intelligibly without illustrating its striking contrast to the years preceding it. The earlier portion of Edward's reign had been a time of extremely active political opposition led, after 1311, by the king's cousin, the earl of Lancaster. The main objective of this opposition was always to obtain control of the king's government, but its methods and immediate targets varied as the king acquired different friends and advisers. In the years 1317–21, as the two Despensers, father and son, gradually obtained a monopoly of influence over the king, they in turn became the main targets for baronial hostility. The crisis which began in 1321 with two successive civil wars ended with Lancaster's execution in 1322, but the 'Despenser regime' became too hated to endure. The rule of Queen Isabella and Roger Mortimer, which replaced it in 1326–30, proved equally insecure and hastened its own collapse by imitating some of the worst features of the activities of the Despensers. The book will conclude with a brief picture of the strikingly different court and political climate which the young Edward III managed to create after 1330, once he began to rule personally. His *coup d'état* against his mother at Nottingham brought to an end ten years of terror for the aristocracy and of recurrent disturbance and civil war for the country as a whole.

The reign of Edward II has chiefly been the preserve of the constitutional and administrative historians, the pupils and academic descendants of Bishop Stubbs and Thomas Frederick Tout respectively, as well as of these great scholars themselves. It attracted this succession of distinguished historians because it seemed to constitute a vital stage in the growth of a limited monarchy in England. The work of these historians, beginning with Stubbs himself, was profoundly influenced by the tone and attitude of some of their most important inspirers, the St Albans chronicles. Professor Galbraith has reminded us that the medieval ideal of a limited monarchy in England was based mainly on the wishful thinking of the pro-baronial chronicler, Roger of Wendover: 'The constitutional attitude which marks the St. Albans history to the very end, was first set out by him. Henceforth for two centuries the St. Albans history is, as it were, an *apologia pro baronibus*. Like the Whig interpretation of history in modern times, the constitutionalism of the St. Albans historians has exerted a great and continuous influence on the modern interpretation of our medieval history.'[1]

Bishop Stubbs, who had thoroughly absorbed this viewpoint, not surprisingly found the fourteenth century a constitutional anti-climax after the resounding issues and great men of principle which the thirteenth century had produced. His reflections provide a deceptively plausible picture of the age.

We pass from the age of heroism to the age of chivalry, from a century ennobled by devotion and self-sacrifice to one in which the gloss of superficial refinement fails to hide the reality of heartless selfishness and moral degradation – an age of luxury and cruelty. This age has its struggles, but they are contests of personal and family faction, not of great causes; it has its great constitutional results but they seem to emerge from a great mass of unconscious agencies rather than from the direct action of great lawgivers or from the victory of acknowledged principles. It has, however, its place in the history of the constitution; for the variety and variations of the transient struggles serve to develop and exercise the permanent mechanism of the system; and the result is

sufficiently distinct to show which way the balance of political forces,
working in and through that mechanism, will ultimately incline. It is a
period of private and political faction, of foreign wars, of treason laws and
judicial murders, of social rebellion, of religious division, and it ends with
a revolution which seems to be only the determination of one bloody
quarrel and the beginning of another.[2]

Stubbs, who gave much thought to what England's constitution
would have been without the concession by King John of
Magna Carta, never really considered the constitutional and
political implications of an England ruled permanently in the
way which Edward II and the Despensers would have liked.
He grotesquely underestimated and misunderstood the motives,
character and vigour of these men at the height of their power
when he thought that 'the grievances of the people' were 'the
result of dishonest administration, chicanery and petty malver-
sation, not of bold and open attempts at tyranny'.[3]

The firm belief by Stubbs and his followers that the middle
ages brought a slow but sure growth of limited monarchy had
two unfortunate side effects. Firstly, it raised to the level of
great constitutional issues arguments which the magnates
bandied about only as transient weapons in a bitter political
struggle against a king whom they hated. Secondly, it meant
that these historians neglected to study the Despenser regime
because it suppressed open political opposition and produced
no constitutional theories, in contrast to the earlier years of the
reign, the period of the Ordinances of 1311 and then of the
'middle party' whose political achievements so impressed Tout.
But recent close study of the 'opposition' before 1322 has
shown that this contrast is unreal and has established that
personal connections and family feuds rather than principles
guided most magnates through the dangerous maze of the
court. Their alliances and enmities were characterised by great
fluidity and opportunism rather than adherence to anything
like 'parties'.[4] 'See how often and abruptly great men change
their sides' wrote the author of the *Vita Edwardi*. Careful
examination of the careers of less prominent men leaves one to
ponder not only whether questions of principle operated in that
dangerous political climate but whether loyalty did either.
Knights carefully engaged themselves to serve more than one

master and moved with ease from one magnate to the following of his deadliest enemy.

Until recently, the historiography of the reign not only tended to transform political feuds into constitutional conflicts but also neglected that last part of the reign, which did not seem to provide any support for the belief that England was being inevitably turned into a limited monarchy by the outcry of a united baronage against a weak and fickle ruler. The attention of historians, riveted to the period of active opposition to the crown, peters out with the defeat of this opposition at Boroughbridge in 1322. Their interest, focused on parliament's development as an occasion for obstructing the king's wishes, fades away when parliament no longer dares voice its opposition under the Despenser regime. Yet, if the reign is to be studied as a chapter in the parliamentary history of England, the Despenser dictatorship deserves a peculiar place in that chapter. These last years of Edward II's reign show that the very existence of parliament was precarious in spite of the effective use to which the opposition had occasionally put it in the previous years. When that opposition was driven underground parliament fell completely under the control of the king and ceased to be effective as a mouthpiece of any opposition whatsoever.

England gradually turned into a limited monarchy after John's reign for wider reasons. The loss of a large part of Henry II's Angevin continental empire had placed the king of England in a much weaker position in relation to his magnates than any other outstanding western European monarch. The king's estates, though larger than those of any single magnate, ceased to be sufficient for his needs. Royal castles did adequately balance those of the magnates, but they had become enormously sophisticated buildings and the cost of their upkeep and garrisoning was high. The king's inadequate revenue made him quite unable to afford a standing army or to finance foreign wars of any importance without the consent of the magnates to exceptional taxes. After the reign of King John, the kings of England could no longer afford to maintain a properly paid bureaucracy of local officials and local government had to be left in the hands of local landowners exposed to varying amounts of pressure from the major magnates. It was through these local officials, recruited mainly from the lesser landowners, that the king had to raise the shire levies in military emergencies. He could never be sure that they would not be paralysed by the local notables. In the civil war of 1321–2 the sheriff of Hereford in fact sided with the rebels and was hanged for it, dressed in his sheriff's robes.[5] Edward was able to gain a quick victory on this occasion largely because loyalist Welsh leaders, who hated the Marcher lords more than they did the government at Westminster, used the pretext that the Marchers were prominent among the rebels to devastate their lands and overwhelm their castles. In March 1322, however, it was the shire levies of Cumberland, outraged by Lancaster's apparent collusion with the Scots, who gave the king his decisive victory over the earl by intercepting and defeating Lancaster at Boroughbridge. In 1326 the shire levies in a negative sort of way again played a decisive role though the evidence leaves many questions half-answered. When Queen Isabella invaded her husband's realm bent on removing the Despensers, the shire levies of eastern England, who alone could have destroyed her before her army grew, failed to defend the realm against her. On the contrary, their leaders like Richard Perrers, sheriff of Essex and Hertfordshire, soon appear among her party. The stand taken by the earl of Norfolk against his half-brother was no doubt decisive in giving Isabella an initial foothold on the east coast. The king's other chief representative in those parts, John Howard, head of the great family destined to dominate East Anglia for centuries, apparently did nothing, save for subsequently claiming his war wages![6] There is some evidence that a portion of the shire levies in southern England did attempt to march to the king's aid but they clearly evaporated as a force before they found him.[7] Edward's attempt to repeat the successful Welsh military intervention of 1321–2 failed. As far as the North Wales supporters of the king were concerned, Edward's own official there, Robert Power, chamberlain of North Wales, may have thwarted this.[8]

The barriers to enduring authoritarian rule in England came from the smallness of the country and the integrated nature of the English aristocracy. In contrast to a larger country like France, it was very difficult to isolate a rebellion and carry on

the government in London for any length of time. Even the far
north of England, or the valleys of South Wales were only a few
days' gallop from London, and the disaffection there could
present an immediate threat to the king. This meant that
political fortunes could rise and fall rapidly, as they did in this
period. The smallness of the country also meant that family
connections cut across regional divergences. The king could
not unduly favour or maltreat one family without stirring up
a swarm of its friends, kinsmen and supporters, scattered
throughout the rest of the country. The king himself could not
easily build up a block of support to cope with these widespread
and integrated family alliances of his opponents. However, the
magnate opposition to Edward II clearly saw an attempt to do
so in the build-up of the younger Despenser's power in South
Wales and the March. Edward's own support from the Welsh
leaders, combined with Despenser's authority in South Wales
and the March, threatened to create a powerful and dangerous
military grouping with which no opposition would be able to
deal. Under Edward I the March had been the centre of
opposition to royal authoritarianism. Under Edward II it
looked like becoming the bastion of royal support.

The military power of Edward and the Despensers was the
more terrifying since it was accompanied by formidable
financial means. The confiscation of magnates' lands after the
rebellion of 1322, although much treasure was lost to plunderers,
still made the king enormously wealthy. He was storing as a
reserve more than a year's normal revenue. Much of the
confiscated property was let out on short-term leases only, or
retained in the king's hands, and this created a new balance
of wealth in the country which entirely favoured the king. No
king since John had been in this happy position. He and the
Despensers also had at their service two leading Italian banking
companies who could place vast resources of ready capital at
their disposal. The story of the last years of this reign is the tale
of how he misused this opportunity. For instance, although
hatred of the Despensers deprived him of political and military
support, there is no sign of a systematic attempt to build up a new
group of supporters. Neither did the king make lavish grants of
land outside the small circle of Despensers' close friends nor

did he hire mercenaries on a grand scale like his ancestor King John. A number of foreign knights appear at court from the beginning of the reign and we find Flemish mercenaries manning the Tower in the last year of the reign,[9] but neither represented an appreciable body of support.

The study of Edward's personal rule and of the supremacy of the Despensers in the years 1321–6, though it has proved of inferior interest to recent constitutional historians, greatly attracted writers of the late sixteenth century.[10] This was so perhaps because the extraordinary polarisation of Edward's favour, and the evil policies to which it led, had obvious parallels in the atmosphere of suspicion and favour at the court of Queen Elizabeth in her later years. Marlowe's play *Edward II*, written during this period, has captured the essential atmosphere of the regime perhaps better than any historian has since been able to do.

After the subject of evil royal favourites became virtually obsolete with the execution of Charles I and the proclamation of a Commonwealth, the study of the honourable origins of parliamentary opposition naturally became of more topical interest. It has remained true until the present day that historians have been more interested in the significance of magnate opposition than in the implications for political development of Edward II's behaviour and intentions. The 'discovery' of administrative history by Professor Tout at the beginning of the century began to redress the balance. He was particularly impressed by the reorganisation of the records of the exchequer in the last years of the reign as part of an attempt to speed up and improve the auditing of accounts. But his emphasis on the much-admired administrative achievements of the regime needs critical review. 'There is nothing astonishing in intelligent champions of strong monarchy being greater reformers than a conservative aristocracy', says Tout. 'It is enough, however, to show that the Despensers and their followers were not mere creatures of court favour but politicians with ideas, which however unpopular among the magnates, were valuable and attractive in themselves.'[11] It is necessary to refute this straight away. There is not the slightest evidence to show that the

Despensers themselves were interested in or involved with administrative reform. No letter exists which suggests this though a considerable amount of correspondence of the younger Hugh survives. The letters under the privy and secret seals from Edward himself ordering reforms in the exchequer show that these reforms came quite naturally in response to two things.[12] One was the king's boundless greed, and the other was the administrative crisis caused by the sudden responsibility imposed on the exchequer for the great mass of confiscated rebel lands. Edward made no mention of initiative or suggestions by the Despensers.

Tout's outrage at the neglect of England's administrative history, in spite of the unique quantity and quality of the sources available, caused him to focus too exclusively on this question. The great advances which had been made in the administrative history of medieval France also greatly impressed him and increased his indignation at the neglect of the subject in England.[13] He reconsidered the reign in the light of its administrative achievements and asked, and sometimes answered for the first time, many questions about how the government was functioning behind the political feuding; which organs of government the king preferred to use and why the magnates wanted to control them; how particular offices developed and how their efficiency increased. The stolid efficiency of the bureaucracy, the endurance of the clerks whose holidays were stopped so that they could compile lists of forefeited estates,[14] the persistent hard work of the chief officials harassed by hysterical and bad-tempered letters from Edward, who wanted quick results,[15] are indeed admirable. But Tout's appreciative judgement of the character of the Despenser regime and its 'achievements' on the basis of its administrative performance and innovations has distorted our understanding of the true nature of their corrupt dictatorship.

One deterrent to a fresh reconsideration of the Despenser regime has been the nature of the evidence. While there is a superabundance of evidence of one sort, namely formal government records, there is a shortage of the intimate royal correspondence which might give us a better understanding of some of the motives and ideas of the king himself. Curiously

enough we are better served in this respect for Hugh Despenser
the Younger than we are for King Edward II, though very
occasionally Edward's personality emerges suddenly in a few
of his irate personal letters addressed to the exchequer. The
younger Despenser was an outspoken correspondent and made
many revealing remarks even in his letters to his officials with
whom he had a good personal relationship, especially his
sheriff of Glamorgan, John Inge. In one such letter he exhorted
him to watch Despenser's affairs so that Despenser 'may be
rich and may attain his ends of which John has good cogni-
sance'.[16] Arrogant, although obviously intended humourously,
was his remarkable statement a few years later that 'even I
cannot control the wind' alluding to delays in the arrival of
ships in Gascony.[17] One wonders if he remembered it when
paying a chaplain to give prayers for a fair wind as he and the
king were attempting to flee by ship from South Wales in
October 1326.[18]

In the case of the king himself, personal evidence which
might explain important political decisions is distressingly
scanty. When fragmentary remains of once more complete
collections chance to survive, such as a small, paltry file of
letters under his privy seal, we realise how inaccurate our
knowledge of events can be and how our understanding of
people's characters can err. This file, written just after the
king's retreat from Scotland, which followed the disastrous
campaign of August–September 1322, illustrates both points.[19]
It proves, as other evidence only suggests, that the Scottish
campaign was brought to disaster by the activities of Flemish
pirates who intercepted supplies; the bitter tone of the letters
also makes clear how deeply committed Edward was to
intervention in Scotland. It makes nonsense of the suggestion,
never attached to any solid evidence, that Edward was half-
hearted in his desire to defeat Robert Bruce. He failed to defeat
the Scots for reasons other than lack of determination to do so.
But this file was a chance survival, a tiny fragment of a huge
series of privy seal letters which were also recorded once in
registers.[20] The loss of these letters is as serious for the study
of the political history of medieval England as is the complete
disappearance of exchequer 'books of loans' which dealt with

the office's transactions with money lenders for its financial history.[21] From the description of the state of the Public Records kept in the Tower of London as they were in the seventeenth century, 'peeping out of Heaps of Dust and Rubbish a yard or two in Depth', we can well understand why some groups of documents have vanished.[22]

The one-sided nature of what survives means that we have a great deal of evidence to show what men did and very little for why they did it. For some periods two recent biographers of leading magnates of Edward II's reign are able to give almost day-by-day accounts of their whereabouts and activities. Yet the precise reason why Lancaster became such a bitter opponent of Edward remains elusive, just as does the extent of Pembroke's loyalty to the king during the civil war in 1321.[23] The gap between the vast quantity of evidence which tells us what men did and the tiny bits of evidence which give us real insight into why they did it, apart from the occasional snippets of lay and ecclesiastical correspondence, is to some extent filled out by the chroniclers. But the narrative sources have their own special shortcomings. The English writers of this period were not as a rule prepared to discuss the motives of those about whom they were writing. In discussing personalities they usually confined themselves to conventional descriptions and superficial characteristics. Very rarely do we have such a revealing scrap of information as the statement by the author of *Vita Edwardi Secundi* that a hereditary enmity existed between the Despensers and Mortimers since the younger Despenser was under a vow to avenge the death of his grandfather, Hugh Despenser the Justiciar, for whose slaughter at the battle of Evesham as far back as 1265 he held an earlier Mortimer responsible.[24] Inadequacy of coverage by most chroniclers makes the task of the historian more difficult than does the bias of some who, for partisan reasons, are excessively preoccupied with boosting the reputation of certain people. An extreme example is the very apologist, almost hagiographic, French 'Brut' and, to a lesser extent, the other pro-Lancastrian chronicler of Henry Knighton of Leicester.[25] Both eulogise Lancaster but also provide invaluable information. Significantly there are no chroniclers who attempt to eulogise Despenser.

At the two extremes of revelation and discretion lie two chief narrative sources for the reign, both contemporary. The so-called Monk of Malmesbury who wrote the *Vita Edwardi Secundi* was almost certainly a royal official and a secular priest rather than a monk.[26] His prejudices and powers of description make him the Procopius of the reign and, like Procopius' *Secret History*, his narrative must have been composed in secret. It is most regrettable that our only manuscript of it stops abruptly in 1325. At the other extreme lies the infuriatingly careful Adam Murimuth who, significantly, earned the epithet *discretus* from the powers-that-be in his own time. Murimuth was a royal councillor who reports in his chronicle with quiet, anonymous smugness on the success of English embassies to the papal court which he himself had led. From letters to and about him, we know that he was a close friend of Walter Reynolds, archbishop of Canterbury, and the careful and all-knowing prior of Christchurch, Canterbury, Henry Eastry, who remained loyal to Edward until relatively late in the reign. When it is realised, however, that Murimuth was also closely connected with the two greatest episcopal opponents of Edward II, Henry Burghersh, bishop of Lincoln, and Adam Orleton, bishop of Hereford, it becomes clear that he successfully walked on both sides of the corridors of power, no mean achievement. When Roger Mortimer deposed Edward II, he chose Murimuth as custodian of the temporalities of the murdered bishop of Exeter. One can scarcely turn the pages of an episcopal register of the period without finding that Murimuth had a foothold in the diocese or a connection with the bishop. Yet his chronicle is a flat and factual narrative carefully interspersed with qualifying remarks, especially 'so it is said'. Only occasionally does a personal prejudice break through the smooth official front, such as the catty remark about Louis de Beaumont, bishop of Durham's club foot. His additional jibe that many Frenchmen were so deformed[27] was rather extraordinary coming from an ambassador to France.

One can supplement these narratives with a number of chronicles of special local value. The London chronicles are particularly fascinating and vital for the city's role in national affairs while those of the north of England are valuable for their insight into the Scottish war.[28] Most other regions produced narratives which contribute something new to our picture of what happened. A newly rediscovered continuation of Gervase of Canterbury gives some unique information about what was happening in Kent.[29] A local chronicle in the Bodleian library has greatly enlarged our understanding of the war in the Marches of Wales in 1321–2.[30]

As far as the royal archives are concerned, we are fortunate in dealing with a period when the volume of business was becoming so great as to necessitate a more efficient organisation of the records, such as took place at the exchequer between 1322 and 1326.[31] On the other hand the stage had not yet been reached when the government was compelled, by the sheer bulk of material, to keep many records only in a more summary form. This begins to happen by the beginning of the fifteenth century. The recurrent political upheavals of the reign also resulted in massive confiscations of the estates and records of several leading families, most notably those of Lancaster in 1322, of the Despensers in 1326, and of Mortimer in 1330. This large quantity of chronicle and record material presents an opportunity to retell what happened during one of the most dramatic and dangerous periods of English history.

2

Introduction:
The king and the magnates before 1318

The opposition to Edward II displayed the typical medieval
baronial attitude to royal government. It was an ambivalent
one. On the one hand the magnates proclaimed that the rights
of the crown must be integrally maintained and they protested
against alienations of royal property. On the other hand they
were ready to resort to violence and rebellion against these
same kings whose authority was the linch-pin of the whole
order of society which the magnates professed to uphold.
During and after the reign of Henry III, and before the dynastic
civil wars of the fifteenth century, they mostly justified their
opposition to royal government by claiming that they were
attacking not the king's proper authority but one perverted by
the counsel of evil favourites. Favourites were, in any case, a
considerable threat to magnates' possibilities of bettering
themselves, or even of surviving. Those magnates rich and
important enough to frequent the court were always haunted
by the fear that their power, based on a quasi-monopoly of
royal favour and patronage, might be eroded by the arrival
of newcomers or monopolised by one or two individuals. This
meant not only the loss of land grants but of possibilities of
finding the best marriages for themselves and their children.
For such favours they were dependent on the king as their
feudal overlord. If the favourite not only absorbed a lot of royal
wealth himself but also developed a hostile or contemptuous
attitude to the nobility, this could not be endured. In the early
part of the reign opposition was quickly formed to Gaveston.
The magnates reacted particularly swiftly and sharply to him
because his heavy hand on patronage came from a source
completely outside the old channels of influence. He was a

Gascon and, although a man of noble rank, came from no great family and had no strong connections in England. Yet he obtained the title of earl of Cornwall, that had hitherto been reserved for members of the royal family, as well as one of the best marriages of the day, to the king's own niece. One has to bear in mind, too, that there had been virtually no promotions to earldoms of men outside the Anglo-Norman aristocracy since Stephen's time. Their chagrin was the more understandable since Gaveston maintained an attitude of total hostility towards them. He bestowed upon the best-known figures at court a series of insulting nicknames and, what was probably even more serious to their self-esteem, trounced them in a tournament.[1] However, the baronial reaction to the Despensers' monopoly of the channels of power and influence was no less vigorous, although they were traditionally members of the magnate group which had helped to rule England since further back than living memory. This time their hatred was stimulated less by affront and more by fear.

The personal nightmare of any medieval landowner, whether a great magnate at court or a substantial knight in a far-flung part of England, was that one of his neighbours should become so powerful that he would be able to ride with armed men into his ancestral lands and disseise him of them. This could happen in one of two circumstances. The first was that the neighbour became a royal favourite so that nobody dared to challenge him. The second was that the character of the king had so diminished the royal authority that the neighbour no longer feared the king's wrath or that of his ministers. Both nightmares became a reality under Edward II and were particularly experienced by the neighbours of the younger Despenser.

Edward's striking characteristic of concentrating all his love and favour on one man was remarked upon by contemporaries. The shrewd author of the *Vita* said, 'Our king was incapable of moderate favour. . .and so Piers was accounted a sorcerer.'[2] Sir Thomas Gray, who perhaps of all chroniclers was most favourable to Edward and who himself attended the court, said the same thing. 'He was too familiar with his intimates, shy with strangers, and loved too exclusively a single individual.'[3] It is strangely fitting, in view of his infatuation for individuals, that one of our last recorded transactions between the king and Hugh Despenser was a royal order to hand over to the favourite the king's copy of the romance of Tristan and Iseult, the most famous of all the tales of infatuated and doomed love.[4]

To launch into an account of the Despenser regime and Edward's fall without sketching the disasters of the early years would be impossible. Edward and the Despensers, in fact, ruled under the shadow of enmities made long before. In a way the years 1321–6 are the story first of the apparent defeat of those enemies and then their slow transformation into a force that finally overwhelmed the regime. Edward himself inherited a host of enemies, both personal ones and those who had hated his father. He was himself, like his father, a passionate and difficult man. Towards the end the two clashed in a violent quarrel. The atmosphere created at court during Edward I's declining years because of the terrible feud between the king and the prince over Gaveston can have done nothing to earn respect for the new prince.[5] Most of the magnates belonged by then to the prince's generation rather than to his father's and most of them must have known him well, both because there was no privacy at court and also because they had served on campaigns together. The future Edward II did not distinguish himself on campaigns and started his reign with no great psychological advantage in contrast to his father who succeeded to the throne fresh from his victories over his father's baronial opponents and newly returned from a crusade.

Edward II not only started his reign as a man who inspired misgivings, he also inherited a formidably difficult political situation from his father. It was double-edged. The threat came partly from the magnates who resented Edward I's extension of their military and financial obligations to fight his wars.[6] Secondly, the aged king had been faced with the hostility of his archbishop of Canterbury who feared for the church's privileges at the hands of this ruthless monarch. By 1302 the two forces had combined into a group which exactly fore-shadowed the type of opposition at the beginning of Edward II's reign and which then came to be known as the 'Ordainers'. Like the Ordainers of 1310–11 they formed themselves into a committee, in this case of thirty-five, under the leadership of

Archbishop Winchelsea, with the intention of opposing the king's demands. They also assumed the more general responsibility of enquiring into the state of the realm and the church. In 1305 Edward I cleverly broke up this opposition with the aid of his old crusading friend, the new Pope, Clement V, who translated some of its more important clerical members abroad. After his father died, however, Edward II realised the difficulties of ruling with his archbishop of Canterbury in exile and, pretending magnanimity, he recalled Winchelsea. The archbishop rapidly resumed his bitter enmity to the crown. A third serious legacy from Edward I was a large debt and this burden may explain Edward's subsequent rapacity even when he was well-off.

When Edward I died on 7 July 1307, while mounting a great campaign against the Scottish leader, Robert Bruce, his successor, Edward II, was twenty-three years old. The new king immediately recalled Gaveston. Thereafter opposition developed rapidly and was led, not surprisingly, by the man to whom Gaveston's exile had been entrusted by Edward I, Henry de Lacy, earl of Lincoln.[7] A few days after Edward's marriage on 25 January 1308 to Isabella, daughter of Philip the Fair, king of France, Lincoln was among a group of magnates who attested a letter to which a recent writer has given the name, 'the Boulogne Agreement'. This document recorded that the magnates who had sealed it had taken an oath to maintain the honour of the crown, to repair abuses which had tarnished it up to that time and to redress oppressions committed against the people.[8] There is no evidence that the king approved of the way in which these magnates assumed responsibility for the honour of the crown and government. Without quoting the king's approval, advice or authority, they took upon themselves the king's own responsibility for maintaining the honour of the crown and administering justice.

The opposition showed its hand clearly enough one month later, at the king's coronation on 25 February. It was no less than a revolutionary move. The Coronation Oath had remained formally unchanged since Richard I's investiture though, if E. H. Kantorowicz is right, it may have been expanded in practice.[9] But an additional fourth pledge, publicly proclaimed and set down, was something new. Like his ancestors before him, Edward swore to hold 'church and people in good peace, put down evil-doing and temper justice with mercy'. He was now also required to 'uphold and defend the laws and righteous customs that the community of the realm shall choose'. Such a provision was a direct attempt to control the king's future legislation and also a prelude to a reform of some of the measures imposed by Edward I.[10] The term 'community of the realm' was the traditional name, employed by the baronial opposition to Henry III, for the ultimate consenting body.[11] It must have smacked to Edward, as it does to us today, of control of his activities by a baronial council. This was soon to become a reality.

This oath has had a distinguished after-history. Its meaning has been the subject of dispute since the time of the seventeenth-century antiquarians, William Prynne and Robert Brady, via the pens of Frederic William Maitland and Bishop Stubbs in the nineteenth century, down to the recent writings of H. G. Richardson and Bertie Wilkinson. In 1308 the earl of Lincoln took it quite literally. At a great council of magnates, held on 3 March, he moved that the king be requested to give effect to his Coronation Oath by pledging himself to agree to ratify beforehand anything which the magnates might resolve.[12] To those who think that Lincoln's mind may still have been solely on parliamentary procedure, we should point out that the king's reaction was to change the castellans of the chief fortresses in the land, removing three of the signatories of the Boulogne Agreement and handing over castles to court favourites including Gaveston himself and the elder Despenser. He also fortified the Tower, prepared Windsor for a siege and laid plans for seizing the earl of Lincoln by force.[13] By April 1308 the country was in a state of near civil war.

In the space of a few months, the formal protests of the coronation had turned into preparations for violence. To those who know the subsequent story of the reign, the list of the great nobles who officiated at Edward's coronation is a tragic one.[14] His brother-in-law, the earl of Hereford, who carried the sceptre with the cross, was to die, a proclaimed traitor, from the thrust of a Welshman's lance at the battle of Boroughbridge.

The earl of Lancaster, his cousin, who carried the blunted sword *Curtana*, was executed publicly with the blow of a sword some days after the same battle. Lancaster's brother, Henry, who carried the rod adorned with the dove proved himself worthy of this symbol by managing to avoid open rebellion against Edward, though he came near to ruin in 1328–9 under the regime of Mortimer and Isabella. The bearers of the other two great swords of state, the earls of Warwick and Lincoln, both died before the beginning of the Despenser regime, but both spent the last years of their lives in bitter enmity to the king, attempting to oust Gaveston. Of the four bearers of the royal robes, one, Roger Mortimer of Wigmore, summarily executed two others, the earl of Arundel and the elder Despenser. Mortimer himself, after deposing Edward twenty years later, was then executed by Edward's son in 1330. Among the distinguished visitors to the coronation came a man who was to play an important part in later events, Charles of Valois, Queen Isabella's uncle. By the last years of the reign he was noted for his hatred of the English. It was his successful overrunning of the English duchy of Gascony in 1324 which began the final chain of events leading to Edward's overthrow in 1326. He and the other French visitors to the coronation were outraged at the king's infatuation with Gaveston. To us preference for the company of a man of his own age whom he had known much of his life to that of a girl of twelve does not seem so strange, but the king's behaviour dangerously flouted social conventions. It is possible that the marriage was already fraught with friction. One source suggests that Edward had never wanted to marry Isabella in the first place.[15] He was reputed to have preferred a Spanish princess, perhaps out of sentiment for his dead mother, Eleanor of Castile. His father had arranged the French marriage at the time of the negotiations which brought to an end the Anglo-French war over Gascony. These negotiations also gave Edward I a second, French wife. It would have been difficult to repudiate the betrothal subsequently without insulting the dangerous Philip the Fair, in spite of Edward's possible inclination to follow his own wishes after his father's death.

At the parliament of April 1308 the magnates arrived for the first time in the reign in arms. At this assembly they once more demanded that Edward should fulfil the fourth clause of the Coronation Oath, enact what the magnates had demanded and remove Gaveston.

'The people rate him as a man attainted and judge and pray the king that, since he is bound by his Coronation Oath to keep the laws which the people shall choose, he will accept and execute the award of the people.'[16] Edward refused to part with Gaveston. The battle of nerves and threat of war lasted until June. Then finally the magnates obtained the king's agreement to Gaveston's exile in an assembly held at the Temple where they again arrived heavily armed. The royal favourite departed with the additional threat of excommunication should he return. At the end of the summer, over a year after he had succeeded to the throne, Edward wrote with great frankness to his friend, Pope Clement V, begging his forgiveness 'for not having sent messengers to him since he received the government of the realm because there has been disturbance and dissension and the king has not yet fully enforced unity'.[17] Such was Edward's own judgement on his first year's rule.

Gaveston was allowed to return in 1309 and the conflicts about his prominence at court soon revived. When the magnates refused to attend a parliament in February 1310 unless Gaveston was banished for good, it was Thomas of Lancaster who took the lead. We do not know why he quarrelled with Edward. The author of *Vita* says that Lancaster was incensed because Gaveston removed a protégé from office.[18] Lancaster's biographer, Dr J. R. Maddicott, has pinpointed his departure from court quite suddenly in November 1308.[19] Until then he was in constant attendance on Edward. Even for fourteenth-century chroniclers Lancaster was an enigma. The almost hagiographical *Brut* chronicle and the local Leicester chronicle, written at a house patronised by Lancaster's family, both provide rosy and unreal pictures of the earl.[20] To the author of *Vita* he was a dangerous man, and a characteristic which this writer mentions more than once was his vengeful nature.[21] Later on in the century, the chronicler Higden recorded that there were already differences of opinion about his worth and described on the one hand his immorality, maintenance of evil-doers and his vindictiveness and on the other hand his alms-giving, high respect for churchmen and consistency of political conduct. He concluded with the reflection that there was even great dispute among ordinary people as to whether he should be accounted a saint or not.[22] The meticulous unravelling of his career by Dr Maddicott has revealed many new facts and certain facets of character of which Higden was probably unaware. His consistency of opposition to Edward is conspicuous. So was his relentless pursuit of Earl Warenne, who abducted his wife. Lancaster conducted a private war against Warenne in the north of England in 1317 and 1318 and temporarily imprisoned him. Lancaster's ultimately fatal struggle with the Despensers probably arose originally out of the much smaller matter of a quarrel over a wardship. He was certainly a friend to some churchmen, and the clergy of St Paul's, London, seem to have had some success in promoting a cult of their former benefactor. To judge from his surviving correspondence his relations with his brother Henry were cold. With his neighbouring landowners they were apparently not good since they refused to join him in an attack on the Despensers in 1321. He then himself, later in the same year, refused to help the Marchers relieve their common ally Bartholomew Badlesmere, who was being besieged at Leeds castle in Kent by the king, and just before his final battle with Edward II at Boroughbridge, in the north of England in March 1322 the leader of his household retainers, Robert Holland, deserted him.[23]

Whatever his character and motivation, Lancaster's presence amongst the king's enemies was invaluable to them and after this first appearance in February 1310 he slowly moved into the position of their leader. When the next assembly of magnates met in March 1310, it reiterated the old cry of maintaining the honour of the crown and attacked the king for his heavy and unjust exactions for the Scottish war. It also, on 20 March, established the Committee of the Lords Ordainers to enforce the policies of the magnates, since it was clear that Edward could not be relied upon to carry out his promises without a supervisory body. One source maintains that Edward was forced to agree to the appointment of the Ordainers under the threat of deposition as an alternative.[24] It is of considerable importance that in the view of at least one contemporary this sinister spectre should again be at large in a land where it had not been seen since John's reign.

Edward proclaimed a Scottish campaign for 8 September 1310. Robert Bruce's strengthened position and the incursions of his followers into northern England made it highly necessary. A campaign also provided an excuse to Edward to rid himself of two distasteful obligations. The first was to travel to France to do homage to the French king for Gascony. The other was to remain in London while the Ordainers were organising complaints against his misrule. The campaign made possible the removal of the main government offices to York. This infuriated the earl of Lincoln, but death carried him from the scene on 11 February 1311. His heir, and now the holder of five earldoms, was Thomas of Lancaster. Future events were to confirm the view of chroniclers that Lancaster in addition to Lincoln's vast lands, inherited Lincoln's political position as hammer of Gaveston. As well as being son-in-law to Lincoln, Lancaster was also closely connected with the other opposition leader, the earl of Warwick, who was a near neighbour in the Midlands and to whose eldest son he was godfather.[25] After Lincoln's death, Lancaster's opposition became extremely strident. He refused to cross into Scotland to do homage and fealty for his new earldoms when the king was campaigning there. It was a considerable psychological victory for him when Edward crossed the border to receive his fealty and also allowed his vow of homage to wait until later. It was only the beginning of a war of nerves and words, which would lead to violence and the murder of Gaveston the next year and eventually to civil war.

While the king was campaigning, the Ordainers carried on preparing their demands for reform. They eventually produced a document of considerable size, comprising twenty-four clauses. If effectively enforced, it would have maintained Edward under the tutelage of a baronial council. This Edward was able to frustrate most of the time, but for the next eleven years the demands that the king should submit to the Ordinances provided a rallying cry for his opponents. Predictably Edward showed himself reluctant to summon the parliament which would confirm the Ordinances. When finally persuaded to do so, Edward repudiated beforehand, in a notarial act drawn up by French lawyers, any clauses of the Ordinances which he should deem prejudicial to his ancient authority. It was only the arrival of the magnates in arms, by now the usual prerequisite for obtaining Edward's consent to anything which he did not want, which forced him to observe any of the Ordinances and, above all, to expel Gaveston. The attempt to cripple Edward financially by the twofold method of expelling the king's Florentine bankers, the Frescobaldi, and prohibiting the collection of the New Custom which had been a valuable source of royal revenue since Edward I first imposed it in 1303, failed speedily. In April 1313 the king officially recognised as his banker a Genoese, Antonio Pessagno, whose massive loans of around £140000 between 1312 and 1319 kept Edward financially afloat during the crucial years of magnate opposition.[26]

The story of Gaveston's return in less than two months, his flight north with the king and his surrender at Scarborough castle are well known.[27] He was subsequently seized from his formal custodian, Aymer de Valence, earl of Pembroke, to whom the Ordainers had entrusted him, by their most violent member, the earl of Warwick. Whether the Gascon favourite received any sort of trial before his summary execution on 19 June 1312 is not certain. Warwick, who had originally taken Gaveston to one of his own castles, passed the captive on to Lancaster for execution on Lancaster's lands. He thus passed the buck and remained prudently absent. Gaveston was executed by one of Lancaster's Welsh retainers. Edward later pardoned this man, but he never forgave Lancaster. His immediate grief, which some chroniclers say was mitigated by the birth of a son and heir to the queen, was followed by constant remembrance. He changed the dedication of a religious house at Langley, originally founded as a chantry where masses could be said for his Plantagenet ancestors, into a shrine for Gaveston.[28] For the rest of the reign the wardrobe accounts attest that he remembered his friend's birthday and the day of his death with masses and offerings. He also immediately collected an army. Lancaster also mustered his forces near St Albans. The mediation of the earls of Richmond and Gloucester prevented the fighting but the threat of civil war haunted the whole of the next year.

Edward summoned the magnates to a parliament for 23 September 1313. Lancaster believed, not for the last time, that Edward intended to murder him and allegedly arrived with one thousand armed men. The earl of Warwick arrived with an impressive body of troops and the earl of Hereford with a small, but no doubt frightening, army of Welshmen. Once in parliament, however, the king not only castigated the magnates for Gaveston's murder but also for the seizure of Gaveston's property at Newcastle, a vast rich hoard including former royal treasure and a huge number of the tremendously valuable war-horses. The magnates for their part demanded the implementation of the Ordinances, pardon for Gaveston's murder and admission from Edward that his friend had died a traitor under the Ordinances. Edward daunted by their appearance with an army, gave the pardon in October 1313, but refused to admit that Gaveston had been guilty of treason. Deadlock over the return of Gaveston's property was only broken by the intercession of the earl of Gloucester and the legates of the Pope.

The removal of Gaveston meant that Edward was able to get wider magnate support than hitherto for the new campaign which he proclaimed in 1314 against Robert Bruce. There followed the disastrous English defeat at the battle of Bannockburn on 24 June which was imputed by chroniclers to demoralisation in the English camp. It was certainly due in part to quarrels within the high command.[29] Edward had entered the campaign with enthusiasm. He caused a preliminary disaster the day before the main engagement by rushing his men into a skirmish with the Scots at Tor Wood. His embitterment at this disgrace may have provoked his famous attack on the young earl of Gloucester as a traitor and prevaricator, when Gloucester proposed to postpone the major onslaught on Bruce in order to rest the men and to honour the feast of the Nativity of St John. Such a delay meant that the garrison of Perth, which had promised that it would only hold out against the Scots until St John's Day, would probably capitulate to them. There appears also to have been a quarrel between Gloucester and the earl of Hereford, Lancaster's ally, over who should lead which wing of the army. In the battle Gloucester was among those who fell. His death removed one of the most influential figures from English politics. The great campaign to which Edward had taken a poet to sing his triumphs, ended in a flight from the battlefield and a universal lament for Gloucester. The captured poet was forced to write his verses for the Scots. The Despensers were amongst those who fled the field with Edward.

The king had allegedly toyed with the idea of capturing Lancaster at his fortress of Pontefract on a victorious march home. Instead the defeat at Bannockburn inaugurated a period of great influence for the earl. At the York parliament of September 1314 Edward was forced to fulfil the part of the Ordinances which he particularly abhorred, the removal of various court favourites and the replacement of his own officials by nominees of Lancaster, but the situation was no calmer after Lancaster obtained the upper hand, and the next March a desperate group of clergy tried to make the granting of a clerical subsidy conditional upon peace between the king and the barons.

The years 1315–18 were filled with magnate feuds fought against a background of famine and epidemics in the country, of which the king and nobles seemed scarcely aware.[30] When the earl of Warwick, Lancaster's staunch ally and close friend, died in 1315, there were rumours that Edward had poisoned him. When an erstwhile supporter of the earl of Lancaster, Adam Banaster, rose against the earl at Lancaster, in October 1315, he thought fit to raise the royal standard, so hopeful was he of Edward's support.[31] It is not surprising that Lancaster's elevation in February 1316 to the position of chief of the king's council proved very short-lived. It was one of those paper arrangements, much desired by the clergy who wanted peace, but in effect part of a political charade played between the king and Lancaster at this time. It passed almost unnoticed by the chroniclers because, like the resumption of lands of royal favourites later in the spring, it was wholly ineffective.

In 1316 disorder in the country became widespread. In Wales a rising took place in Glamorgan in the wake of the death of the last Clare lord of the area, the earl of Gloucester, at Bannockburn.[32] In Bristol, the population, driven desperate by famine, revolted against the imposition of a tallage and held the castle against the king.[33] The disorder in the north, complicated by the devastating Scottish incursions, became a European scandal when in September 1317 Sir Gilbert Middleton of Mitford, a household knight, probably as part of a feud with two other great northern magnates, Henry de Beaumont and Louis de Beaumont, bishop of Durham, attacked them together with two papal legates in their company. These legates, Cardinal Luca Fieschi, a member of a great Genoese family, and Cardinal Gauscelin, were despoiled of all but their shirts and arrived outraged in Durham to be placated with large royal pensions. A number of Lancaster's retainers were among the attackers.[34] In spite of the shock which this generated, it was the least serious of Edward's problems in the north at this time. Far more dangerous were the Scottish raids which were developing from border fights into invasions across the border, carrying destruction and plunder far into England.

The idea that a 'middle party' attempted to heal the breach between Lancaster and Edward, which was only encouraging acts of brigandage like Middleton's, has been refuted by Dr J. R. S. Phillips.[35] He has effectively proved that the group of men previously thought to have comprised such a third party standing between the king and magnates were, in fact, staunch royal supporters. Attempts at effecting a reconciliation between Edward and Lancaster were made fruitless by the dramatic abduction by Warenne of Lancaster's wife on 11 April 1317. Such a private feud between Lancaster and Warenne was dangerous enough, but Lancaster also believed that the king had been party to the plot and that it had been organised at a council meeting in February. In the latter part of 1317 Lancaster was launching attacks on Warenne's manors in the north and those of a current royal favourite, Roger D'Amory. Lancaster also again refused to come to court saying that he feared treachery. The king gathered troops at York in September 1317 while at the same time offering Lancaster a safe-conduct to come to parliament. It appears that he was tempted to attack Lancaster's stronghold at Tutbury but was restrained by Pembroke. It was not until the following summer that Lancaster finally agreed to come to court well-armed not only with safeguards from the king but from his other opponents as well, and on condition that the king's current favourites, Roger D'Amory, Hugh Audley and William Montague were removed from court. It was into this vacuum of favour created by their temporary departure from court that the younger Despenser stepped in 1318.

3

The rise of the Despensers

A discussion of the position and properties of the Despensers before their emergence in 1318 as the king's most influential councillors requires a study of topics that may at first sight seem relatively unimportant. But without such an enquiry their subsequent careers would be much less intelligible. By failing to consider in sufficient detail this phase of their lives before 1318 historians have created myths that must be dispelled once and for all. The reconstruction of the slow, tenacious building up of a magnate fortune may seem a dull, technical subject. But this formed the very core of the interests of the men who mattered most in medieval England, something about which they incessantly schemed and gossiped. When their schemes conflicted too violently, local faction or even general civil war might erupt, as it did in 1321 because the Despensers finally overreached themselves.

Attempts to explain the power of the Despensers in the later years of the reign of Edward II have usually concentrated on the emergence of the younger Hugh Despenser as Edward's last favourite. But this underestimates the importance of his father, the elder Hugh, from the beginning of the reign. Only private correspondence and other personal records of a kind that we lack would explain why the elder Hugh was one of the very few magnates who remained consistently friendly to Edward II. As far back as 1301 the young Edward, then still only prince of Wales, had been describing him as 'one of our friends'.[1] In a period filled with friction between the prince and his father, the elder Despenser knew how to retain the confidence of Edward I without forfeiting the prince's good will. Through this he was the chief architect of his family's rise to power.

The Despensers had first come to prominence in the twelfth
century as the leading vassals and also as household officials
of the earls of Chester. It was from this household office that
they derived their name. The elder Despenser's maternal
grandfather, Philip Basset, came from a family of leading royal
officials descended from two prominent judges of Henry I.
Philip had served as a royalist chief justiciar during the turbulent period of baronial challenge to Henry III after 1258.[2] The
elder Despenser's father, another Hugh, married Philip's only
daughter, and heiress to the rich Basset inheritance, and he,
in his turn, also became chief justiciar. He was killed fighting
at the side of Simon de Montfort at the battle of Evesham, but
the royalist partisanship of Philip Basset saved the justiciar's
infant son from ruin and he grew to become one of the most
trusted servants of Edward I. He clearly possessed some of the
personal distinction of his two justiciar ancestors from whom he
inherited both his own ancestral Despenser holdings and the
still larger Basset estates.[3] These made him one of the major
landowners in the Midlands and the south of England and
close neighbour and feudal vassal of Thomas of Lancaster. It
was this wealth which both made him an important creditor
of Edward I and induced the king to buy from him the marriage
of his only son, Hugh the Younger, for the huge sum of £2000.[4]
In 1306 the king used this eligible heir as husband for his eldest
granddaughter Eleanor, sister of the young earl of Gloucester.
By this time, a year before the old king's death, the elder
Despenser had also already established himself in the favour
of the man who was to succeed to the throne.

His early friendship with the future Edward II meant that
on the new king's accession Despenser was given custody of the
key castles of Devizes, Marlborough and Chepstow and there
is no evidence that he ever moved from the position of the
highest favour in the king's eyes. In trying to interpret correctly
Hugh's subsequent activities and position we encounter, however, one difficulty. Our best narrative source for the career
of the two Despensers, the *Vita Edwardi*, was apparently being
written after the evils of their influence began to be manifest
after 1318. There is a danger that its author is projecting
into an earlier period the reputation which the Despensers

fully deserved only at a later date and that he is exaggerating the nastiness and importance of various earlier incidents.
For instance, he writes in his narrative of 1313 of the elder
Despenser as a man hated by the whole realm and as a disin-
heritor of magnates.[5] The latter charge, at any rate, cannot be
substantiated by any other contemporary evidence. The author
of *Vita* singles the elder Hugh out as the only magnate who
stood by the king in defence of Gaveston.[6] In 1309 he was acting
as a formal messenger between the king and the court of the
King's Bench and he was obviously a highly presentable royal
servant, well-suited to be sent on diplomatic missions.[7] In 1309
the king wrote to the Chancellor explaining that he was in
process of trying to persuade the elder Hugh to undertake a
mission to the French court.[8] This notable royal diplomat,
soldier and creditor was appointed an Ordainer, though he
was probably a royal partisan on the committee. By 1313 he
was described as the implacable foe of Lancaster and his record
down to 1317 was so thoroughly loyalist that it is difficult to
distinguish his political behaviour from that of the king whom
he served.[9] As the author of *Vita* expressed it 'apud regem
latuit'.[10] This same author, early in his narrative, stressed the
growth of Despenser's hostility to Lancaster and the Mortimers
and complained bitterly of the evils which Despenser had
perpetrated as Justice of the Forest, an office which he already
held under Edward I. In 1314 Despenser was one of those whose
removal from court was demanded by the magnate opposition,
but one can find little in his conduct which could have augured
that he would die on the gallows, howled at and execrated by a
Bristol mob. But, as will emerge later on, one cannot go to the
other extreme of accepting the chronicler Geoffrey Baker's view
that he was a knight of great worth who was destroyed merely
by his inordinate affection for his son.[11]

The same chronicler, after making this comment, provides
us with a pen-portrait of the younger Hugh. He remarks that
he was a fine figure of a man. But he also notes the younger
Despenser's impetuosity, pride, ambition and greed. These
qualities brought disaster upon him and upon his king, whose
chief favourite and adviser he was from 1322 to 1326. The
younger Hugh was the son of Isabel, widow of Payn Chaworth,

a considerable landowner in South Wales and Gloucestershire, whom his father married in 1283. She was the daughter of William Beauchamp, earl of Warwick. Chaworth had left her with a daughter, Maud, who married Thomas of Lancaster's younger brother, Henry, early in Edward II's reign.[12] It is possible that this close family relationship to Despenser may have saved Henry's life and his lands after his brother's rebellion in 1322. He is not the only relation of the Despensers to emerge finally as their enemy, as Henry did in 1326. We should also include in this category members of the Courtenay, Giffard of Brimpsfield and Segrave families.

The elder Despenser did not make spectacular land acquisitions under Edward I or early in the reign of Edward II, and it looks as if the repayment which he received for his considerable services was the good marriage for his son and heir. However, such territorial acquisitions as the two Despensers made before the younger Hugh emerged as a royal favourite in 1318 are of particular political importance in showing why the baronage viewed the rise of these two men with such mistrust. In 1297 the elder Hugh appears to have seized a tiny croft with four and a half acres at Curtlington, Oxfordshire. His step-grandmother, Ela countess of Warwick, had held this but the reversion was due to one John Page of Curtlington. Page's son did not recover it until the fall of the Despensers in 1326.[13] Still in the reign of Edward I, in 1306, he obtained the manor of Doddington, also in Oxfordshire, from one John Abel. This he gave to his clerk, Robert Herwedon, but he kept the reversion for himself. By 1321 he had also acquired Datchet and Fulmer in Buckinghamshire from Edmund Pynkeney, who regarded himself as wronged and who temporarily got them back during the Despenser exile. He also obtained Bagshot in Surrey and Merston Maisy in Wiltshire, allegedly unjustly, from Thomas de la Knolle. Wrongful acquisitions of property by great barons were common, but the wealth of manors like Datchet and Fulmer were probably sufficient to give Despensers' contemporaries cause for unease.

The younger Despenser started the reign landless, though his wife, Eleanor de Clare, may have brought him a manor or two at their marriage in 1306.[14] He clearly did not have enough

to support his family comfortably in 1310 because that year his
father handed over to him the manors of Oxcroft in Cambridge-
shire, Kersey in Suffolk and three Essex manors, North Weald,
la Mersh and Wix which were of the inheritance of the elder
Despenser's mother, Alina Basset. He also gave his son the
manor of Bishey in Hertfordshire which he himself had acquired in 1297. He granted him none of the great Despenser
and Basset ancestral properties in the Midlands or Wiltshire,
and Despenser's mother preferred to endow her daughter by
Payn Chaworth with her personal properties. On 14 May 1309
the king made up the younger Despenser's income to just over
£200 a year in what seems to be the only grant he gave him
before Despenser became a royal favourite. He received the
prosperous and well-furnished manor of Sutton in Norfolk
which the king himself had obtained through the sequestration
of the properties of the Templars. It was worth £45 19s. 9½d. a
year in 1326. So Despenser had no mean living, but when one
remembers that the income of his brother-in-law, the earl of
Gloucester was c. £6000 per annum,[15] one realises that in
terms of wealth he started the reign very small fry indeed. It
looked as if, until his father's death, the younger Despenser
would pass his life as a moderately prosperous landowner in
eastern England and it is not surprising that during the first half
of the reign the official records and chronicles have little to
say about him.

It is clear that he did not play an important part in political
life before the battle of Bannockburn. His wife, the king's
niece Eleanor, seems to have been a favourite at court and the
king paid her expenses from early on in the reign,[16] though
there are no signs of similar interest in her two younger sisters.
It is very probable that she, as much as his father, played a
part in bringing the younger Despenser close to the king. Some
historians have assumed that the younger Despenser was an
important figure at the time of the Ordinances. This is a myth,
originating in three pieces of evidence. The most interesting of
these is a malevolent fabrication. It consists of a charge made
in 1321 that he had formulated the doctrine that loyalty was
owed to the crown as an institution rather than to the king as a
person. This caused Tout to attribute to him 'brains enough

to form something like a theory of constitutional law'.[17] The *Historia Roffensis* makes it clear that this charge was the invention of his enemy, Bartholomew Badlesmere, and that it was intended to discredit him.[18] The other two pieces of evidence which seem to support the view that he was an important opposition figure are, at most, of doubtful value. In 1310 his lands were briefly sequestrated by the king because he had gone abroad without permission. This was, however, not an uncommon penalty for such an offence and it cannot constitute convincing proof of Despenser's friendship with the Ordainers.[19] The second piece of evidence which has been taken to indicate Despenser's involvement with the opposition lies in the Ordainers' complaint, on his behalf, that he had been attacked by a member of the court.[20] However, since Hugh's father was a member of the Ordainers' Committee this matter could equally well have been raised by him.

It was probably a simple royal grant of a wardship in 1313 which pushed the younger Despenser decisively into the position of a royal supporter. That year, in common with many other magnates, he accompanied the king to France. About the same time, perhaps because he had come to the king's notice on the trip, Edward granted him the wardship and marriage of William Huntingfield.[21] However, this useful but not unusual grant brought Despenser into the mainstream of political controversy for the first time. The grant was hotly contested by Thomas of Lancaster, who claimed that Huntingfield was his tenant and that the marriage belonged to him. It may be that Huntingfield did hold some lands in chief of the king, aside from what he held of Lancaster; Lancaster lost his claim. The younger Despenser obtained the wardship, but it is quite probable that Lancaster, who had apparently turned against Gaveston for removing one of his retainers from office, should have become incensed against the younger Despenser for robbing him of this valuable prize.

The battle of Bannockburn on 24 June 1314 entirely changed Despenser's fortunes. The death of his brother-in-law, the earl of Gloucester, in the battle entitled his wife to a third share of the Clare estates, and the best part, since she was the eldest daughter. However, there were considerable delays in appor-

tioning the inheritance. The widowed countess received her
dower lands in December 1314, but the apportioning of the
lands to the earl's sisters could not take place because the
widow was believed to be pregnant.[22] She had already borne
the young earl one son in 1312, but he had not long survived
his baptism.[23] In May 1315, when the countess could no longer
plausibly be thought capable of producing an heir by her dead
husband, Despenser, with characteristic brutality, seized
Tonbridge castle in Kent from her. This was an extraordinary
escapade and a presentiment of things to come. He initially
admitted that he had taken it 'of his own authority'. In June
he revised this version to allege that he had taken the castle for
the king.[24] In any case he had completely overreached himself
because the castle was held of the archbishop of Canterbury
to whose custody it had to be returned. As great magnates
were not, as a rule, ignorant of the tenurial position of major
fortresses, this was, presumably, a piece of exceptionally opti-
mistic high-handedness. It is noticeable that by now either the
younger Despenser or his father were constantly in attendance
at court as can be seen from their attestations to royal charters.[25]
They were clearly keeping a close watch on their interests as
the time for apportioning the Gloucester inheritance drew
nigh. During this tense time the younger Despenser was also
responsible for attacking a fellow peer at the Lincoln parliament of 1316. We do not know the identity of his victim nor
the reason for the attack.[26]

Despenser's behaviour over Tonbridge may have been a
reaction to the king's refusal to hand over his wife's inheritance,
but the delays were quite understandable. By the time it was
clear that Matilda de Clare was not pregnant, the lordship of
Glamorgan and Bristol could not be safely entered by royal
officials wishing to assess their value. They were seriously
disaffected and on the verge of major rebellions. There had
already been a serious uprising in Glamorgan, shortly after the
earl's death which had caused a huge amount of damage.
Removal of the ancient Clare authority which had lasted a century, combined with the poor harvest of late 1315–16, were the
major causes of a second rebellion which broke out in January
1316. It was led by a Welshman from upland Glamorgan

who had been an official of the Clares, Llywelyn Bren, one
of the most important landowners in Senghengydd. In Bristol
the same famine, part of a general disaster in north-western
Europe, exacerbated disaffection caused by the tallage of 1312
and the city rose against the king not long after the Llywelyn
Bren rising had been put down. Under these circumstances it
is, perhaps, not surprising that the king was not willing to give
the order to apportion the lands until April 1317. Another
delaying factor was undoubtedly the necessity to find consorts
for the two other girls who inherited these vast and dangerous
properties. Margaret de Clare, tragically married before to
Gaveston, was given by the king to Hugh Audley, who had distinguished himself in the war against Llywelyn Bren. The third,
Elizabeth de Burgh, whose first husband, the earl of Ulster's
son, had also been murdered, was married off to another of
the king's current favourites, Roger D'Amory. These marriages
did not take place until April and May 1317 respectively and
Despenser received livery of his portion of the lands on 15
November 1317.[27] He had petitioned for them three times
already but without success, though, perhaps as a consolation,
in July 1317 the king granted him the manor of Carlton in
Lancashire, confiscated from Gervase Avenel who had committed treason by supporting the Scots.[28] The lands which
Despenser and Eleanor received in November 1317 were
appreciated in the official valuation at £1507 13s. 9¼d., of
which £1276 9s. 9¼d. worth was situated in Wales.[29] Three
days later Despenser received custody of the castle and town of
Dryslwyn and the lordship of Cantref Mawr in West Wales in
lieu of an annual fee of 600 marks due to him.[30] In December
the king gave him a respite from paying the relief on the
Gloucester inheritance, which would have been considerable.[31]
Whether this was again in lieu of repayment of debts or a sign
of increasing royal partiality for Despenser, it is impossible
to say.

A local Glamorgan chronicle maintained that Despenser's
aim from the start was to get the portions of the other co-
heiresses and the title of the earl of Gloucester.[32] Certainly,
from his immediate attempt to extend his control over the lands
of the other co-heiresses, it looks as if the younger Despenser's

sudden accession to huge properties had thoroughly whetted his appetite for lordships and manors. Before the husband of the next heiress, Margaret Audley, had even obtained formal seisin of part of his share, Gwynllwg, Despenser had already taken the homage and fealty of the tenants.[33] The king's attempts to get Gwynllwg back for Audley do not suggest that Despenser was firmly in his position as royal favourite yet. In any case Despenser had his way here. The sureness of Despenser's grip on Gwynllwg was perhaps due more to the fact that it had been traditionally part of the lordship of Glamorgan, administered since 1247 from Cardiff,[34] rather than to the love of Despenser's lordship. By December 1318, now more securely ensconced in royal favour, Despenser was able to engineer a favourable exchange of this desirable lordship in return for some less valuable English manors which he gave to Audley.[35] Gwynllwg was worth £458 10s. 6¾d. a year.[36] About the same time the king also strengthened Despenser's control in South Wales by confirming his grant of the castle of Dryslwyn and the lordship of Cantref Mawr. This acquisition of royal lands was one of the charges brought against Despenser in the indictment of 1326, though, in fact, Despenser had received only a life interest. In general, Despenser's strategy was not to control royal castles or lease royal lands, except when they had special strategic value for him. He was interested primarily in adding to his hereditary possessions which could be passed on to his three sons, Hugh, Gilbert and Edward.

In the period between the handing over of the Gloucester inheritance in November 1317 and the July council of 1318 the Despensers moved into their place as chief councillors and royal favourites. It was probably some time after the beginning of the year that this happened because they do not yet appear among those receiving New Year's gifts from the king in 1318.[37] A unique reference in the Bridlington chronicle, which describes proceedings at the Leicester council of April 1318, reveals how important they had become by that date. As part of Lancaster's terms for a reconciliation between him and the king, after a period of virtual civil war precipitated by the flight of Lancaster's wife with Warenne, Lancaster demanded that the Despensers should be retained in his service for life, bringing

with them the large force of 200 armed men. This suggests a
desire to enrol into his service two of the most important figures
at court whom presumably he did not yet regard with utter
hatred. There is no evidence that anything came of it.[38]

In the summons to the July council at Northampton the
Despensers for the first time led the list of magnates below the
rank of earl. According to one chronicler, whose reliability at
this point it is unfortunately impossible to confirm, the younger
Despenser was the subject of an important controversy at this
assembly.[39] This chronicler maintains that already at some
earlier date he had been appointed to the office of the king's
chamberlain and that his bad conduct in it had caused such
discontent among the magnates that this was the major reason
for calling the Northampton assembly. According to this version, Despenser was then confirmed in his office after a dispute
with the magnates who were pressing for his removal. Be this
as it may, he certainly appears as chamberlain at the York
parliament of October 1318 while his close associate, Bartholomew Badlesmere, formerly the retainer of his brother-in-law,
the earl of Gloucester, figures during this parliament as the new
steward of the household. In November 1318, shortly before
the final additional grant to Despenser of Gwynllwg, the king
also put the seal on Despenser's authority in the March by
granting him and Eleanor all the regalities, liberties and free
customs which the Clares held in the lordship by hereditary
right, to be held without impediment by the king or his
ministers. This nullified the quit-claim of hereditary rights in the
lordship which Gilbert de Clare had made to Edward I in 1290
and in return for which he had received back his special
Marcher privileges only by royal grant.[40] An important part
of the March, seedbed of magnate opposition under Edward I,
now threatened to become a bastion of royal support and
Glamorgan was to be used as a launching ground for Despenser
aggression against the king's Marcher opponents.

4

The civil war, 1321–2

The slide from December 1318 onwards into the civil war of
May 1321 must have been a terrifying experience for those
who lived through it, especially as the Scots were ravaging the
northern border. The younger Despenser was creating a
frighteningly novel situation. He was seizing any neighbour's
lands that he desired and covering himself with royal grants to
achieve virtual immunity. The violence and desperation of his
opponents is easy to understand. His new Welsh tenants were
also restive and the rapidity with which his lands were to fall
to his enemies in 1321 reveals the reluctance of his new vassals
to fight for him and his Clare wife.

By 1319 two situations had arisen which decisively drove the
Marchers into opposition to Despenser. One was border
skirmishing between John Giffard of Brimpsfield's tenants of
Cantref Bychan and Despenser's men in Cantref Mawr. On
the Marcher side there was clearly anxiety that Despenser
intended to expand in this direction. Despenser was probably
nervous because of his suspicions of his Welsh tenantry there.[1]
John Giffard of Brimpsfield was an important man, the owner
of relatively few manors but very rich ones and he himself was
known as John the Rich. He was also very well connected and
came from a family with many branches, one of which had
recently produced an archbishop of York and a bishop of
Worcester.[2] His wife was a granddaughter of Hugh Despenser,
the justiciar, and he is a clear example of how local enmities
could cut across family connections as well as reinforce them.
Until he fell foul of the Despensers, he had been a trusted
servant of Edward II and helped to put down the Llewelyn
Bren rising as well as acting as custodian of Glamorgan after

the earl of Gloucester's death. The king had later prosecuted him on unspecified grounds for his conduct as custodian of the lordship.[3] It is quite possible that the younger Despenser was behind this prosecution as he was also responsible for the proceedings against another custodian, Payn Turberville. There may have been conflict between Despenser and Giffard themselves before their men started to fight on the border between their territories.[4]

However, it was Despenser's more whole-hearted attempt to get hold of another Marcher lordship, Gower, which provoked the most serious trouble. Gower had been held by the Braose family since the beginning of the thirteenth century. The last male Braose in the senior line, William, was a profligate and, although he settled the lordship on the husband of his eldest daughter and his former ward, John Mowbray, lord of Axholm, he proceeded to try to capitalise on it in his own lifetime by selling the reversion! Humphrey de Bohun, earl of Hereford, was one interested party. Another was Roger Mortimer of Wigmore. Both shared common descent from Eva, daughter of the most famous knight of the thirteenth century, William Marshal, earl of Pembroke. Despenser did not belong to this hitherto exclusive Marcher club and his attempt to join in the bargaining for Gower brought about the alliance of the other two contenders and besides roused general Marcher opposition to him.

Hereford was the leader of this opposition and the only one of Despenser's Marcher opponents who was of the first rank in either family, wealth or lands. He was the king's brother-in-law and the owner of the great Bohun lordship of Brecon, Hay and Huntingdon in the March. Son of one of Edward I's most formidable opponents, he himself had been no friend to Edward II in the Gaveston affair. At Bannockburn he had unwittingly helped to precipitate the defeat of the English by quarrelling with his relative, the earl of Gloucester, over strategy and precedence, an event which led to a desperate charge to the death by Gloucester and to Hereford's own capture. Among his fellow captives were John Giffard of Brimpsfield and Maurice Berkeley, who came from an old Gloucestershire family. These were to be two of his chief allies in the fight against the Despensers. Hereford's wife, the king's sister, so fretted during his captivity that the king gave her all the Scottish captives to promote the speedier ransoming of her husband.[5] He returned home in time to lead the suppression of the Llywelyn Bren rising in 1316. He apparently collided with the younger Despenser over an incident in this war, because he later numbered among the charges against the Despensers the younger Despenser's seizure of Llywelyn Bren and his illegal execution. Hereford's family certainly later gave help to Llywelyn's widow and sons.[6] It was Despenser's acquisition of Gower which turned him into a desperate royal opponent who was determined to defeat his enemies or go into exile in Hainault where he had family connections and some money.[7]

Roger Mortimer of Wigmore was particularly nervous of Despenser's growing power in the March because the younger Despenser apparently coveted some of his castles.[8] He may also have felt himself ill rewarded by their meteoric rise, since he was the only magnate of the day who had really had outstanding military success over a long period during the troubled early years of Edward II's reign. These had been punctuated otherwise by nothing but military disaster. Mortimer's success had been in Ireland. He was the head of a family which had come over from Normandy with William the Conqueror and whose possession of the formidable castle at Wigmore in the middle March is already recorded in Domesday Book. As well as being descended from William Marshal he was also descended from the Welsh princes. His paternal grandfather, Roger Mortimer, had played a decisive part in assuring the royalist victory at Evesham in 1265, where Hugh Despenser, the justiciar, had been killed, and had acted as one of the regents of England at the beginning of Edward I's reign while the king was still away on crusade. His two sons, Edmund Mortimer of Wigmore and Roger Mortimer of Chirk, had later profited from Edward I's favour and from the confiscation of Welsh rebel lands to enhance their territorial position in the March. They were both involved in the killing of Llywelyn ap Gruffydd, prince of Wales, near Builth in December 1282. It was Roger Mortimer of Chirk who had carried the prince's head to Edward I in

London. It is important to recall this when one remembers the
energy with which the Welsh chieftains were to pounce on the
Mortimer-led Marcher coalition in 1321. Roger Mortimer of
Chirk had added to his unsavoury reputation amongst the
Welsh when two little boys, heirs to the principality of Powys
Fadog, were found drowned in his charge. Suspicions seemed
to be substantiated when he obtained the grant of part of their
lands from the king. Not surprisingly, the Mortimer properties
in West Wales at Narberth and St Clears were burnt by the
Welsh when he was in Gascony in 1299. During the last years
of the reign of Edward I while his nephew, another Roger
Mortimer of Wigmore was a minor, he was the effective head
of the family. Royal favour continued with the accession of
Edward II. The new king made him Justiciar of Wales in 1308
and later granted him the major strategic castles and lordships
of Blaenllyfni and Bwlch-y-Ddinas. Until 1321 there is no
evidence that he was anything but a faithful servant of the
crown.

There is some evidence that the younger Roger Mortimer
of Wigmore's animosity towards King Edward may have
originated earlier than that of his uncle. He had been given,
as a young man, into the wardship of Peter Gaveston. An
outraged entry in the Wigmore chronicle states that the heir
had to pay 2500 marks to escape from the favourite's feudal
control. Mortimer had already greatly increased his territorial
possessions by an early marriage to Joan de Joinville, the
granddaughter of the famous French chronicler of the Crusade
of St Louis, Joinville. She had brought him part of Ludlow and
Ewyas Lacy in the March and important Lacy lands in Meath
in Ireland. He was not able to bring these Irish lands under his
control without a great deal of fighting. His rivals, the Irish
Lacys, were among those who persuaded Edward Bruce to
invade Ireland. Bruce defeated the Irish Justiciar, Edmund
Butler, at Connor in September 1315. The next year, after
Mortimer had arrived to fight for his wife's ancestral lands,
Bruce defeated him at Kells in the spring and later drove him
out of Meath. Mortimer's activity there, however, caused
Edward to make him Warden and Lieutenant of Ireland on
23 November 1316. The following year he arrived with an army

at Youghal, Co. Cork. He pushed Bruce north, drove the Lacys from his lands and reduced Leinster and Meath. His unique successes among the military disasters of the Scottish campaigns must have given him a place of high regard among the baronage. Edward also recognised this in 1319 when he made him Justiciar of Ireland.

This military reputation and his lordship in the dangerous Marcher area which, of necessity, had always produced good fighting men, made him a dangerous enemy even though he was not a particularly wealthy man. He was a neighbour and cousin of Hugh Audley, who had been Despenser's first victim, and who likewise came from an ancient Marcher family, partly Saxon in origin. The elder Audley had been justice of North Wales at the beginning of the reign. Mortimer was also related to Maurice Berkeley of Berkeley castle in Gloucestershire, whose grandmother was a Mortimer. The Berkeleys were one of the most notable families of the southern March and of Gloucestershire. Descended from a mid-twelfth-century Bristol merchant and trusted servant of Henry II, they had gradually established a great lordship in the area and built a strong and beautiful castle not far from the Severn estuary. Maurice may have had a private grievance against the Despensers. His second wife, Isabella, was the daughter of Gilbert the Red, earl of Gloucester, which made her the much older half-sister to Despenser's own wife, Eleanor. Contemporary sources sometimes turn her into the full sister or confuse her with Elizabeth, another half-sister, who had married the earl of Ulster and subsequently Roger D'Amory. But Isabella had been disinherited when, as part of the arrangements surrounding Gilbert's second marriage to Edward I's daughter, the Clare inheritance had been entailed on the children of that second marriage.[9] Berkeley and, through him, Mortimer were related to the important families of south-western England who were to ally with the Marcher cause, the Mautravers and the Verduns, while the heir to the Courtenay inheritance was married to Hereford's daughter.

It was under the shadow of the growth of this Marcher opposition that Edward attempted in 1319 to conduct another Scottish campaign. Its aim was to recapture Berwick and it was

the first and last campaign in the reign of Edward II in which
the earl of Lancaster took part. Two attacks on Berwick were
repulsed and, in the disappointment and demoralisation which
followed these defeats, camp frictions and gossip brought a
further deterioration in relations between the king and the earl.
On 14 September the terrible news arrived that the Scots had
outflanked the English army and plunged deeply into Yorkshire.
The citizens of Yorkshire, bravely realising that they had no
alternative, had organised their own resistance and gone out
to meet the Scots. From the number of clergy slaughtered the
encounter earned the derisive Scottish nickname of 'the Chapter
of Myton'. Two days after this tragedy, Lancaster left the army.
It is possible that he left to cut off the Scottish retreat or to
defend his own estates, but rumour had it that he had been
bribed by the Scots to the tune of £40 000.[10] Contemporary
references to collusion between Lancaster and the Scots keep
reappearing and the apparent immunity of his lands from their
attacks seemed to substantiate suspicions. No doubt Despenser
took a prominent part in alleging that Lancaster had sold himself to the Scots. We have a letter to John Inge, his sheriff of
Glamorgan, in which he said that 'before Edward had been
there eight days news came to him that the Scots had entered
his land with the prompting and assistance of the earl of
Lancaster. The earl acted in such a way that the king took
himself off with all his army to the great shame and grievance
of us all.'[11] Allegations such as these explain the statement in
the *Vita* that Lancaster 'blamed Hugh for the disgrace which
attached to his name at Berwick'.[12] Lancaster did in fact have
some reason to move off if there was any truth in the story that,
when the town might be captured, the king intended to award
custody of the castle to the younger Despenser and of the town
to his other favourite, Roger D'Amory. It was also said he that
intended to celebrate the victory by revenging himself on
Lancaster, by imprisoning him, for the murder of Gaveston.

Edward's departure to do homage and fealty to the new king
of France during the following summer of 1320 interrupted
hostilities with Lancaster and halted for a while the slide towards a confrontation with the Marchers. In the autumn

parliament things remained quiet as Lancaster failed to attend
the assembly in October, but events in Gower were coming to
the boil. The point of no return was in fact reached on 26
October when John Mowbray entered Gower without a royal
licence and was challenged by the younger Despenser. Hereford
entered the fray and the *Vita* explains the Marcher case over
Gower using him as its mouthpiece. Hereford is made to say
that Despenser

> . . .proposed that the land of Gower, for certain reasons fabricated in
> order to be prejudicial to the laws of the March, should be subordinated
> to the royal treasury, because John Mowbray had entered it without the
> king's licence, although it was held from the king in chief. And the lord
> king who promoted Hugh's designs as far as he could, decided that an
> action should lie against the said John, to the damage of the law of the
> March. John opposed this, as also the earl of Hereford, pointing out the
> general disadvantage, humbly petitioning the lord king that he would not
> introduce a new law contrary to customs used and approved from time
> out of mind. Hugh Despenser stubbornly insisted that the lord king had
> always enjoyed this prerogative in Wales as in England, that no one
> without the king's licence should have entry upon any fee held of the king
> in chief; and, if on the other hand, this should be attempted by anyone,
> the fee so seized should be assigned to the royal treasury. Others cited the
> law of the March and customs which could not be infringed. Hugh took
> no heed of the law and custom of the March, and appeared to accuse the
> barons who alleged such things of talking treason.[13]

There is an echo here of criticism that the king was breaking
his Coronation Oath to keep ancient laws and customs.
Hereford's position as the son of the man who had defended
the law of the March against Edward I is not surprising.

On 14 December 1320, after local resistance, Edward took
Gower into his own hands.[14] The magnate opposition slowly
moved away from court. Audley left at Christmas. Lancaster
refused in January 1321 to attend the eyre in the city of London.
Throughout January and February the king was sending out
orders to the Marchers to keep the peace and not to hold
assemblies. In February, however, it was reported to Despenser
that all was quiet in Glamorgan. He and the king set out for
the Welsh border on 1 March and, as they approached, on
8 March the king ordered the Justice of Wales, Roger Mortimer
of Chirk, to have the royal castles in readiness. Despenser was

also ordering his agent John Inge to do the same with the
Despenser castles and to take hostages from amongst his Welsh
tenants, if trouble seemed threatening. A meeting of Lancaster's
supporters at Pontefract in the last week of February led
observers to think that he would intervene for the Marchers.[15]
Events began to move fast in April. The king took advantage of
Audley's refusal to come to court to seize his lands. They were
in royal hands by 9 April. Hereford replied to the royal summons to meet the king on 5 April that he dared not come for
fear that he would be murdered, an excuse which had previously been used by Lancaster. Hereford demanded a parliament where he and Despenser could put their cases and receive
judgement. Meanwhile, Lancaster should have the keeping of
Despenser and would mainprise to bring him before the king.
To Edward, recollecting promises about the safety of Gaveston,
this must have sounded sinister. He reminded the earl that
Hugh had been accepted as chamberlain in the York parliament by the peers of the realm amongst whom Hereford himself had been. No complaint had been made against Hugh in
parliament and it would be a bad precedent to remove a royal
official without just cause. To Hereford's refusal to obey a royal
summons and his excuses for failing to appear, the king replied
that he had been given a safe-conduct. Edward added that he
had summoned parliament and that it would be against Magna
Carta, his Coronation Oath and the Ordinances to put Despenser in anybody's custody without cause, especially as Despenser
had agreed to appear and answer complaints.[16] Edward
summoned the complainants to a council at Oxford on 10
May.

The Marchers were not interested in answering summonses
to meetings. On 1 May intelligence that Despenser's properties
would be sacked had reached the king and he forbade the
Marchers to touch them. But they began the attack on 4 May.
Newport fell on 8 May after a four days' siege, Cardiff capitulated more quickly on 9 May and Ralph de Gorges, one of
Despenser's favourite knights, was injured in the battle. On
13 May Gower fell. Devastation was widespread. The systematic
destruction carried out suggests the action of vengeful men who
knew that they could not permanently keep these properties

for themselves. Lancaster did not come south although his troops were among those at Cardiff. As holder of Denbigh, Bromfield and Yale he was himself a Marcher lord and there were signs that he was trying to build up a party in Wales.[17] It had been the powerful position of the Marcher lords, backed by their poor and warlike tenantry, which had provided some of the most effective internal opposition to Edward I. The control of the March by a royal favourite was not something which Lancaster could allow to happen. However, Dr Maddicott has recently made it clear that Lancaster was unable to get the same full support from the northern magnates as the Marchers were able to gather together.[18] The meeting at Sherburn summoned by Lancaster for 28 June was not so much a quasi-parliamentary assembly as a military rally and the presence of so many knights was due not to Lancaster's constitutional preoccupations with broadening the basis of support but to the fact that many of them are identifiable as his retainers. Even an assembly so constituted shrank from giving Lancaster support for an unprovoked attack on the Despensers.

Much of the summer passed without any further confrontation between the two camps. Then on 1 August the Marchers set out for London to demand the exile of the Despensers. They arrived dramatically clothed in green but with their right arms covered in yellow and they bore the royal arms in addition to their own. This splendid display was intended to reassure the king of their personal loyalty but was also symbolic of their determination to rid the country of the Despensers.[19]

There are two indications that they did not feel on very safe ground in their prosecution of the Despensers in the summer of 1321. Firstly they felt it necessary to justify their position by bringing with them a tractate containing the properly approved ancient customs when they came to parliament.[20] Its possible contents will be discussed later. The second pointer to their uncertainty was that they thought it necessary to manufacture a completely fictitious charge against the younger Despenser. They accused him of evolving an oath at the time of the Ordinances which stated that homage and fealty could be withdrawn from the king when he acted against reason and that force

should be used against an unreasonable monarch.[21] This was
an attempt to discredit the younger Despenser as a dangerous
revolutionary according to the ideas of the day. It was alleged
that with this traitorous doctrine he attempted to lure Richard
Grey, John Giffard of Brimpsfield and one R. de Shirland from
their allegiance to the king. This charge was apparently
manufactured by the most recent recruit to the baronial cause,
the erstwhile Despenser supporter Bartholomew Badlesmere,
and it was challenged as a fabrication by Hamo Hethe, bishop
of Rochester, who refused henceforth to have anything to do
with the baronial cause.[22]

The devastation of the Despenser lands had put the magnates in a position of temporary control and authority which
could not be permanently sustained, as they had absolutely
no right to most of these properties. They made a show of
some sort of legality by putting Glamorgan under the control
of the husband of one of the younger Gloucester co-heiresses,
Roger D'Amory. Their inability to reconcile their lawful
authority with their actual military success in the March, and
even more their ambiguous position in parliament, which the
king traditionally controlled, may lie behind the ferment of
ideas which produced the *Modus Tenendi Parliamentum*. Professor
J. S. Roskell has recently conjectured that this remarkable tract
was brought by Hereford to the August parliament and this
suggestion would fit best the known facts.[23] The authorship and
purpose of this short document is one of the great puzzles of
medieval English historical literature. It was effectively ignored
by Stubbs and Tout until it was resuscitated by the great Tudor
specialist, Pollard. Its probable origin was traced by Morris
to the reign of Edward II, while its brief but amazing pages
provided material for a book by Maude Clarke.[24] One approach
to the early manuscripts has been to stress the documentary
company which they kept. Thus the *Modus* has been regarded
as a piece of political propaganda by Lancaster's party because
copies of it are often, though not always, found associated
with a tractate on the stewardship of England. This is obviously intended to push Lancaster's claim to exercise the
greatest authority in England, under the king, through his
hereditary claims to that office.[25] It is hard to believe that two

great earls like Lancaster and Hereford were wholly behind the *Modus* with its statement that 'two knights who come to parliament for their counties should have a greater say in conceding or refusing [an aid] to the king than the greatest earl in England'. But the leading enemies of Edward would find very useful a document which attempts to compel the attendance of the king in parliament 'because it is a damnable and dangerous thing to the whole community of parliament and the realm that the king should be absent from parliament'. Also very acceptable would have been the provision for a special committee to adjudicate difficult cases 'if through discord between the king and the magnates themselves, the peace of the realm should be endangered'.[26] Very likely this document was the work of a clever paper politician who had not drafted exactly what his employers needed. Fascinating though it is, in the absence of an official record of the proceedings of the summer parliament of 1321, we do not know whether it affected that assembly. For the purpose of this book it is useful because it reveals how the desperate political situation could create advanced theories of reform in the mind of an undoubtedly well-informed man, probably a churchman, and certainly a man well acquainted with the machinery of the king's central government.

The remaining charges against the Despensers can be discovered from a number of different texts formulated at different stages in the process of trying to obtain their exile.[27] The magnates complained particularly that the younger Despenser had used his position as chamberlain to install his father near the king, although the elder Despenser had not been one of the lords chosen by the York parliament to be in constant attendance on Edward. Together the two Despensers had used their position near the king to 'encroach' on the royal power. The opposition also complained that father and son refused to allow anyone access to the king at all unless one or other of them were present. This charge is substantiated in the pages of the *Vita* and it is interesting because it suggests that their hold over Edward was not wholly secure. The Despensers were said to have replaced good officials by their own corrupt nominees, and in particular, to have appointed justices who did not know the law of the land, among whom Hugh Despenser the Elder

himself, Ralph Basset, Ralph Camoys and John Inge were
named. They added the serious charge that they had used false
jurors to pervert the law and oust Hereford, John Giffard of
Brimpsfield and Robert Mohaut from their lands. They
charged the younger Despenser with murder and usurping
royal authority. The charge of murder concerned the killing of
Llywelyn Bren whom the Marchers had delivered to a royal
agent. Despenser had then taken him and executed him at
Cardiff. The charges of illegally taking Audley's and D'Amory's
lands and of purposing to obtain the whole Gloucester inheritance were repeated. They also claimed that the elder Despenser had illegally obtained custody of the lands of the earl of
Warwick, although by grant of parliament Edward had
promised the dead earl's executors that they should control
them. They attacked the two Despensers for being party to the
unreasonable confiscation of Gower for which the heir, John
Mowbray, ought to have been allowed seisin by a reasonable
fine. They accused them of misappropriating confiscated
Templar properties and of demanding a fine from ecclesiastics
before they were allowed to recover their temporalities. They
rounded off the charges with the specific case of John Latchley
who was alleged to have been illegally removed by the younger
Despenser from Colchester gaol, where he had been imprisoned
for an offence against Lady de Vescy, the sister of Henry de
Beaumont and of Louis de Beaumont, bishop of Durham.
Latchley, in return for his freedom, had to hand over his lands
and pay a fine to the younger Despenser.[28]

Faced with a determined and united baronage, the king's
usual main supporters were for the time being quite helpless.
One of the most reliable was probably Edward's youngest
half-brother, Edmund of Woodstock, and on 18 July, a few
days before his twentieth birthday, he was promoted to the
earldom of Kent and endowed with suitable additional revenues. But he was of no importance politically. Pembroke was the
ablest of the earls who might normally have been expected to
rally to the king's side, but in this crisis he played an ambiguous
role which earned him the distrust of the king and of the
Despensers, as Pembroke discovered to his cost after the royalist
victory in 1322. Arundel, who had recently become the younger

Despenser's brother-in-law, Warenne and Richmond, had wealth and many armed followers, but they were likely to be helpful only if they were offered some convincing assurance of success.

Pembroke seems to have given an oath to the opposition to support the exiling of the two Despensers.[29] He now advised the king to accede to their demands and warned him that otherwise he could lose his throne. Bereft of support and faced by this threat, Edward on 14 August came to parliament and with a grim face agreed to the exile of the Despensers. There was no precedent for exiling members of the English aristocracy. The violence of baronial hatred had led to this improvisation which before had been used only for foreign favourites like the Poitevins under Henry III and for Gaveston. On 20 August the king had to pardon the barons for attacking the Despensers' lands. The baronial revolt against his favourites may have been accompanied by a bureaucratic one. It is difficult to believe that Stapeldon's resignation, or dismissal, from the treasurership on 25 August[30] did not have something to do with their exile. Since he did not later on support their return wholeheartedly we can only suppose that he was temporarily out of favour with both sides. Edward was hard up at this time and did not have the money to fight an effective campaign against this formidable coalition of enemies.[31] As events of the next few months were to show, this was not by itself a decisive weakness. If the king could divide his enemies and fight a succession of geographically limited campaigns, this sort of strategy could be financed. But the time for this had not yet come, in August 1321.

The Despensers did not entirely disappear. The elder Hugh withdrew to Bordeaux, but the younger Despenser, under the protection of Edward's loyal men of the Cinque Ports, played pirate in the Channel, robbed a Genoese vessel, killing its crew, and attacked Southampton.[32] The king remained in the south of England working out the clever strategy by which he was presently to recover his favourites' company. Partly out of guile and partly through financial necessity, he chose to pick off his opponents one by one. He started with the nearest,

Bartholomew Badlesmere, son of the influential Justiciar of Chester and favourite of Edward I, Guncelin Badlesmere. He was an important Kent landowner who, earlier on, had been a retainer of the Clares and for a time had transferred his loyalty to Despenser. He had become steward of the household while Despenser was chamberlain. A marriage alliance between his daughter and Roger Mortimer of Wigmore's son in 1316 may have been responsible for the gradual loosening of his ties with the Despensers. In June 1321, when on a royal mission to the Lancastrian opposition meeting at Sherburn, he was persuaded to join their cause. In the autumn of 1321 Badlesmere was particularly easy prey for the loyal forces. His chief castle was in central Kent where he could easily be cut off from the rest of England especially as several of the king's leading supporters had extensive estates in Kent and the adjoining counties.

On 26 September Edward ordered Badlesmere to surrender Tonbridge castle, one of the former Clare fortresses of which he was a temporary custodian. Badlesmere refused. Instead he hastened to munition his chief Kentish residence at Leeds castle and, after making a pilgrimage to Canterbury to the tomb of Thomas Becket, the famous opponent of royal tyranny, he rejoined the Marchers at Oxford.[33] Probably he would have stayed to defend his castle and called for Marcher help if he had had a suspicion of what the king would do next. Edward himself came into Kent, made the same pilgrimage to the tomb of Becket and moved east to the Isle of Thanet to meet the younger Despenser. But he sent the queen to Badlesmere's castle to demand admittance hoping, no doubt, to enter it without the expense and trouble of a military campaign. Badlesmere's wife was not so easily fooled and refused Isabella admittance, as her husband had instructed her to admit nobody. Edward's plot certainly placed Isabella at risk. Fights broke out between her servants and the castle garrison and a number of the queen's servants were killed. For once Edward appeared clearly in the right and this insult to his wife may have compelled former waverers, like Pembroke, to rally to him. One report has it that the Marchers refused to come to Leeds out of respect for Isabella.[34] On 17 October a preliminary force under

Pembroke, Norfolk and Richmond arrived to besiege the castle. Edward himself came and obviously found the experience somewhat boring, for he sent for his hunting dogs.[35] However, he subsequently fixed the date of the opening of the civil war at the beginning of the siege of Leeds. He procured such limited money as he had (*c.* £600) for the besieging army and on 23 October reinforcements arrived. Most of Badlesmere's other lands were in the hands of royal keepers from 28 October.[36] The castle itself fell on 31 October. Now followed reprisals which astonished and terrified Edward's opponents. Its garrison, headed by Badlesmere's knight Walter Culpeper, was executed on the spot. This was apparently the first application of martial law to internal discords. Badlesmere's wife and children were sent to the Tower.

The Marchers had never moved to relieve the castle. This was partly because they were halted by a delegation led by the archbishop of Canterbury and the bishop of London together with the ubiquitous Pembroke. They offered to mediate with the king.[37] How far this was a deliberate delaying tactic organised by Edward, it is impossible to say. The rebels may also have been halted in the Thames Valley by the news that Lancaster would not join them. He would fight no battles for Badlesmere. There was reported to be a feud between them. Lancaster, by virtue of being also earl of Leicester, was hereditary steward of England. He believed that this gave him the unchallengeable right to appoint the working, temporary stewards of the household. Badlesmere, who had become steward at the time when his erstwhile ally Despenser became chamberlain in 1318, was hardly Lancaster's choice. If this was the reason for the failure of the Marchers to go to Leeds, then ultimately their cause was lost through Lancaster's feud with Badlesmere.

The execution of the Leeds garrison opens a new episode in English history when opponents of the king could seriously expect to lose their heads if they were defeated. At the time it gave Edward the assurance to recall the Despensers. As a magnate council or a full parliament was neither practicable in a country fighting a civil war nor desirable, since Edward's enemies were likely to dominate it, an officially inspired appeal to the loyalist clergy was thought sufficient justification to recall

them. It proved by no means easy to obtain.[38] Edward's creature, Archbishop Walter Reynolds, who had recently proved so
useful in delaying the Marcher advance to Kent, summoned a
convocation to Canterbury for 1 December. He managed to
collect only five of the seventeen possible bishops. There were
naturally defaulters from among the staunch supporters of the
Marchers like Adam Orleton, bishop of Hereford, a close friend
of the Mortimers, and Henry Burghersh, bishop of Lincoln, the
nephew of Badlesmere. Murimuth, the chronicler, in his
usual tight-lipped way, blamed the lack of attendance on the
danger of the roads, without specifying whether it was troops
or the inclement winter weather which constituted the danger.[39]
He also blamed the shortness of time allowed between the
arrival of the summons, sent out on 14 November, and the date
of the assembly's meeting, two weeks later. Edward did not
give up. He sent letters to twelve of the absentee bishops
requesting their opinion on the proposed reversal of the
Despensers' exile.[40] He received at least two replies which did
not give him *carte blanche* for recalling them. One, not surprisingly, was from the saintly Thomas Cobham, bishop of Worcester. The other, perhaps because of his removal from office
in August, was from Walter Stapeldon, bishop of Exeter. He
advised the king to put the matter before parliament since the
Despensers had been exiled in parliament. Edward was furious
with Stapeldon and ordered him to send a different reply and
come to the king at once.[41] This episode should be borne in
mind when one considers how far Stapeldon was a creature of
the Despensers and how far he was simply a loyal royal admini-
strator. The Despensers, from their refuges, duly petitioned the
bishops for revocations of their exile. Such bishops as were
present, influenced perhaps by the presence of Richmond,
Arundel and the king's secretary, Baldock, and a royal order to
do nothing *rege inconsulto*, responded favourably.[42]

The Marchers were meanwhile making a hasty visit to
Lancaster in the north to try to obtain more active support
and a counterpetition was sent to the convocation demanding
that the parliamentary exile of the Despensers be upheld.
Lancaster accused the Despensers of piracy and charged the
king with supporting them in it. He also accused them of seizing

magnates' lands in breach of Magna Carta. He gave the king until 20 December to answer but Edward had done with negotiating with him.

As soon as he had received convocation's favourable ruling, Edward recalled the Despensers. He revoked their exile on 8 December and justified this by quoting Magna Carta and his own Coronation Oath. The same day he set out for Cirencester and a military campaign.[43] At Cirencester he spent Christmas and received the submission of the first of his Marcher enemies, John Hastings, lord of Abergavenny, who had never been a particularly recalcitrant foe and was married to younger Hugh's sister. On 27 December he left Cirencester to attack John Giffard of Brimpsfield's main castle and from there he moved north. He sent a detachment of troops to try to take the numerous castles of the Berkeleys clustered together around Berkeley castle and on 28 December a formal order for their seizure was issued together with one for Giffard's lands.[44] Corresponding orders for the seizure of other Marcher lands were not sent out until 4 January.[45] Whether this was because he hoped a few of them might still join him is not clear. The smallness of the sums sent out from London and the necessity of loans to pay for his household requirements together with the need to pay out huge sums to Pembroke, Arundel, Warenne and Richmond, meant that Edward was still very short of cash. The arrangement for financing the campaign have a very hand-to-mouth look about them.[46] One small payment ordered on 13 December is particularly interesting. It was made by a warrant of privy seal issued at Newbury in Berkshire as the king was moving westwards. It asked the Bardi of Florence to pay £12 12s. 8d. for the cost of military equipment delivered to Gruffydd Llwyd, a favoured North Wales notable.[47] It suggests that he had been sent from the king's camp back to North Wales to organise the attack from there on the Marcher barons. This was an integral part of Edward's subsequent strategy. Alternatively it might merely mean that Edward was sending military supplies to Gruffydd in North Wales. Either way it confirms that the king was behind the preparations for a surprise Welsh attack on the castles of the rebel Marcher lords. This supplements other evidence. A month before the king had sent mandates out both to Gruffydd and to his nephew Rhys ap Gruffydd, a South Wales potentate, to levy the Welsh and prepare to fight. It all clearly formed part of a well-formulated strategy.[48]

Edward's route north was difficult because the Marchers took the royal town of Bridgnorth, strategically based on a high cliff dominating the western bank of the river Severn. They also destroyed the bridge, which made it impossible to cross the river swollen with the winter's flood waters. Seeking another crossing, Edward moved north to Shrewsbury, where he was forced to raise a loan of £400 from local merchants.[49] It was apparently at Shrewsbury that he received news of the successful Welsh attacks on Marcher lands. By this time, Mold, Chirk, Clun, Welshpool and Holt had been taken. Gruffydd Llwyd and his men had devastated the Mortimer lands and intervened so decisively in Brecon that even the earl of Hereford's most faithful officials had to submit to royal authority.[50] His nephew, Rhys ap Gruffydd, a favoured Welshman of the south, had similarly intervened with a forty men-at-arms and 3000 infantry in Cantref Bychan, Gower, Narberth and Builth.[51] One can imagine the delight of these Welsh leaders who were now able to practise their ancient feud against the Marcher lords under the patronage of the king of England – and in his pay! It was the first time since Wales had been conquered that an English king had seen the potential of using his Welsh subjects against his magnate enemies in this way. The result of these activities was that the Marchers were left without the wherewithal to fight and their communications with their castles were cut off. Not surprisingly the Welsh petitioned, using strong language, against the restoration of the Mortimers. They claimed that the Mortimers, if restored, would destroy them and that they would not be able to stay in their lands.[52]

The Mortimers surrendered on 22 January at Shrewsbury, after safe-conducts to come to the king had been granted to them. They had hoped for, and perhaps been promised, better treatment, but they were sent away under heavy guard to prison in the Tower. At least, contrary to the usual policy of Edward and the Despensers, their lives were spared. This may have been because the younger Despenser, a sworn foe of the

Mortimers, had not yet rejoined the king. Hereford, who had also been about to surrender, on hearing of their fate fled to Gloucester which was still holding out. The king slowly followed in his tracks taking some of the Welsh, who had rejoined him, with him. On 6 February, when Gloucester had capitulated, the king received Maurice Berkeley's submission. His castles had offered more successful resistance than anybody else's. Berkeley and the elder Audley were incarcerated at Wallingford. The younger Audley continued his flight with Hereford and D'Amory. Their plan was to rejoin their last unscathed ally, Lancaster. Until this point, he had sent no help.

On 13 February the king summoned additional levies to meet at Coventry on 28 February to proceed against the remaining rebels and the Scots.[53] The rebellion in the March had not been completely suppressed. In the second half of February, Gruffydd Llwyd and Giles Beauchamp attacked Lancaster's lands in Denbigh. By 26 February these were safely in their hands as royal custodians. Perhaps because of these vestiges of resistance, Edward was very unsure of the adequacy of his military forces and clearly uneasy at the prospect of facing the most powerful rebel of all, his cousin Lancaster. On 16 February he appealed to the clergy to send troops.[54] More surprisingly still, on 18 February he wrote to the towns of Agenais asking them to send troops as quickly as possible, as they had offered. He even asked the king of France for soldiers![55] Another factor which accounted for his nervousness was the knowledge that many Englishmen were certainly refusing the royal summons to fight. Edward ordered a commission to enquire into these acts of disobedience.[56] He was now, however, less troubled by shortage of money, partly because he was beginning to receive money from the rebel lands, and the treasuries and provisions of the Marchers helped to pay for the campaign against Lancaster.[57]

The muster date was later changed to 5 March. The timetable of at least one royal supporter is known. William Roos of Helmsley received the summons in faraway Freston in Lincolnshire within four days, on 18 February. He took a week to collect together a substantial contingent of squires with 60

C

hobelars. He arrived at the king's camp at Burton on Trent on 1 March.[58]

On his way north the king took Lancaster's great castle of Kenilworth, apparently without a struggle, though its great moated area, which could be flooded like those at Berkeley and Caerphilly, could have made it capable of enduring a long siege. On 2 March the king was joined by the Despensers at Lichfield. They brought their own troops. Lancaster, on the other hand, was about this time deserted by the commander of his household knights, Robert Holland. The latter was motivated perhaps by fear for the safety of his daughter, who was a hostage of the king. Holland was followed in his desertion by a large contingent of Lancaster's men.[59] By 9 March the king was at Tutbury, which Lancaster had abandoned on his flight towards his most northerly castle of Dunstanburgh. This flight northwards confirmed the impression, perhaps substantiated by treasonable correspondence with Robert Bruce allegedly found at Tutbury, that he was in league with the Scots. In his flight he encountered his former retainer Andrew Harclay who was proceeding south to meet the king with the Cumberland levies. Lancaster attempted to win them over but they remained loyal to the king. Lancaster's way was blocked over the river Ure and he had to fight. Hereford was killed in the battle and Lancaster was captured soon after it. A letter of the Pope of 19 February which had exhorted Edward to maintain his reconciliation with the barons was swiftly followed by one exhorting him to ascribe the victory to God.[60]

This prompt appearance of Harclay's Cumberland contingent and other northern shire levies was a testimony to Edward's power and Lancaster's unpopularity in the north of England. This is underlined by the defection of Lancaster's retainers and some sources place another former Lancastrian stalwart, William Latimer, by the side of Harclay at Boroughbridge.[61] Even without these defections Edward could not have been defeated on this occasion. In addition to his own household followers, he had the shire levies of northern England. These northerners may have been hostile to Lancaster because of his rumoured alliance with the Scots, who had so often devastated their homes. Also with him were the troops of the loyal earls and of his favourites, the Despensers. The second half of the reign is the story of how this military advantage was lost. Having removed the Lancastrian opposition which had recurrently threatened to paralyse the realm, the royal adherents among the magnates had made possible an even more dangerous phenomenon, a royal tyranny.

The aftermath of civil war:
Imprisonments and executions

'Oh Calamity. To see men lately dressed in purple and fine linen now attired in rags, bound and imprisoned in chains', wrote the author of *Vita Edwardi* at the sight of the men imprisoned after Boroughbridge.[1] The Bridlington chronicler greeted the terrible executions which followed the battle with a quotation from the Apocalypse.[2] The series of executions of the king's opponents began a reign of terror in England. It was the first time in a fifteen-year-long rule, dogged hitherto by opposition to the king's favourites and his policies, that Edward had been in such an unchallengeable position.

The execution of Lancaster in its political significance stands apart from the others. For the first time a member of the highest rank of the English aristocracy and of the royal family was executed for his rebellion and treason against the king. Lancaster had been charged with treason before his participation in the battle of Boroughbridge. On 11 March 1322 the king, together with the earls of Kent, Richmond, Pembroke, Arundel and Atholl, had denounced the rebels, in their absence, as traitors.[3] After his capture Lancaster was taken first to York and then to his own castle of Pontefract. On 20 March he appeared before a commission of peers. The *Brut* chronicler attributed Lancaster's abrupt trial to the Despensers. According to him, it was they who had sought 'how and in what manner the good earl should be dead without judgement of his peers'. This was only one expression of the contemporary unease that he was illegally done to death. The Lanercost chronicle was equally explicit in its condemnation of the regime's executions, carried out 'without holding a parliament or taking the advice of the majority'. Such unease was predictable when one

considers the novel process used against him.[4] At his trial he
was allowed to make no defence. He apparently exclaimed that
'this is a powerful court, and great in authority, where no
answer is heard nor any excuse admitted.'[5] Lancaster was in
fact being subjected to the usual summary process of martial
law during which the defendant was never allowed to make a
defence once his offence had been recognised by witnesses. It is
very probable that what Lancaster tried to say at his trial was
the same retort that his apologists used when seeking in 1327 the
nullification of the process against him: that martial law was
illegal under these circumstances, firstly because, since the
courts were sitting it was not definable as 'time of war', and
secondly that the king had never unfurled his banners against
the earl.[6] This is confirmed by the Bridlington chronicler who
stated that the king had been about to unfurl his banners after
crossing the Trent in pursuit of Lancaster when he had been
dramatically stopped from doing so by the younger Despenser.[7]
The favourite's fear may have been that if time of war were
proclaimed and the king lost the last battle then he and his
father would immediately have lost their heads under martial
law. Dr Keen has shown that these legal proceedings were not
a perversion of the common law, 'isolated and unconstitutional
travesties of justice, but present an unbroken series of trials in
which a more or less regular procedure was applied consistently,
in accordance with the rules of known law'.[8] These rules had
not, however, been normally applied to members of the English
aristocracy for their civil disturbances and, if the evidence of
the Bridlington chronicler is correct, strictly speaking Lancaster was illegally done to death, as martial law should not
have been used. However, since in the eyes of contemporaries
such an execution of a nobleman was unprecedented, their
unease was understandable. To the Lanercost chronicler,
Lancaster was executed 'without parliament and without
consideration of the majority or wiser council'.[9]

Lancaster was executed with such speed and lack of publicity
that many chroniclers were left in doubt as to who had tried
him or, as we should probably say, were present at his court
martial. The *Eulogium Historiarum* names only three.[10] These
were the elder Despenser, Robert Baldock, and the earl of

Arundel, whose heir was married to the younger Despenser's daughter. At the other extreme the Bridlington chronicler names seven earls: Kent, Richmond, Pembroke, Surrey, Arundel, Atholl and Angus, 'together with barons, bannerets and other magnates of the realm sitting'.[11] Even the official record is curiously unreliable. It omits to mention that Sir Robert Mabelthorp, a royal justice, was present although *Le Livere de Reis de Brittanie* includes his name. However, it was he who gave the judgement in the king's name, for he subsequently found it necessary to obtain a pardon for this, three months after Edward's deposition.[12]

It is probable that Lancaster's condemnation as a traitor had only been pronounced five days before Boroughbridge because it was only then that Edward had become convinced that he had evidence of his alliance with the Scots, which was allegedly found in Tutbury castle after its capture. A long list of charges against him was read out at Pontefract but his treason really consisted in this alliance. Civil disturbances and even rebellion against the king had not before been grounds for executing a magnate, only for dispossessing him. John, in spite of his brutality, had not, with one exception, executed his baronial opponents. Henry III, after the civil war which ended in the battle of Evesham, did not execute those who survived the battle. One chronicler remarked that the execution in 1321 of the Leeds garrison had terrified the king's baronial opponents and well it might, for it was unprecedented.[13] The English monarchy had clearly been brutalised by the serious Scottish and Welsh rebellions against its rule. The novel punishment of hanging, drawing and quartering had invariably been employed against defeated rebels from these countries. Before the Despensers were entrenched in power it was only used against noblemen in two cases. The first was against Sir Thomas Turberville in 1295 for treasonable collaboration with the French. The second occasion was against Gilbert Middleton in 1317 after he had robbed and humiliated two cardinals. The application of these penalties on a wide scale was as new as the use of martial law against members of the nobility. The baronial point of view, in direct conflict with martial law's application to civil discord, was, to adapt the last clause of

Magna Carta of 1215, claiming that the baronage had the right to coerce a king who did not rule according to law.

Edward also adopted the novel expedient of despatching his victims for execution to the areas where they held lordship. This was intended to terrorise their followers. It did that but also caused scandal and horror.[14] A group of northern retainers of Lancaster was put to death at York on the same day as Lancaster met his end at Pontefract. They were William Touchet, Warin de Lisle, Thomas Mauduit, Henry Bradbourne, William Fitz William and William Cheney. William Sully, formerly a household knight of Isabella, Roger Burghfield, John Page, Ralph Ellington, John Mowbray, the claimant to Gower, Roger Clifford, a Marcher and a northern lord, Jocelyn D'Eyville, the descendant of John D'Eiville, the rebel leader of the Disinherited under Henry III, and Hugh Lovel were despatched at the same time. For some reason three of Lovel's squires were executed with him. In other parts of the country, Henry de Montfort and Henry Wilington were executed at Bristol, John Giffard of Brimpsfield, a cousin of Despenser, at Gloucester as was Henry le Tyeys, from a wealthy Lincolnshire family and brother-in-law of another victim Warin de Lisle. Francis Aldham was executed at Windsor and Bartholomew Ashburnham at Cambridge. In Wales Stephen Baret, who had presumably led the resistance to the Despensers in Gower, was executed there and William Fleming, another Lancastrian retainer, was executed at Cardiff.[15]

One chronicler clearly differentiates between the execution of Lancaster by decapitation because of his royal blood and the hanging of the rest. A detailed description in a local chronicle of the execution of Badlesmere conveys the terrible manner of his death. He was dragged by a horse a huge distance through Canterbury to the cross roads at Bleen. There he was hanged and afterwards decapitated. His head was stuck on the Burgate of Canterbury to remind those passing under it of the penalties for rebellion.[16] It is possible that John Giffard of Brimpsfield was also decapitated since, though no other member of the large Giffard family was executed, a decapitated skeleton has subsequently been found in a tomb of the right

date in Boyton church.[17] Some, however, certainly died by
hanging, because in 1324 the clergy finally persuaded the king,
by petition in parliament, to allow their rotting corpses to be
cut down.[18]

The seemingly indiscriminate choice of victims was probably
as terrifying as their manner of death. The Marchers who had
surrendered on terms months before Boroughbridge were
spared but condemned to imprisonment. They could hardly
be accused of allying with the Scots which was basically the
most serious charge which could be levied against those who
had reached Boroughbridge. However, there were exceptions
even in the treatment of the Marchers. Roger D'Amory, dying
of wounds received in the battle, may have been pardoned
because Edward gave him an honourable burial. On the other
hand, Roger Mortimer of Wigmore, who had surrendered on
terms at Shrewsbury, was suddenly condemned to death after a
year's imprisonment. It was to avoid death that he escaped
from the Tower.[19] The younger Hugh Audley, who had been
captured sometime after Boroughbridge, although he had been
a leading opponent of the Despensers, was spared because his
wife, Edward's niece and Eleanor Despenser's sister, pleaded
for him.[20] Historians have managed to sort out from the
proceedings against the Contrariants essential stages in the
development of the English state trial and law of treason. To
contemporaries the crown had broken all customary conventions in dealing with its opponents and in arbitrarily executing
some of them.

The chroniclers give different numbers of those imprisoned.
The author of *Vita* says that 100 were imprisoned after Boroughbridge alone.[21] Another gives a more exact figure of 62.[22] In
fact the number is difficult to give exactly as some, like John
Charlton, soon made their peace and received back their
lands. However lists of those in prison occasionally come to
light. This was usually when they were being transferred from
one place to another, which the king repeatedly did for greater
security. Roger Mortimer of Chirk and Roger Mortimer of
Wigmore, together with Thomas Gurney, Jocelin D'Eiville,
John Fitz Simond, Hugh Eland, Edmund Darel, John Vaux,
Bartholomew Burghersh, John de la Beche, Walter Selby,

Geoffrey de la Mare, John Page, Richard Peshale, Henry Ashburn, John, the son of John Mowbray, and Giles Badlesmere, were kept in the Tower in February 1323.[23] Maurice Berkeley and the elder Hugh Audley were kept in Wallingford. Others were scattered in more obscure castles throughout the country. John Blaket was at Sandale, John Wroxhale at Conisborough, though both towards the end of the reign were moved to Windsor, presumably because these far fortresses were in danger of being taken. At this same late date William Denham and John Kensington were sent to the strong fortress of Corfe and William Hedersete from the Tower to Castle Barnard.[24] We do not know how these men fared in prison. Most were allowed 3d. per day for their maintenance,[25] which would have meant a poor diet by the standards of a nobleman in the fourteenth century. Roger Mortimer of Chirk, exceptionally, received 6d. a day. He died before the end of the regime, as did Maurice Berkeley after attempting a dramatic escape from Wallingford castle.

The prolonged imprisonment of noblemen was strange enough. More curious, brutal and seemingly unnecessary was the detention for long periods of the wives and children of the Contrariants. The queen herself had to remind the administration to pay for the maintenance in the Tower of Lady Mortimer of Wigmore.[26] She was separated from her children, who were scattered about the country. The daughters, Joan, Margaret and Isabel were despatched to the priories of Sempringham in Lincolnshire, Shuldham in Norfolk and Chicksands in Bedfordshire respectively. Two of her sons were imprisoned in Windsor while a third was in the custody of the sheriff of Hampshire.[27] In May 1324 they were reunited in Odiham castle, a strong fortress belonging to the elder Despenser. At Windsor the two Mortimer boys had the company of the three sons of the dead earl of Hereford, the king's own nephews. Happily, at least in diet, they evidently did better than their elders. They received in all ten shillings a day for food and their table included lamb, pork, mackerel, salmon, lampreys, capon and sturgeon.[28] The wives and children of other Contrariants were treated infinitely worse. John Wroxhale's wife, imprisoned with him at Conisborough, received only 9d. a day for herself and an unspecified number of children. Isabel de la Beche and Margaret Blaket received even less, at 6d. a day.[29] One hopes that the allotment of money was on the basis of the number of their children rather than social status. Equally unprecedented was the imprisonment of elderly relations. Margaret Mortimer, mother of Roger, may have used her liberty to stir up trouble at Wigmore,[30] but one wonders whether the aged countess of Lincoln, mother of Alice, countess of Lancaster, could have done much harm. She was carried off to prison with her daughter.[31]

It is probable that some statement about the executions was made at the York parliament which met shortly afterwards on 19 May, but there is no reference to any such statement in the surviving official agenda for this meeting.[32] An unofficial source, a fragment of a chronicle, states that the parliament's first business was the revocation of the process of exile passed against the Despensers in the Contrariant-controlled parliament of August 1321. The second item, the chronicler maintains, was the formal recording of the process against Lancaster.[33]

One of the notable features of this York parliament was the extension of its membership to include representatives from two areas hitherto not represented which had given Edward strongest support in the recent troubles. Writs of summons were sent out to the Cinque Ports, whose sailors had helped the younger Despenser during his exile, and to the Principality of Wales, which had furnished the troops who had brought the Marchers to heel. But the magnate section of the assembly must have seemed a strange place, with so many familiar faces of the old king's old opponents missing because they were either in prison or had been executed.

The official agenda for the York parliament states that the first two items of business would be the repeal of the Ordinances followed by the incorporation of their 'good points' into a statute. The repeal allowed the king, among other things, to levy again the 'new custom' on the imports and exports of foreign merchants, which was sure to add several thousand pounds to the king's ordinary revenue. It began to be collected again on 21 July 1322.[34] Not everything on the agenda was implemented. Item four points to one notable failure and behind this may lie considerable opposition. Since the discontinuance of the general eyres after 1294 nothing had been done to exploit for the king the goods of fugitives and felons. At York the king was proposing to create new arrangements for this purpose, so that he could derive an annual revenue from these windfalls. He was affronting important vested interests among the local officials and other notables. That this was a highly contentious matter is confirmed by its subsequent history. In 1337 Edward III tried again to exploit these potential assets and instituted a preliminary inquiry into what had been happening to confiscated chattels. The next parliament, a few months later, forced him to discontinue the inquiry and to abandon his proposals.[35] All this suggests that even at the York parliament of 1322 Edward II may have been unable to overcome all opposition.

Modern historians of this assembly have been specially concerned with a general statute enacted by it. In this Statute of York Edward II provided that there should be no restraint whatsoever upon him for the future: 'And it [is decreed] that henceforth and for ever at all times every kind of ordinance or provision made under any authority or commission whatsoever by subjects of our lord the king or his heirs relative to the royal power of our lord the king or of his heirs or contrary to the estate of the crown, shall be null and have no validity or force whatever; but that matters which are to be determined for the estate of the king and of his heirs and for the estate of the kingdom and of the people shall be treated, granted and established in parliament by our lord the king and with the consent of the prelates, earls and barons, and of the commonalty of the kingdom as has been accustomed in times past.'[36] A vast literature has developed around these words,[37] but there is little doubt what the priorities in Edward's mind were: the statute gave him, through its wide terminology, licence to denounce any independent part being played in his affairs or those of the kingdom by anybody else. Instead 'the statutes and establishment duly made by our lord the king and his ancestors prior to the said ordinance shall remain in force'. These statutes and establishments are claimed to have been made by the king and his ancestors without any reference to the consent of anyone else and from the formal, legal point of view, there was, of course, no reason why participation by anyone else should have been mentioned. But it is clear that Edward was expressing a very authoritarian outlook and that the 'consent' which he was prepared to seek from the prelates, earls, barons and the community of the realm was preferably limited to formal consent. There is no reason to imagine that because consent was sought, dissent would be lightly tolerated, at least in important matters. The probable alternative to consent which Edward implied was silence. As long as the Scottish war continued Edward still needed parliaments to secure new taxes but after the conclusion of a truce with the Scots in the spring of 1323 even this necessity disappeared. The destruction of his enemies and the possession of their vast lands had given him an unusually strong financial and political position: lack of consent became irrelevant.

Throughout his reign Edward II, like all English kings down to 1688, considered his parliaments a highly regrettable necessity. He postponed or cancelled them whenever possible, limited them to dealing with specific issues or stopped them from transacting inconvenient items of business. In 1311 he had delayed the parliament which confirmed the Ordinances by going on a pilgrimage to Canterbury. The next year the Lent parliament was postponed because of his absence. In 1313 he stayed away from one parliament, using the excuse of a possibly fictitious illness, and deliberately came so late to the next that by the time that he arrived the magnates had stormed away in anger. He stayed away as long as possible from the Lincoln parliament of 1316. It was an event, therefore, thought worthy of comment by an observer when Edward listened patiently to discussions in an assembly in 1320.

Until 1321 the baronial opposition might use parliaments as convenient occasions for putting pressure upon the king, but they were not interested in vindicating the importance of parliament as an institution. The very idea that it was on the way to becoming an institution is an invention of modern scholars. 'As Tout points out, it is remarkable from one angle how little parliament came into the story of opposition to Edward II. Conflict revolved principally around influence at court, the personnel and conduct of the king's ministers and the composition of the king's council.'[38] This is especially true of the Commons' part, even though after 1311 it was becoming fairly frequent to include the elected representatives in parliaments. They seem to have done nothing more than agree with whoever happened to predominate at any one moment. This is confirmed by the careful statistics of Sir Goronwy Edwards which show that there is nothing to distinguish the run-of-the-mill membership of the parliament which exiled the Despensers from that which registered their recall in 1322.[39] As has been already noted, the only remarkable difference lay, of course, in the composition of the magnate section of the assembly.

The schedule surviving for the York parliament of 1322 shows that even in this assembly, which was intended to register the king's victory over his opponents, the king wanted the council to consider beforehand the issues which were to arise 'in order to allow the people who come to the parliament to depart the sooner'.[40] Reluctance to hold parliaments at all characterises the period 1322–6. Of the five assemblies summoned between the York parliament of 1322 and that which deposed Edward in January 1327, Edward changed the place and date of meeting of three of them. Two were limited assemblies without burgesses to which the term 'parliament' would cease to be applied in official records after 1327. In 1325 a royal memorandum, which has recently come to light, differentiated quite clearly between the sort of assembly (consultative) which the king preferred and a proper parliament which he did not want, when he wrote that the magnates should be summoned 'pur conseiller et noun pur parlement'.[41] He merely wanted advice as to whether he should or should not cross to France to render homage to the French king. Writing of the events of the same year the author of the *Vita* commented on Edward's dislike of parliaments: 'The harshness of the king has today increased so much that no-one, however great and wise, dares to cross his will. Thus parliaments, colloquies and councils decide nothing these days. For the nobles of the realm, terrified by threats and the penalties inflicted on others, let the king's will have free-play.' He forcefully finishes this bitter critique with the words, 'Thus today, will conquers reason. For whatever pleases the king, although lacking in reason, has the force of law'.[42] If this regime had persisted very much longer parliament might have virtually disappeared from the vocabulary of English politics.

6

The aftermath of civil war:
Confiscations and the territorial settlement

The royal victory of 1322 meant a social dislocation and territorial revolution which has hitherto passed without much
comment. Only detailed research into the landholding position
county by county could bring its significance and long-term
effects into sharp relief but the general picture of momentous
upheaval is clear.[1] It was accompanied by widespread plundering of Contrariants' property and a general breakdown of law
and order. Riots and disturbances occurred which were apparently unconnected with the main civil war of 1321–2. A striking
example was the attack by several hundred Cambridge towns-
folk on the colleges some time shortly before May 1322. This
was obviously the culmination of a good deal of town–gown
troubles. A crowd led by the mayor himself 'attacked and
spoiled divers inns of the masters and scholars of the university,
climbed the walls, broke the doors and windows, mounted by
ladders into the solers and assaulted the said masters and
scholars, imprisoned some, mutilated others and killed Walter
de Shelton, parson of the church of Welton, carried away all
they could of the books and other goods of the masters and
scholars, so that no person dare to go to the University of the
said town for study'. It is true that Edward II had called the
universities of Oxford and Cambridge the 'twin jewels in his
crown' and that he favoured the scholars of King's College,
inviting them to spend Christmas with him, but these disturbances were probably not directed specifically against the
king's protégés. This is rather an example of the complete
breakdown of law and order giving men an opportunity to vent
old feuds unconnected with the main civil war.[2] Similar
dangerous but apparently unconnected incidents were the

attacks on Hanseatic merchants on both the east and the south coasts.[3] Like the royalists, who found it necessary to request special commissions into the devastation of their lands by Contrariants, the scholars of Cambridge and the Hanseatic merchants only secured their commissions of enquiry in the early summer.

In the meantime the king issued the most sweeping commissions to capture suspected rebels. The names of their adherents were also enrolled on the rolls of the court of King's Bench and they provide us with more than a thousand suspects with huge concentrations in the Marches of Wales.[4] This is not surprising since presumably retainers of the Contrariant leaders were automatically suspect. In particular Edward regarded Lancashire and Cornwall as peculiarly disaffected.[5] These extensive proscriptions of rebels, mostly very obscure people and some of them poor and landless men from whom the king could not even collect a fine, resulted in at least 117 enduring seizures of land.[6] Few of the king's opponents made an easy peace with him. The cases of John Charlton, Bogo de Knoville and Robert Wateville were exceptional: although they were fined, they were employed at court on confidential missions and in important military functions. The majority of those who escaped with their lives and, after paying fines, recovered some or all of their properties, remained fundamentally unreconciled to the new regime.

It was only on 8 July, nearly three months after the battle of Boroughbridge, that the king announced a procedure for dealing with those whom he had captured or who had surrendered to him. On that date he ordered a powerful commission of the Chancellor, the Chief Justices of the two benches, the Keeper of the Rolls and a King's Serjeant to deal with the 'important prisoners'.[7] The head of the commission was instructed that he should deal with the prisoners as follows:

> He should receive security by their oath and bond of loyal behaviour towards the king and none the less by mainpernors under a penalty according to the forms below written, and that after such securities have been made he should cause the said prisoners to be delivered, and that they should come to the king to have delivery of their lands; and that from the less important prisoners he should receive like security by oath

and other things contained in the said bond or letters, and cause enrolment to be made by way of record on the rolls of Chancery for their loyal behaviour towards the king and their ransoms to be paid to the king, and that he should likewise receive by mainprise security from them of their behaviour under a certain penalty, and of their ransom to be paid, and that after such securities have been received he should cause their bodies to be delivered from prison and their lands to be delivered to them; and that he should cause poor persons, who have nothing, to be delivered of the king's alms.

The rebel, in this case Richard le Waleys, a Yorkshire follower of Lancaster,[8]

then made the following oath that in a war waged in the land by certain magnates against the king, he was with the said magnates against the king, and for that reason has rendered himself to the will and forfeiture of and to the king of his body, lands and tenements, and the king has granted him his life, lands and tenements by ransom, he desiring to act so that the king can assure himself of him as the king's liege man in all points, of his own free will and without coercion has made oath on the Holy Gospels to be obedient, intendant and of aid to the king as his liege lord in all things in all his enterprises whatsoever they be, and to aid, maintain succour and defend with all his power without any excuse the king's body, honour, estate, royal dignity and lordship in time of peace and in time of war against all men who shall live and die, and also all those whom the king shall wish to aid, maintain, succour and defend, in every way that it shall please the king to enjoin him; and whenever the king order him, he will come at the king's order without any excuse if he be not disturbed by sickness or any other reasonable excuse, and will not ally himself to any against the king, his estate, honour, royal dignity and lordship nor any against whom the king shall wish to aid, maintain, succour and defend as aforesaid, and if any persons disobey the king and make alliance or enterprise against him or other whom he shall wish to maintain and defend, the said Richard will exert all his power to repress such disobedience, alliance and enterprise and for greater security hereof he binds to the king his body, lands and tenements, goods and chattels within the king's power, and grants that if he contravene or transgress in any of the said points, the king may take and detain his body in prison at his will and do with him as with one attainted of deceit and crime, and seize his lands and tenements, goods and chattels as forfeit, quit of him and his heirs for ever; further for greater security hereof he has found mainpernors who have mainprised that he will loyally with all his power observe the points aforesaid and have bound them and their heirs to the king by letters patent in a sum payable at the king's will if Richard contravene or trespass in any of the points aforesaid.

This double fine, both exacted from the rebel to ransom his lands, and waved over his head as a threat to his mainpernors to assure his loyalty, was potentially crippling. It is curious that rebels managed to secure mainpernors from among the very men who had fought against them. The civil war had temporarily cut across, but not destroyed, previous links of friendship and personal allegiance. Edmund Hakelut is a striking instance. A Marcher, he found as one of his mainpernors his fellow Marcher and former rebel, John Walwayn, who had been a close friend and executor of the earl of Hereford as well as a former royal official.[9] But the other mainpernor was none other than Sir Gruffydd Llwyd, who had led the attack from North Wales on the Marcher properties and had forced Walwayn to surrender Hereford's lands.

It is noticeable that the heaviest fines were imposed on a group of Lancaster's Yorkshire retainers. Nicholas Stapelton agreed to pay 2000 marks and Adam Swilington 1000 marks.[10] The only non-Lancastrians who suffered fines as large were Gilbert Talbot, Otto Bodrigan and John Wilington.[11] Gilbert also had to hand over some lands to the younger Despenser while John Wilington received back only three out of his four manors in return for his crushing fine. The younger Despenser received the fourth. However, before Wilington received back the lands they were farmed, probably on his behalf, by his younger brother, Reginald who had remained loyal.[12] His other brother had been the Henry Wilington executed at Bristol. Both the Contrariant members of the Wilington family had been associated with the Berkeleys. The fines of the other Marchers were smaller. Whether this was because of their earlier surrender or for other reasons it is impossible to say. There is no evidence that fines were graded according to a man's ability to pay. They were large, round, arbitrary figures.

Most rebels could probably claim a close relationship with somebody in the king's camp and may have been helped by their more fortunately placed brethren. There are many striking cases of divided families. The most notable is Henry of Lancaster, brother of the earl, Thomas. Most of his lands were initially seized. They were quickly returned and he was subsequently employed by the regime. He was abroad at the time of the rebellion and it seems unlikely that the initial seizure of his lands was any more than the automatic reaction of the government against one so closely related to the leader of the rebellion. Henry does not seem to have been on close terms with his brother, and, had he played any part at all in the rebellion, it is unlikely that he would have escaped his brother's fate or that his marriage to Despenser's half-sister would have saved him. In the D'Amory family, although Roger was one of the chief rebels and husband of one of the unfortunate Gloucester co-heiresses, his elder brother, Richard, remained loyal. Like Henry of Lancaster, Richard D'Amory at first suffered confiscation and he was briefly thrown into Oxford gaol.[13] However, since in the summer he appears in the highest military post of the royal household, the Stewardship, and since there is no record of a fine paid by him, we can only surmise that his arrest was the work of a bungling sheriff. The sheriffs had good reason to be cautious. If any Contrariant escaped, Edward threatened, they would suffer the same penalties as their escaped prisoner and the king planted spies to control their activities. The confusion and mistrust implicit in this is typical of the new regime throughout its short existence. The Grandisons, Mauduits, Charltons, Sapys, D'Eivilles, de la Beches, Bureses, Leyburnes, Percies and Knovilles were also divided by the civil war. A striking case of how relations in the royal camp could help a Contrariant is the large and far-flung Yorkshire clan of Darcy. The king granted the bodies of two members, Philip and Norman, to three members of the family who had remained loyal, Robert, John and John 'le Cosyn', 'to be delivered or otherwise at their will'.[14] There are also some surprising royal allies – the Mohuns of Dunster for instance. Although related to both the Mortimers and Berkeleys, they remained loyal. Just as in the time of the baronial revolt under Henry III, 'it would be very unwise to assume a friendly alliance from the mere existence of a blood or marriage tie. These links represented only a convenient range of social contacts and a number of potentially useful relationships. Where they were reinforced by other motives they might result in political alignment but the number of divided families show that family claims were frequently overruled by more pressing considerations.'[15]

The people whom we have been discussing were all well-known rebels. The king also sent out commissions to enquire into less well-known rebels who had escaped. In the cities it was the mayor's responsibility to ferret them out.[16] Otherwise it was the sheriff's responsibility to summon a local inqui-sition. It is not difficult to imagine how much scope this must have given for preserving one's friends and relations and for presenting to the indicting jurors the names of more unpopular members of the community. Thomas Langdon of Berkshire later complained that John Inge, the younger Despenser's sheriff of Glamorgan, had treacherously indicted him although he was loyal.[17] William de Greye claimed that Despenser had indicted him for being a follower of Lancaster simply because he had been a bailiff of Cardiff when the baronial allies had made Roger D'Amory custodian of the city. Despenser also accused a group of Swansea burgesses of being followers of John Mowbray and forced them to ransom them-selves after four weeks in gaol during which he kept them in irons.[18] High-handedness or error by the sheriff could have the same result. The sheriff of Leicestershire, as early as February 1322, seized the lands of two men within his shrievalty, Ralph Stanlowe and Oliver Waleys, although they were fighting in the royal service, at first manning Nottingham castle and later besieging Tutbury.[19] The sheriff of Lancashire was wrongly indicted for sending men to help Lancaster.[20] It is not difficult to see how, under the conditions of civil war, uncertainty crept in. The king himself, until the last moment when the war broke out, was uncertain of the allegiance of some of his main parti-sans. The most famous example is that last-minute defector from Lancaster's side, Robert Holland, whose betrayal of his master deprived the earl of some of the best Lancastrian soldiers.

Another case is that of the little known Cardiff man, William Fleming. On 14 February Edward presumed that he was loyal and commissioned him to collect troops for the royal army.[21] Six days later he sent out an order to seize Fleming's lands.[22] He was to be one of two Welshmen executed after Borough-bridge.

Those fined were sometimes lucky enough to escape the full penalty or mitigate it in one of a number of ways. Firstly, they might appeal to the king to pay instalments. John Wilington, fined the massive sum of 3000 marks, had obviously been troublesome in importuning the king to ease the instalments. When, in November 1323, the king agreed that he should pay £300 in six monthly instalments at the exchequer, he made it a condition of the concession that the arrangement would lapse if John demanded any further alleviation of the conditions or mitigation of the penalty.[23] Richard Waleys paid much lower instalments of 100 shillings yearly at the exchequer. In this and several other instances the instalments were very modest. It is clear that in all such cases the fines simply represented a security for good behaviour. Attermined fines were usually paid punctually as a default would have caused the immediate exaction of the entire debt and the seizure again of the defaulter's lands. Many cases of reduced fines appear scattered through the Patent Rolls. The king may have been more willing to make concessions in the early summer of 1322 because he needed men to serve on his Scottish campaign. Gilbert Ash, a former retainer of Roger Mortimer of Wigmore, found mainpernors to go to Scotland, but later on he was acquitted from taking part in the campaign and put in charge of the lands of another rebel, Gilbert Talbot.[24] Failing the king's charity or his need for soldiers, a third method of avoiding imprisonment and surviving the fine was to seek the patronage of a favoured magnate. John Dalton, Lancaster's oppressive bailiff of Pickering, was also one of the liveried dependents of Henry Percy. This was a case where serving as a retainer to more than one lord, a not infrequent occurrence, could be vital. Through the intercession of Percy and his wife he obtained a pardon in June 1324,[25] and even became Keeper of Works in the Tower.[26] Other royalist magnates bought men's services by so interceding for them.

The 158 particularly large fines alone amounted together to £15000. Edward certainly meant to collect much of the money. To apportion many of the fines in instalments was a practical way of ensuring that payments could really be collected and served also as long-term political blackmail. It was characteristic of his greed that he should have used the defeat of his enemies to exact such large sums. The instalment system implied that he had no inkling of the precariousness of his regime and never imagined that it would be of such short duration.

Some Contrariants, out of special favour, were allowed to postpone payment altogether. Bogo de Knoville is an interesting case in point. Having been received back into royal service[27] he had clearly paid nothing, because the king remitted half of his fine as late as 16 October 1326, when he was already fleeing from Queen Isabella's invading forces.[28] It is also symbolic of the unreal world in which Edward and the Despensers lived that, even in their last extremity, they should still have demanded half the Contrariant fine from one of their few remaining supporters.

Edward could afford to allow payment in instalments since, even allowing for the wholesale plundering of his opponents' properties, he was still glutted with their assets and possessions. Plundering was a major problem. For one thing, royal officials had to distinguish between what had been taken before the king's enemies surrendered and goods illicitly removed after their possessions came into the king's hands. For instance, when Edward issued a commission to William Herle and Geoffrey Scrope to make an inquisition in northern England into Contrariant possessions that had been plundered, he had to remind them not to molest William Anne, the staunch royalist and former constable of Tickhill, for his depredations before the surrender of the rebels.[29] Edward was also in the disadvantageous position of not knowing precisely what was the nature and value of the Contrariants' assets and it must have been very difficult to assess what had been plundered. Marauders in royal service complicated matters. Thus they sacked Kenilworth and Wigmore, to name only two of the most important Contrariant properties. Prominent among the plunderers were some of the king's closest friends and most warlike followers. To this category belonged Oliver Ingham, Nicholas Kingston and Robert Ewer, who stole a huge quantity of carcasses from John Giffard's estates with the help of one of Giffard's own former bailiffs. Higher up the social scale, the earl of Pembroke himself ordered one of his bailiffs, John Waltham, to set off for a Contrariant manor in order to bring back supplies of corn to the earl's manor of Newbury. The earl of Arundel received plundered goods from the estates of Roger Mortimer of Wigmore which were later treated as a royal gift to the earl.[30]

To find out what should have belonged to him before this orgy of plunder had occurred, Edward demanded, whenever possible, the Contrariants' own lists of their possessions and to this we owe the survival of these baronial records until today. He also organised treasure hunts, especially in neighbouring abbeys, for their jewels and other precious possessions, which mostly went to swell the great treasure hoard which Edward kept in the Tower of London or the collections of valuables stored in the king's wardrobe.

There would have been few people alive who could personally remember the seizure of the rebel lands after the battle of Evesham and the fate of the 'Disinherited' Montfortians,[31] but this other black period for the English aristocracy must have been in the Contrariants' minds as they grimly faced their future in 1322. In 1322, as in 1265, the whole country suffered grave dislocation from confiscations and pillage. Like the 'Disinherited' Montfortians in 1265–7, several Contrariants supported themselves by plunder until their capture, or in some cases, until the end of Edward's rule. John Wyard, who first appeared raiding and looting during the campaign of 1322, joined Robert Ewer's rebellion in 1323 and was, the next year, implicated in more raids in Worcestershire. His lands had been granted to one of Despenser's closest friends, Simon of Reading.[32]

At the other end of the scale, we can quote the remarkably audacious raid of some relatives of the leading Contrariants. This took place when the younger John Mowbray, Jocelyn D'Eiville and Hugh Eland, with a large force of 24 men-at-arms and 400 foot, attacked villages in the Honour of Tickhill in 1326 and carried out large-scale plunder.[33] This happened on the eve of the invasion of Queen Isabella and by this time Mowbray and his colleagues had spent some time 'on the run' and gathering men. A smaller scale and more typical example, combining possibly a personal with a political feud, was the attack led by a gang under Philip and John de la Beche on lands of Aubyn de Clinton at Yattendon. They took, not surprisingly, armour, in addition to money and jewels, allegedly to the value of £200. What is particularly interesting about the case is that Aubyn stated that 'he did not dare to pursue his action at common law'.[34] Edward's inability to protect his supporters and neutral members of the gentry from such attacks and plundering must undoubtedly have caused much resentment and may have been a contributory factor which lost him support in 1326.

The Contrariants' desperate recourse to plundering arose from the fact that these remnants of resistance, unlike the survivors of the Montfortian party in 1265, did not negotiate from positions of freedom and strength. The Montfortian leader, John D'Eiville, had held out in East Anglia aided and supplied by sympathetic local people. Ultimately he and his men were rescued by their former ally turned royalist, Gilbert, earl of Gloucester, who forced a compromise on the Lord Edward which brought the restoration of the rebels' lands in return for fines assessed according to a fixed tariff. The rebels then had had help from the sympathetic clergy in paying these fines. Under Edward II the situation was entirely different. There was nobody who dared intercede for the Contrariants and no possibility of negotiation or of a Dictum of Kenilworth. The rebels were an entirely defeated party, their leaders with few exceptions imprisoned, executed or in exile abroad. They were also disinherited but had no formal right to buy back their lands which had escheated to the king.

The judges sentencing the Contrariants shared, to some degree, the outlook of the writer of the passages in Bracton dealing with treason, including the dictum that the offence of treason was so atrocious that the traitor should suffer 'the last punishment of bodily pain, the loss of all his goods and the perpetual disinheritance of his heirs so that they be admitted neither to the paternal nor the maternal inheritance'.[35] It was in this most extreme doctrine of punishment for treason which Edward II practised contrary to the precedent set down under Henry III, though Edward was extremely inconsistent. As we have shown, rebels were deemed to have lost their lands for ever. The properties of those who did not come to terms with Edward remained in his hands. Even after his overthrow they were not automatically returned to the families of their former owners, though where the members of these families were on the victorious side in 1326 they usually regained most of their losses. However, the lands of the families wiped out by the civil war and including Lancaster's personal acquisitions, like the lordship of Denbigh, were retained by the crown. Some of these properties were later regranted to new owners and ultimately served to endow some of Edward III's friends and companions in arms. The seizure of the Contrariant lands is thus an important incident in the permanent redistribution of some important lordships. Because it raised sharply all the implications of the law of treason and of the terrible effects which it could have on the position of the relatives, dependants and tenants of the condemned traitors, it is an important episode in the social history of the English aristocracy.

There was no consistency in the treatment of rebels' wives. A number of wives, as we have shown, were imprisoned with their husbands. Presumably they were regarded as rebels themselves and received nothing. Some widows of the executed men, for example Margaret, widow of Henry le Tyeys, also failed to get their dower lands.[36] In other cases, including the most prominent widow, Alice, countess of Lancaster, they received their dowers and jointures. The fact that the Despensers then devoted considerable chicanery to seizing some of these Lancastrian dower lands is irrelevant to the legal issue. An important fact is that, to judge by surviving fragments of the records of the surveyors of Contrariants' lands, dower lands were excluded from the extents drawn up by them.[37] To give Edward credit, there is one case where he gave the manor of one Contrariant to the widow of another, Badlesmere's retainer, John Penreth, because she had no other means of keeping herself and her children.[38] Those who suffered most were the wives of the surviving but imprisoned or fugitive Contrariants who, since their husbands were alive, were not entitled to any dower. Their sorry plight does not, however, usually reach the records.

The process of administering the lands was a complicated one and was all the more difficult because it was carried out against a background of looting. In some cases there was such chaos and destruction in the former rebel lands that, when they came to be handed back, this proved extremely difficult. Two cases from Powys in the middle March of Wales illustrate this. On 20 May 1323, a royal letter shows that not only had the widow of Griffin de la Pole of Powys not been able to get seisin of her dower lands, but she had been captured by a gang of her Welsh tenants.[39] On 11 September 1322 the king pardoned the lord of Powys, John Charlton, and orders were issued to hand back his lands. By the next July Charlton had still not obtained reseisin. The king stated that this was because of 'dissensions among Charlton's tenantry'.[40] Quite clearly Edward had never obtained complete control over the lands and reading, perhaps too closely, between the lines, one cannot help wondering whether Charlton was not pardoned so quickly because his lands, without him, were ungovernable. In this case the civil war merely accentuated long-term trouble in the area.

In most cases the taking over of the rebel lands proceeded much more smoothly. During the first half of 1322 the officials of the king's chamber were gradually put in charge of this rapidly growing accumulation of confiscated properties. At first it was all a matter of improvised expedients, with some lordships entrusted to particular keepers while other lands were in the hands of sheriffs or of specially appointed regional custodians. The most important of these was Roger Belers, a leading deserter from Lancaster's service, whose meteoric rise to royal favour is sketched in another chapter.[41] He was initially put in charge of the main block of Lancaster's vast estates in the Midlands.[42] On 9 May Belers and Richard Rodeney were together appointed as chief auditors for all the confiscated properties and in late June they began to hold preliminary views of the accounts of all the temporary custodians. On 4 July Belers and Rodeney were ordered to pass on these views to four pairs of newly appointed regional auditors who were to complete the audit and assure that all the revenues and other assets seized or collected in the first months of confiscation were properly answered for.[43]

Side-by-side with this review of the proceeds of the initial seizures, more permanent arrangements began to be made for long-term exploitation of the rebel properties. On 18 May the various regional custodians were ordered to value the properties in their charge and to draw up extents of them in the customary form. But, in addition, the extents were to contain information that would determine the future handling of these estates. The custodians were to enquire in particular 'which lands are forfeitures to the king without claim and which have claims lodged against them; which are worth keeping in the king's hands for stock and other profits, which would be better let to farm to tenants and at what rates and terms; also as to those lands kept in the king's hand, at which farm they should be let; also how much great wood and underwood could be sold without waste or destruction and what other profits could be made thereof'.[44]

The extents drawn up under the supervision of Robert Aston, a regional keeper in Gloucestershire, have been studied in detail recently.[45] They cover properties valued at £303. If they are at all typical, these extents show that in the late spring and summer of 1322 men did not dare to assert claims against the king, but were also reluctant to lease the confiscated properties or to make concrete offers for them. Aston believed that the larger properties, of which there were seven in Gloucestershire, could be most profitably exploited by the king himself, but they would need restocking. This confirms that during the civil war they had suffered greatly from indiscriminate removal of animals and other saleable assets.

On 20 July Belers started a fresh career as one of the barons of the exchequer and a few days later the supervision of the Contrariant lands was transferred from the chamber to the exchequer.[46] This also meant the subordination of the special auditors of confiscated lands to the exchequer. They continued to act locally in their appointed regions holding enquiries and their duties can be reconstructed from a succession of mandates sent to them under the exchequer seal in the autumn of 1322 and subsequent months.[47] At the exchequer itself several more auditors of foreign accounts had to be employed to draw up final accounts for all these new acquisitions. The first Exchequer

Ordinance of June 1323 made this change permanent.[48] It also provided for the appointment of a special third remembrancer for the keeping of records of confiscated lands and organising at the exchequer all business connected with them.[49] The roll of memoranda kept by him appears to be lost.[50] By January 1326 his department had drawn up on royal orders a calendar of all Contrariant lands.[51] This too seems to have disappeared, but a summary of all the leases of confiscated lands still survives and may be the work of this official and his staff.[52]

The intensified enquiries set on foot by the exchequer and other subsequent investigations reveal, that, in addition to the depredations during the civil war, the king had suffered considerable losses through the inefficiency or corruption of some of the early surveyors of the confiscated estates. Two examples arising out of the activities of a particularly notable man will illustrate the rest. Henry Hanbury, the associate of Roger Belers in Staffordshire and Derby, sent to enquire into rebel lands there, was said to have received 40 marks from Robert Broughton as a bribe not to take £200 worth of land into the king's hands. When justices came round to enquire into such abuses, nobody dared prosecute Hanbury. In league with a justice, Ruald de Richmond, he actually freed William Kneveton from Herston castle, though Kneveton had been found guilty of suborning men fleeing to join the king into returning to the rebel army. Kneveton's ransom was reckoned at 500 marks and the total loss which Hanbury caused the king was put at 1000 marks in lost fines and revenue.[53]

The calendar of confiscated properties still remaining in the king's hands after Michaelmas 1325 permits a detailed study of their exploitation.[54] The first surveys, made in 1322, were regarded as inadequate by the exchequer and a second series of extents was compiled in 1323 under the control of its senior officials. Walter Norwich, the chief baron, was personally responsible for many of them. These new extents usually valued the Contrariant properties much more highly, sometimes even more than doubling the original estimates. This is particularly noticeable in the case of some large properties which were subsequently retained for direct exploitation by royal agents.[55]

Judging by what happened in Gloucestershire, there was a change in royal policy at about Easter 1324.[56] Until then the government had been eager to reap quick profits while incurring the minimum of costs. That meant leasing everything that could be leased. In Gloucestershire 'labour services were usually commuted, demesne buildings and mills were leased, growing grain crops and hay were sold and uncultivated arable was sold as pasture'.[57]

New instructions were issued in March 1324. Thereafter all properties worth less than £40 a year were still to be leased, but estates of higher value were henceforth to be restocked with animals and exploited directly by royal keepers.[58] In Gloucestershire this did not involve any change as virtually everything had already been leased, mostly for periods of seven years. But the calendar of forfeited estates shows that in other parts of the country some valuable estates were after Michaelmas 1325 in the hands of royal 'approvers' entrusted with the task of raising their value.[59]

The position of the people taking up leases of Contrariant properties was bound to remain somewhat uncertain. In some cases the king changed his mind and restored properties to relatives of the defeated Contrariants. Under medieval English law, and indeed for many centuries afterwards, leaseholders were not entitled to any compensation for any improvements made by them and the political precariousness of their tenure must have been a discouraging factor. Only one case has come to light hitherto, where a political reversal of confiscation was followed by compensation for improvements. When Alice de Lacy, Lancaster's widow, was restored to some of the Lacy properties in November 1323, she was ordered by the king 'to satisfy the farmers of the lands for their expenses' since they took up their leases.[60] The king had consistently treated Alice very harshly and this was but one more instance of scant regard for her.[61] It is, perhaps, not surprising that prominent supporters of the regime figure repeatedly among the holders of leases. They included the elder Despenser,[62] the Treasurer Stapeldon,[63] Ingeram Berenger[64] and Robert Wateville,[65] two important followers of the Despensers, and William Cusance, a prominent clerk of the younger Despenser and subsequently keeper of the wardrobe of Prince Edward.[66] Even in the case of these favoured people, it is noticeable that they usually had to take up leases at fairly high rents. The exchequer of Edward II's last years was expected to drive hard bargains. The second series of extents, drawn up by Walter Norwich and his subordinates, formed the normal basis for the fixing of all leasehold rents from Easter 1324 onwards. Repeatedly rents were even fixed at figures over and above this second and higher valuation.

The royal confiscation automatically terminated all the temporary leases made previously by the displaced Contrariant owners. Probably, in many cases, it was easiest for the royal custodians to renew leases to the old tenants provided that they had not been personally involved in the rebellion or had made their peace with the king. However, we have record of small tenants whose leases were deemed to have lapsed through the forfeiture of their lords and who were possibly ruined thereby. For example, the manor of Titchwell in Norfolk, belonging to Thomas Lovel, had been forfeited to the king. It was valued at £20 and was leased for £21 a year. As an appendage to it the sheriff had seized the holding of Robert Harlewyne valued at 10s. It consisted of two-thirds of a messuage, 4 acres and 4 roods of arable, 1 acre of meadow and 7 acres of marshland. They remained in the sheriff's hands 'because of the forfeiture of Thomas Lovel'.[67] At Langeford in Wiltshire the forfeiture of Nicholas Kingston led to the seizure by the king of a tenement worth £3 16s. a year which Kingston had leased for life to Simon Lecche. In 1325–6 it was being directly exploited for the king, together with other neighbouring Wiltshire properties.[68]

The royal confiscation also stopped the payment of perpetual rent charges and other long-term obligations. Sometimes, after due enquiry, the king was prepared to sanction their resumption. 'These restorations, however, took months, and sometimes years', and in the meantime the recipients lost their income.[69]

The downfall of the Contrariants ruined or impoverished multitudes of ordinary people. Here are two examples taken from one single file of ancient petitions, but many more are to be found in this hitherto uncalendared class of records. Roger Marchinton, who had leased from Lancaster the manor of

Ashburn for a period of ten years at the large annual rent of £93, had been forced to relinquish it during Lancaster's lifetime. Roger had been impoverished by the recent murrains of sheep and cattle and was unable to pay the annual rent. Lancaster had allowed him to give up his tenancy, but the royal officials controlling Lancaster's lands had continued to exact rent from Roger.[70] An exceptionally heart-rending case was that of Constance, widow of William Haliday. Here hardship was being caused by the enforcement of the king's legal right to ignore the obligations of those whose lands he had seized. Lancaster owed Constance's deceased husband £26 13s. 4d. for arms purchased. She begged the king to honour the debt because she had been left with fifteen children. Her plea was endorsed, on the king's behalf, with the words 'the king does not hold himself obliged to pay the debts of the earl.'[71]

Many cases occur of hardship caused by confiscation of lands held by relatives. One example is supplied by the tribulations of Isabella, wife of Thomas Dodswell, whose father, Perys Crok, had held Olveston and Berwick in Gloucestershire. After his death two-thirds of these two manors had gone to her brother, Roger Crok, who had died serving with Roger D'Amory, all his lands being forfeit. The other one-third had been assigned as dower to her mother. Unfortunately her mother had married another Contrariant, William de Llanfihangel, who was a follower of Maurice Berkeley, and he had died in prison after surrendering with his master at Gloucester. Her mother had obviously never obtained back her share of the two manors and, through the misfortune of politics, Isabella was deprived of the whole of her paternal inheritance.[72] Another example is the case of Nicholas Kingston, whose widow, Anastasia, was deprived of her dower lands though her husband had died before the rebellion, and they were simply swallowed into the exchequer as part of the seizure of the properties of Nicholas' heir, his brother John, another Contrariant.[73] This was obviously a gross injustice.

Examining the surviving records of the seizure, including three massive rolls of enrolled accounts, and enormous series of particulars of account lying behind them, one is amazed at the industry of the exchequer. The surviving royal orders to exchequer officials reveal quite clearly that this was the responsibility of the king himself. At the time, this bureaucratic efficiency must have seemed just one aspect of the nightmare through which disinherited noblemen and disseised tenantry felt that they were living.

7

Royal finance, 1321–6

The financial history of the reign of Edward II has never been adequately studied in its own right and historians have developed surprising misconceptions about it. It is true that Edward inherited a mass of debts from his father and that during the earlier part of his reign he was at times seriously embarrassed by lack of money. Stubbs and Tout assumed that Edward was an unbusinesslike man, never interested for long in the detailed working of his financial administration or of any other branch of his government. In reality, Edward's early financial difficulties created in him an obsessive preoccupation with wealth. This bore fruit in the last, most autocratic part of his reign, when Edward displayed a minute and obsessive interest in his finances which was perhaps politically unwise but certainly resulted in the accumulation of vast reserves of treasure.

Edward's initial financial difficulties were aggravated by some of the Ordinances of 1311, notably by the abolition of the supplementary 'new custom' charged since 1303 on the imports and exports of foreign merchants. His main bankers, the Frescobaldi of Florence, were driven out of the country at the demand of the Lords Ordainers and were virtually ruined by 1312. This did not, however, prevent Edward from acquiring a new, and most resourceful banker in Antonio Pessagno of Genoa, whose advances between 1312 and 1317 reached a higher annual average than those of any Italian banker previously employed by the English crown.[1] Pessagno financed the invasion of Scotland in June 1314 and it was not through lack of money that this ended in the disastrous defeat of Bannockburn.

D

Edward was reasonably solvent, though not affluent, between 1315 and 1320, but the political difficulties of 1321 again put a serious strain on his finances.² His triumph over the Contrariants in the civil war of 1321–2 was financed on a shoestring. He was determined never to be in the same situation again. The achievement of great riches became as much his objective as had been the annihilation of the detested Lancaster and other opponents. The York parliament of May 1322, by abrogating the Ordinances of 1311, restored the 'new custom' on the trade of foreign merchants. Edward retained in his hands the lion's share of the properties of his vanquished enemies, so that by 1324 they were yielding more income than did the ordinary farms of the shires and other traditional land revenues of the crown. Both the old and the new resources were administered with unusual rigour and a minute attention to the enforcement of all royal rights. The driving force came from the king, as is attested by a stream of impatient and menacing letters of privy seal addressed to his treasurers and other financial agents. The reforms at the exchequer and the reorganisation of its records, which alone have attracted the attention of modern historians, were the necessary result of this relentless pressure. Already by the end of 1322 huge reserves of treasure were piling up. The war with France in 1323–5 could be financed without any need for extra taxes and its mismanagement was due to other causes than lack of money. On the eve of his fall Edward possessed reserves surpassing a year's revenue, but he had become too greedy and mean to use these vast resources sensibly. His oppressive enforcement of royal rights was spreading dismay and fear. It became a major cause of the unpopularity of his rule. Edward's position in this respect resembled perhaps most closely that of Henry VII in his later years, but Edward could not reckon on Henry's hard-won immunity from foreign attack. Edward had some small mercenary castle-garrisons in his pay in 1326, but he did not use his ample wealth, as King John had done, to recruit a larger mercenary army. Such a force might have given Edward a chance to resist for a while Queen Isabella's invasion in the autumn of that year. When that invasion came, a few weeks sufficed to show that vast riches could not save a king who had forfeited the support of most of the country's notables and whose henchmen were regarded with hatred by a large part of his subjects.

The long years of financial uncertainty planted in Edward's mind a number of definite ideas. He tried to apply some of them during periods of relative stringency before 1321, when there was some justification for harsh measures. But the same 'hard' policies recurred after his victory in the civil war and he continued to pursue them to the end of the reign. He had an obsession about secrecy in his financial administration. No unauthorised persons, who had not been sworn to secrecy, were to be allowed to see exchequer records or were to be admitted to any premises where his financial affairs were being trans-acted. He wanted to limit as far as possible the amount of discretion that his officials could exercise, so that all financial concessions to his subjects should become a matter for his personal decision and review. He was convinced that his financial officials did not work hard enough, that their devotion to his service was not as boundless as it ought to be and that their activities should be rigorously supervised. Historians have noted with approval the considerable amount of experiment and reform in Edward's financial administration during the last years of his reign. They have failed to observe how much of this sprang from the king's distrust of his officials and his conviction that they were not augmenting royal revenue as fast as they ought to do.

Many of Edward's commands to the exchequer were clearly contrary to the preferences and habits of its officials. The repetition of these disturbing directives under several different treasurers confirms that they stemmed from Edward's personal ideas. Virtually identical phrases recur in Edward's letters of privy and secret seals from at least 1318 to 1325. These policies ran counter to the traditional wisdom of his professional fiscal experts. To take some examples from the years before the civil war, on 28 November 1318 Edward ordered that all assign-ments on royal revenues were to be suspended. Henceforth no assignment was to be conceded to anyone without the king's explicit personal order. Edward's letter justified these drastic measures by the need to send all available money to the king's household and for discharging other necessary expenditures 'so that the king is no more decried throughout the country for failure to pay his way'.[3] The exchequer officials believed that this was a short-sighted solution to the king's difficulties. On 5 February 1319 Edward was persuaded to countermand this order and the exchequer was specifically permitted to assign suitable revenues to royal creditors whenever it had to negotiate fresh loans.[4] The exchequer officials were convinced that they must have such discretion and that without it the king's credit would suffer.[5]

In October 1319 Edward tried to restrict the exchequer's habitual practice of allowing crown debtors to repay their debts by reasonable instalments.[6] We know from a later letter of the king's council that the exchequer regarded this as the most sensible method of recovering larger debts.[7] Its officials must have circumvented Edward's prohibition, because on at least three more occasions in 1323–5, he tried to reaffirm stringent restrictions on this practice and to insist that payments by instalments must in each case be personally authorised by him.[8]

The same Ordinance of 31 October 1319 stressed that no one except the king's officials, who have been duly sworn into his service, could inspect royal fiscal records. The exchequer was informed that in future specially deputed royal councillors would inspect its records twice a year in order to enquire into the state of revenue and expenditure. They were to report to the king in secret and they were also to check on the conduct of exchequer officials in other matters.

A more detailed account of Edward's finances must begin in 1321. Unfortunately there are no detailed wardrobe records for the crucial period between July 1321 and the end of April 1322, while a continuous series of chamber accounts starts only in October 1322. As has been noted before, Edward appears to have been short of money in the summer of 1321. This contributed to his inability to resist baronial demands for the expulsion of the Despensers. On 15 August, a few days after the exile of the Despensers, Bishop Stapeldon ceased to act as treasurer. It is surprising that the brief record of his 'exoneration' from office on the exchequer receipt roll should not be followed by the customary mention of the amount of money left in the treasury.[9] This suggests that no large reserves were handed over by Stapeldon. There are also other indications of financial stringency. Between March and September 1321 Edward had to borrow at least £1973 6s. 8d. from the Bardi. It is specially significant that their advances included £200 in cash sent to the king's chamber in July and £100 paid on 28 August to one of the king's personal servants on a warrant under the secret seal of the king's chamber.[10] The Bardi were particularly committed to Edward, especially as they were also acting as bankers of the younger Despenser, but the king's credit with other foreign firms stood very low. When early in 1322 loans were requested from various foreign merchants active in England, most of them not only refused to help, but complained of large unpaid debts already due to them from the king. The Ballardi of Lucca declared that they were virtually ruined because Edward owed them £7000 and more than 5000 marks were due to the Spini of Florence.[11]

Edward's main campaign against the Contrariants started on 8 December 1321, the day of his recall of the Despensers. He began his march westwards carrying a very modest hoard of money. The exchequer had supplied him with £2100 in the first fortnight of December and four of the earls whose retinues were serving in his army received some £1400.[12] Thereafter during most of the campaign Edward's forces must have lived from hand to mouth, sustained by such driblets of revenue as periodically reached them. Between the middle of December 1321 and the final victory over Lancaster at Boroughbridge on 16 March 1322 Roger Northburgh, the keeper of the wardrobe, who acted as Edward's main war treasurer, received at least £7896. As has already been explained, our sources are incomplete. But he certainly received no more than £5066 13s. 4d. in cash sent from the exchequer.[13] As this would normally be the main source of supply, Edward was clearly very short of money. A comparison with the Welsh campaign of 1294–5 might be instructive. In an identical period of winter between the middle of December 1294 and the end of February 1295 the exchequer of Edward I was able to despatch to the armies based on Chester and Carmarthen £23000.[14] The impression of extreme penury in 1321–2 is heightened when particular stages of Edward's campaign are examined separately. By the

time he had reached Shrewsbury on 20 January he was so short
of money that he had to ask three of the local merchants for
loans amounting altogether to £400.[15] During this part of the
campaign the exchequer was able to contribute only a mere
£1066 13s. 4d., sent out in two consignments on 20 and 30
January. At the end of January the treasurer asked for a loan
from all the main groups of foreign merchants active in England
but met with an almost complete rebuff. Only one Florentine
undertook to transmit directly to the king 100 marks and did
so in the course of February.[16] During that month Edward
seems to have been chiefly kept going by loans from the Bardi.
They supplied £1320 at Gloucester in the first part of February
and another £680 at the end of the month.[17] Fortunately,
money and supplies from the captured estates of the Contrariants were beginning to reach Northburgh in the course of
February. Three hundred pounds raised from the estates of
Roger D'Amory and Badlesmere reached him already on
17 February.[18] There was a marked improvement early in
March when £4000 was brought from the exchequer, so that
just before the battle of Boroughbridge Northburgh was able
to make substantial payments to leaders of new contingents
who had joined the king on his progress northwards.[19]

When on 10 May 1322 Stapeldon resumed the office of royal
treasurer he found a mere £1195 9d. in the treasury.[20] Much
greater reserves were being accumulated, however, in the
chamber, which until late July administered all the treasure and
revenues from the properties of the Contrariants. This, and the
fines paid to the king by rebels, must be the origin of the
unusually large amounts handled by the chamber in the summer of 1322. The ordinary revenues of the chamber in the last
four years of the reign averaged annually only about £1500.[21]
Yet between the middle of July and early days of September
1322 the chamber delivered to the wardrobe and paid on
behalf of the exchequer a total of at least £14724 8s.[22] Presumably this was only a part of the chamber's haul from the
Contrariants and other unspecified sums must have gone into a
vast reserve that Edward was beginning to build up. He would
have had even more if widespread plundering of the properties
of his enemies had not occurred during the civil war.[23]

In the spring and summer of 1322 Edward was preparing an invasion of Scotland which ultimately began in August. At the York Parliament in April the king was able to secure for this purpose an aid from the clergy known as the subsidy of five pence in the mark.[24] No general tax was granted by the laity and there is nothing to show that one was sought. The agenda of business drawn up in preparation for the York Parliament is silent on this point.[25] Separate subsidies were secured, however, in the summer of 1322 from London and some other towns.[26] Loans were sought again from Italian merchants. This was destined to be the last occasion when Edward needed to borrow from them on any scale. The Bardi agreed early in June to advance £4000 on condition that the loans provided by them during the civil war were repaid. The Peruzzi lent 1000 marks. All the loans were to be repaid out of the customs.[27] Late in July a messenger was sent from the wardrobe at York to bring back from London the money provided by the Bardi and the Peruzzi and the subsidy paid by the men of London and Norwich. With the addition of other funds supplied by the treasurer he fetched altogether £10000.[28]

As will be shown later, the invasion of Scotland in August–September 1322 speedily collapsed because Flemish ships in the service of the Scots ruined Edward's plans for provisioning his army by sea. Lack of supplies of food for men and horses had been decisive, not shortage of money. All through the campaign the wardrobe received money from the chamber: £6500 between 2 August and 6 September.[29] After the invasion was over the wardrobe still had an unspent reserve of £7000.[30]

In the last months of 1322 preparations were on foot for the renewal of warfare against the Scots in the following year. Edward, who was always ready to economise at the expense of his officials at the exchequer, had ordered a suspension of payments of their customary fees. This could not be maintained and the fees were restored in the case of the most hard-working officials. A letter of privy seal of 2 December left such payments to the treasurer's discretion.[31] In November 1322 Edward secured a grant of a lay tenth and sixth from a parliament at York. It was the heaviest tax of the whole reign. The minimum limit below which townsmen and inhabitants of the ancient demesne were not to be taxed was lowered from 10s. to 6s. Yorkshire, which had been severely devastated by the Scots, was assessed at about half its contribution to the levy of 1315, but most shires paid more than they had contributed at any time since 1301.[32]

On 30 May 1323 a special council at Bishopsthorpe agreed to a long truce with the Scots. Edward could now pursue wholeheartedly one of his main passions, the accumulation of wealth. 'Serve us in such a way that we should become rich' he wrote to the treasurer and barons of the exchequer on 21 September 1323.[33] He had already made a good start. At the end of July £27500, in 55 barrels of £500 each, were being moved from York to London for storage in the Tower.[34] It is probable that the proceeds of the lay tax, now no longer needed for war, constituted the main initial core of this reserve, together with treasures seized from the defeated Contrariants. The assessment for that tax totalled £42394 5s. 10d.[35] Edward also disposed of clerical subsidies likewise originally secured for war against the Scots. In April 1322 Pope John XXII had conceded to him for this reason two clerical taxes, to be collected over a period of two years in 1323 and 1324. The bulk of the revenue from these clerical taxes, which yielded £34172 17s. 8d.,[36] presumably likewise went to swell his reserves. Edward's policies of rigorous enforcement of royal rights and claims were steadily adding to this growing surplus. On 1 May 1324 a further £44000 was added to the store in the Tower.[37] The war in Gascony made a dent in this accumulation of treasure, but not for long. To judge by the known cash payments, at least some £51500 was expended on the war in the second half of 1324 and the early months of 1325.[38] The total cost may well have exceeded £65000.[39] But when on 8 July Stapeldon was succeeded as treasurer by Melton, he was still able to hand over £69051 13s. ¼d.[40] As will be shown later on, these reserves were even larger a year later, on the eve of Queen Isabella's invasion of England. To the end Edward was never satisfied that he had enough money. For example, it had been one of the informal conditions of the papal concession of two clerical tenths in 1322 that John XXII should receive one quarter

of the proceeds. But in November 1324, and again as late as
June 1326, Edward was assuring the Pope of his inability to
pay though promising to do so at some future date.[41]

One striking feature of Edward's years of affluence is the
virtual cessation of the issuing of new money by the royal mints.
The mint at Canterbury was shut after Michaelmas 1323[42] and
the amounts coined at London fell to very little after that date.
The annual value of the coins minted in 1325 and 1326 was
the lowest in the fourteenth century.[43] In order to attract more
silver to the mints Edward would have had to raise the price
offered to merchants and this would have presumably been
repugnant to him. As the owner of a steadily growing hoard
of treasure, he possibly realised that it was in his interest to
maintain the high value of the existing currency by not adding
to the amount in circulation, and his expert advisers were
certainly bound to be aware of this.

A wealthy government does not need to borrow from bankers
but it might use the special facilities that they offered for
carrying out payments abroad or for supplying silver plate,
bullion and foreign currencies. Like the younger Despenser,
who used extensively the Peruzzi of Florence for facilitating his
financial operations,[44] Edward employed in the same manner
the companion Florentine firm of the Bardi. On several occasions in 1323–6, the money that they were obliged to disburse
on the king's behalf had already been previously deposited with
them by the king's treasurer.[45] It may be that the Bardi
themselves preferred this. They were also given special privileges. Of great value was the concession made to them in
December 1322 allowing their firm to sue its debtors at the
exchequer.[46] They could recover there not only loans made
by them to private persons but also the interest due on
their advances.[47] The machinery of the exchequer was
put at their disposal for enforcing any judgements in their
favour.

The financial operations of the Bardi on behalf of the royal
government involved in 1323–6 at least some £13000.[48] The
king also made some slight use of the Peruzzi and the Scala of
Florence and of a few native financiers. There was an advantage
in selling to major businessmen like the Bardi and Peruzzi, or

William de la Pole of Hull, substantial quantities of wool and other commodities from the confiscated estates of the Contrariants or the properties of vacant bishoprics. On 13 July 1323 the Bardi contracted with the treasurer to pay him £250 in return for the delivery to them of the entire wool clips of the great Lancastrian estates of Pickering, Pontefract and Tutbury. The precise quantity was not known but this did not matter. The Bardi offered to pay the high price of £8 per sack and the precise amount that they might owe could be left to a future settling of accounts.[49]

Italian bankers provided special facilities for making payments abroad. When the war with France began in the early summer of 1324, the Bardi, Peruzzi and Scala of Florence transmitted to the constable of Bordeaux the first instalment of urgently needed funds, paying him £2000 in Florentine florins early in July.[50] The Bardi handled most of the business of paying royal envoys going to the French court or to Avignon and financed the permanent English agents at the papal court. When Queen Isabella departed for France on 9 March 1325, she was empowered to draw funds from the Bardi branch at Paris and they supplied her with at least £3674 13s. 4d.[51] In the summer of 1325 Edward was for a time planning to join her in order to render in person homage to Charles IV of France. In preparation for this journey 18 146 French gold florins valued altogether at £3515 17s. 11¼d., were acquired from the Bardi, William de la Pole and a couple of Londoners. The Bardi also supplied silver plate worth £1768 15s. 10d.[52] Perhaps Edward needed this for making gifts at the French court. Early in September he decided not to go abroad and most of the gold florins were still in the keeping of the exchequer at the time of his fall a year later.[53]

We must question the wisdom of some of the measures by which Edward was trying to increase his income in his final years of greatest power. But his affluence certainly owed something to his own personal thrift. Tout, who quite unaccountably missed all the evidence of Edward's wealth, ascribed the low level of wardrobe receipts during these years to the king's alleged financial difficulties.[54] Speaking particularly of the last two years of the reign, Tout surmised that 'something of the falling off may be ascribed to the difficulty of collecting revenue in a time of increasing disorganisation'.[55] He missed entirely thereby one of the most interesting glimpses of Edward's thrifty or even miserly outlook. Freed from responsibilities for financing major wars, his wardrobe after 1323 supplied Edward's domestic needs on a very modest budget. Only in the eighteenth regnal year did its receipts rise to five figures, but out of the £20006 that it handled in that year £13333 6s. 8d. was in fact destined for the war in Gascony.[56] The wardrobe receipts in the nineteenth year of the reign (8 July 1325–7 July 1326), amounting to £6175, are the lowest recorded receipts for any entire year between 1224 and 1399.[57] As we luckily possess for this period a complete set of chamber accounts, with chamber receipts averaging only some £2000 a year, it is certain that Edward's household expenditure was really exceptionally modest at a time when he had much more money than ever before in his life.

An official estimate of the king's revenue drawn up in January 1324 has come to light recently.[58] The document is badly damaged but the total of the king's revenue and other important items remain legible. It is clearly based on elaborate surveys of royal income by the treasurer and his staff and it may have been drawn up in response to Edward's order of 21 April 1323 demanding information about the value of his lands and of the other profits of his kingdom.[59] Whenever possible it is an estimate of net income, after the deduction of all normal expenses. The overall total is estimated at £60549. This is very close to Lord Treasurer Cromwell's estimate of £64815 in 1433,[60] but the situation under Edward II was better, as Cromwell gave the figure of gross income. The estimate of 1324 includes the net revenue from Gascony, estimated at £13000, while in 1433 Gascony yielded very little. Nearly half of Cromwell's total was derived from the customs, which yielded only some £16000 in 1323–4. By contrast in 1324 revenues from royal lands and the farms of the shires formed by far the largest item, contributing altogether £24385. The most surprising feature of this figure is that the revenue from confiscated lands in England alone,[61] given as £12643, surpassed by £900 the income from the ordinary farms of the shires

and other traditional land revenues of the crown, estimated at
£11742 12s. 3d.

The high estimate of the income from confiscated estates is
quite credible. The bulk of it must have come from Lancaster's
estates which Edward largely retained for himself. Lancaster's
estates are estimated by Dr Maddicott to have been worth
slightly over £11000 a year and they allowed the earl to spend
annually at least some £8700.[62] Besides these Edward had
retained a lion's share of other forfeited properties. As Thomas
Gray put it, Edward 'kept himself quite quiet, undertaking
nothing in honour or prowess, but only on the advice of Hugh
le Despenser so as to become rich, keeping for himself as much
as he could seize of the aforesaid barons'.[63]

This comment of a younger contemporary of the king, who
knew and appreciated Edward, confirms that accumulation of
wealth formed the core of Edward's personal policies. His
exploitation of the estates of the Contrariants has already been
discussed in an earlier chapter. His intense personal involvement in everything else that might increase royal income has
hitherto been largely ignored by historians. They have been
particularly interested in the improvements in the arranging
and keeping of records. We can still admire the clarity and order
of the surviving calendars of the muniments of the exchequer
and the wardrobe compiled in 1322–3 and associated with the
name of Treasurer Stapeldon.[64] The exchequer ordinance of
1323 and the companion wardrobe regulations of 1324 have
certainly eased the labours of historians handling the fiscal
records of subsequent years.[65] The contents of the two memoranda rolls were henceforth more rationally divided, the pipe
rolls shed some of their contents that were henceforth transferred to separate rolls. One other reform, not mentioned in
any surviving ordinance, led to a great simplification of the
issue rolls kept at the exchequer of receipt. From April 1325
onwards they began to be arranged chronologically, thus
conforming for the first time to the more ancient arrangement
of the receipt rolls. It became possible henceforth to use
together much more easily these two parallel series of records.[66]

Edward would have been puzzled by the modern preoccupation with these administrative by-products of his pursuit

of riches. He would have been even more surprised by the ignoring of his personal share in these changes and the exclusive attribution of them to his treasurers and other financial experts. Stapeldon and his principal assistants at the exchequer were presumably responsible for the precise wording of the exchequer ordinance of June 1323. The details of the household ordinance of May 1324 must have been drafted by him in co-operation with experienced experts drawn from wardrobe and exchequer. The last exchequer ordinance, of June 1326, which merely repeated or supplemented the earlier regulations, was drawn up by Stapeldon's successor, Archbishop Melton, but we are expressly told that Stapeldon had been consulted.[67] A glance at the royal letters enrolled on the memoranda rolls makes it, however, quite clear that these various enactments merely tried to implement in a practical way the things that Edward had been ordering in a succession of mandates of privy and secret seals. Their wording leaves no doubt that they represented the king's own ideas and wishes. Of particular interest are his detailed complaints about the failure of his officials to carry out some specific measures. As he says on one occasion, he is using the secret seal to make it quite clear that he is personally concerned.[68]

The improvements in the keeping of official records were primarily designed to increase royal revenue. Debts could be recovered more fully and more rapidly, royal rights and claims could be enforced more successfully. Large parts of the exchequer and wardrobe ordinances were specifically concerned with the same objectives. Several chapters of the household ordinance of 1324 deal with controlling of expenditure and cutting out of waste. Edward's characteristic meanness comes out in the order that in future wages and fees of the household should be paid in arrears. It was intended to eliminate as far as possible the practice of allowing prests, that is of making advances subject to a future account.[69] The exchequer ordinances devoted much space to the ferreting out of all debts due to the crown and to the reviewing of all fiscal concessions made in the past. Some of their provisions show, however, a genuine desire to put an end to abuses by royal officials and to redress some of the past injustices.[70] If carried out, they would have

benefited all classes of the king's subjects. They confirm that
Edward was not uninterested in ordinary people, as can also
be glimpsed from instances of generosity to humble men whom
he happened to meet on his travels.

The demands made by Edward on his officials often went
beyond the bounds of what was effectively practicable. An
enormous amount of work was done by them on his orders and
Edward secured a large revenue, but all that was achieved
continually fell short of the king's expectations. The complete
fulfilment of his orders would have required a standard of
honesty, of single-minded devotion to his service and of
unquestioning obedience that were unattainable in medieval
England. Edward grudgingly accepted that his demands
necessitated the employment of a larger number of exchequer
officials. He resented the cost of this and tried to compensate
for the increases in manpower by expecting longer hours of
work,[71] curtailment of vacations[72] and partial reductions in
salaries. In the interest of efficiency he was trying to eliminate
some of the customary perquisites of the officials at the exchequer. The reforming ordinances sought to restrict the
amount of litigation that could be conducted before its barons.[73]
This curtailed one source of their profits. There were past
precedents for this, but only in exceptional emergencies. Now
it was a time of continuous emergency. All exchequer personnel
were severely forbidden to act as attorneys for people rendering
accounts in it.[74] Edward was trying to impose thereby a standard of impartiality expected of a modern civil service, but was
destroying a valuable source of extra profit enjoyed by his
financial officials. They must have been particularly struck by
the contrast between the brutal rapacity of the Despensers and
Edward's other leading henchmen and the restricted oppor-
tunities and unremitting labour that he was trying to force
upon his lesser underlings.

The upshot of all this was that Edward was increasingly at
odds with his fiscal civil servants and many of them must have
come to regard his rule as an oppressive nightmare. The speed
with which Edward was deserted in his hour of need in the
autumn of 1326 by a large proportion of his officials, including
many of his household servants, has been noted by several

historians. Even more striking was the willingness of many of them to serve his supplannter Some historians, and notably Tout, have treated this ass.gn that a per͓ ͻs aimaneivil service had arisen, indifferent to the shifts of political power at the top. There may be some truth in this, but much more important was Edward's mismanagement, if not ill-treatment, of his officialdom.

In late July 1322 the control over the confiscated properties of the Contrariants was transferred from the king's chamber to the exchequer, adding immensely to the volume of its business.[75] This coincided with the return of the exchequer from York to Westminster[76] and with the appointment on 20 July of Sir Roger Belers, formerly one of the two chief surveyors of the Contrariant lands, as a baron of the exchequer.[77] This important follower of Lancaster[78] had deserted his former master in circumstances that are obscure but which endeared him greatly to Edward and earned him a royal gift of £200.[79] According to the writer of the *Annales Paulini* he became one of the king's leading advisers.[80] An element of personal self-seeking by Belers was added to the influences that shaped Edward's fiscal policies and his strictures on the officials of the exchequer, for Belers seems to have been the one member of that body who never lost the king's favour. The exchequer also now absorbed the eight special auditors of the accounts of Contrariants' properties. While there was only one auditor of foreign accounts when the exchequer was at York earlier on in 1322, there were now several more. The exchequer ordinance of June 1323 formally ratified the need for four additional auditors of foreign accounts and nine were in office at the end of the reign. Their annual fees of 20 marks were, however, changed to a variable scale in November 1323, their former fee being henceforth treated as the maximum to which only the most favoured might aspire. The entire scale was reduced again in the spring of 1326.[81]

Edward's request in April 1323 for a statement of his revenues has already been noted. In the same mandate the king demanded a list of all uncollected debts due to himself or his predecessors.[82] This was followed in June by the first exchequer ordinance which was intended, among other things, to speed up the recovery of debts due to the crown. The king returned to the same subject in a mandate of 21 September 1323. All accounts audited since September 1320 were to be diligently inspected and all clear debts arising out of them were to be listed. While making these and other demands on the exchequer, the king was as yet fairly well disposed towards it. He promised that, if its officials would so discharge their duties as to make him rich,[83] he would, in return, prove a good lord to them. But two months later the tone of king's letters became very menacing. Two mandates of 23 and 27 November complained that the exchequer was ignoring a succession of his previous orders both in writing and by word of mouth. He specifically referred to one, unnamed, receiver of confiscated properties who had never yet been summoned to account, though he had handled for a year royal funds amounting to 1000 marks. Edward asserted that this was not an isolated example. He had been dismayed, in travelling through the country, by the many instances of the neglect of his fiscal business.[84] In one specific letter, sent early in January 1324, he complained of the disrepair into which his manor of Feckenham had fallen, as he had noted on a recent journey, and the exchequer was given a long list of things that should be improved.[85]

The king's accumulated dissatisfaction was expressed most bitterly in the mandate of 27 November 1323. On the positive side it required a review of all the royal lands farmed out and the resumption into the king's hands of all leases that had been granted out without sufficient personal warrant from him. It threatened the officials with his extreme displeasure unless they managed to put right all that was amiss. Edward singled out for special attack the chief baron of the exchequer, Sir Walter Norwich, who as the most experienced member of its staff could have been expected to conduct himself in a manner much less displeasing to the king.[86]

Further mandates in January and February 1324 dealt with various other matters which in the king's view had been neglected hitherto. In January an order came for putting into execution the collection of all debts due to the Contrariants.[87] This resulted in prosecutions of many men who had been involved in transactions with the fallen rebels going back sometimes many years into the past. On 19 February the king ordered a rigorous scrutiny of the accounts concerning the former treasurer, Walter Langton, already deceased, as well as of the accounts for the lands of the Templars and for the papal tenths.[88] This new preoccupation of the king with arrears of ecclesiastical accounts may not have been to the liking of the treasurer, Stapeldon, who in the next few months drifted into a conflict with Edward over a new scheme for the division of the exchequer into two sections. Edward's dissatisfaction with Norwich may have contributed to the king's decision to carry this out. The larger section, consisting of the prosperous southern counties, was to be entrusted to Belers. Norwich was to be restricted to the poorer shires north of the Trent together with most of the Midland counties within the dioceses of Lincoln and Coventry. The reform would necessitate the increase of the total number of barons of the exchequer to seven and the appointment of an additional staff of remembrancers and other subordinate officials. The treasurer, Stapeldon, appears to have been as opposed to this change, as was Norwich, and there is nothing to indicate that it was likely to procure any clear benefits. The original orders for division were disregarded and a further peremptory directive had to be sent on 16 June 1324 before the exchequer was duly divided two days later.[89]

A year later, on 3 July 1325, Stapeldon was replaced as treasurer by Archbishop Melton. Soon afterwards the king was complaining again to the exchequer that his previous mandates were still being disregarded. A letter of 10 August 1325[90] reiterated a long list of Edward's past directives and insisted especially that his wishes must be consulted in all matters of some importance. He again expressed his great displeasure with the exchequer, but one has the impression that the tone of his complaints during Melton's tenure of the treasurership was not quite so violent as in the time of Stapeldon.

The replacement of Stapeldon by Melton may have increased still further the importance of Belers. While Walter Norwich had once served for two and a half years as treasurer and had filled the position of acting treasurer on at least four occasions in Edward's reign, when in August 1325 Melton withdrew on temporary leave, his place was taken this time not by Norwich but by Belers.[91] The murder of Belers in January 1326 in circumstances that were never cleared up produced a speedy reunification of the exchequer. This was one of the aims of the second exchequer ordinance of 30 June 1326, which, as already noted, was certainly drawn up in consultation with Stapeldon.

Edward's treasure hoard was growing until the last moment before Isabella's invasion. Between April and October 1326 at least £7457, raised from the estates of Isabella and her adherents, were delivered into the chamber and the Westminster treasury.[92] But his huge accumulations of treasure proved of little avail in this moment of his greatest need because the speed with which one disaster followed another precluded all effective use of his resources.

In August and early September large sums were moved to Porchester in Hampshire: £7000 was sent from the exchequer and £100 by the Bardi,[93] while the younger Despenser received £2000 from his bankers, the Peruzzi.[94] Substantial amounts were paid out to the sailors on the king's ships and to a force of infantry. It was all presumably needed for the mysterious and apparently abortive raid on Normandy which took place some time during this period.[95]

After Isabella landed on the east coast on 24 September, events moved so quickly that considerable sums of money sent to organise the defences of the threatened areas could never be delivered to their destinations. Four hundred pounds provided by the exchequer on a warrant of privy seal of 20 September for the wages of the fleet north of the Thames, was subsequently returned unspent, as was £500 paid out at Westminster at about the same time for taking to the army that was supposed to assemble in the estuary of the Orwell in Suffolk. The same was true of £100 delivered on 30 September to men charged with arraying the shire levies of Sussex and another £100 paid out at Westminster on 2 October for paying the force that was supposed to muster at Colchester in Essex. These two payments were returned unspent to the exchequer on 4 and 6 October respectively.[96] Further inland, sheriffs were still disbursing money on Edward's behalf until at least the middle of October. Geoffrey le Scrope managed to pay on 9 October some levies of southern counties which he then despatched westwards to the king.[97] On 11 October the sheriff of Yorkshire paid 640 marks to Earl Warenne and some of his northern followers assembled to join Edward, but the sheriff's disquiet is revealed by the condition which he attached to one of these payments. The recipient, Henry Fitz Hugh, had to promise that he would return the money if he failed to reach the king.[98]

Before Edward fled from London early in October he had received in his chamber substantial deliveries of arms and armour paid for by the exchequer. Throughout his flight westwards Edward was accompanied by an exchequer official, John Langton, who carried with him at least £29000.[99] At Chepstow, on 20 October Langton secured a formal receipt for the delivery of this sum to the king.[100] At that date £10000 was still intact at Chepstow, but it could be of only very slight use because the forces still adhering to him and within his effective reach had dwindled to very little.

When on 17 November the treasurer, Melton, who had remained loyal to Edward until the end, was compelled to hand over his office to Bishop Stratford of Winchester, one of Isabella's ablest advisers, he also handed over an impressive hoard of treasure.[101] The silver and gold in it were worth £57915 10s. 11½d. As unspent sums of money in the hands of Edward's various military and naval paymasters came back into the treasury during the next few days, the total increased to £61981 4s. 9½d. On the royal estimate of 1324 this amounted to almost exactly a year's income. The new regime of Queen Isabella and Roger Mortimer was to spend this enormous treasure with astonishing rapidity and, by the time of Mortimer's overthrow in October 1330, there was virtually no reserve left.[102]

8

The Despensers' spoils of power, 1321–6

In 1324, when royal troops awaiting embarkation for Gascony were plundering the countryside because Edward was too mean to pay them, the author of the *Vita* castigated the king: 'The king had plenty of treasure. Many of his forbears amassed money; he alone had exceeded them all. Howbeit, the king's meanness is laid at Hugh's door, like the other evils that afflict the court.'[1]

While one may doubt whether the younger Despenser had much to teach Edward where meanness was concerned, it is clear that Hugh's own insatiable greed and rapacity were regarded as the mainsprings of his evil influence upon the king. There is also no doubt that horror and disgust at the Despensers' illegal seizures of land was a major cause of the fall of Edward II. Such a drastic outcome would have been less predictable if, as the chroniclers imply, they indulged in these activities merely watched by a quiescent and indulgent ruler. Edward's own greed makes it likely that he was an active participant in all their deeds and the facts confirm that, in two of the nastiest cases, that of Elizabeth D'Amory and Alice de Lacy, he was closely implicated. This being the case, there was not a landowner in England who could feel his possessions safe from their avarice or have any assurance that he was likely to be able to hand on his property to a young and defenceless heir without danger.

The allegation in the summer parliament of 1321 that the Despensers had been unjustly depriving magnates of their lands was already true. This was to be only a pale presentiment of their extraordinary activities between 1322 and 1326. No other royal favourite in English history was ever able to take such liberties with the properties of the king's subjects and with the laws of the realm. As it was, both father and son received many grants of the lands of Contrariants, especially those of men executed after Boroughbridge but, not content with this, set about despoiling particularly vulnerable heirs of these rebels. Nobody was immune from their rapacity, neither the smallest crofter nor the greatest lord. In 1323 Thomas of Brotherton, earl of Norfolk and the king's half-brother, was forced to rent out to the younger Hugh his lordship of Chepstow, which included a major wine-importing port.[2] He obtained in exchange a rent far below its value and later was forced to sell Chepstow to the younger Despenser for the equivalent of only four years' annual rent. The Despensers failed to appreciate what the fate of their former opponent, Thomas of Lancaster, might have taught them. The lesson of his fall was that the possession of great lands and wealth could not preserve them without the unswerving military support of their retainers together with the retention of the friendship of a part of the magnates and a measure of popularity among the gentry who were in charge of the local levies of troops.

Our main sources for studying the acquisitions of the Despensers are the calendar of their charters compiled by the exchequer after their fall and the voluminous extents of their lands drawn up at the same time.[3] This information can be compared with the petitions of their victims presented in the years after the overthrow of Edward II. The younger Despenser, who started the reign virtually landless, ended it with lands worth at least £7154 14s. 8½d. per annum and with goods on the English portion of his estates estimated at £3136 18s. 7d. This excludes the value of goods on almost all his Welsh properties, for which virtually no evidence survives, and which, since they formed five-sevenths of his estimated wealth, would make this figure more massive still in spite of the earlier depredations on these estates by Llywelyn Bren and later by the Contrariants.[4] He was thus, at the end of his career, worth considerably more than his brother-in-law Gilbert de Clare had been at his death in 1314, when the exchequer had valued his lands at over £6000 a year. His lands were also worth more than the annual value of the second richest see in England, the bishopric of Winchester. He continuously spent on an enormous scale, though part of the expenses of his household at court were financed by Edward. One object of this expenditure is still wonderfully visible today in the magnificent work which he carried out on the Clare fortress of Caerphilly. Built on a remarkable scale and with the highest quality of stonework, surrounded by a moat which is like a great lake, it remains one of the most dramatic fortresses in the British Isles and its siege cost Isabella and Mortimer £500 before the garrison capitulated. At the height of his power, in January 1324, he had a total of £5886 7s. 8d. deposited with the two great Italian banking companies, the Bardi and the Peruzzi. His bank account did not fall into deficit until the very last days of the regime. In the years 1321–6 he was a much more important source of funds for these firms than were the papal collectors in England and his average annual deposits during these years are invariably larger than the sums which the two societies annually transferred in the same period from England to the Papal Chamber in Avignon.[5] Together, he and his father, whose lands at the end of the reign were worth at least £3884 10s. 10¼d., were probably receiving a larger annual income than Thomas of Lancaster, the holder of five earldoms, had been able to enjoy.[6]

After the defeat of the Contrariants Edward made considerable gifts to the elder Despenser whom we may now, after the grant of his earldom on 10 May 1322, call the earl of Winchester. Most of the grants which he received, totalling in all at least £1664 19s. 11¾d. in annual value, including the 'third penny' of Hampshire in support of his earldom, were centred around his existing ancestral properties. Apart from these centres of power in the Midlands and Wiltshire, he was also now developing a third area of control in the home counties of Surrey and Sussex, very close to the city of London and centred on the manor of Kennington where he often stayed.[7] It is significant that in this case, as in that of most of the land-grants, the king gave as life-grants or in perpetuity only the properties of dead Contrariants. Thus Winchester received blocks of D'Amory, Giffard, Badlesmere, Tyeys, Lisle, Bohun and Kingston properties. The younger Despenser concentrated almost entirely on augmenting his vast lordship in South Wales and the March. Surprisingly, we find that the grants to the younger Despenser in England amounted to lands worth only £499, against total royal grants to both Despensers between 1322 and 1326 of properties worth £2153 19s. 11¾d., almost entirely from the estates of dead Contrariants. These are immense sums, to which it is impossible to put a modern equivalent. Other royal supporters, even of the status of Arundel, Richmond or the king's two half-brothers obtained comparatively little. Edward retained the bulk of the lands of dead Contrariants, including especially almost all of Lancaster's properties, and most of the lands of those who remained alive, in prison or in exile. As mentioned elsewhere, he was deriving more income from them than from his inherited crown properties.

However extensive, these grants of confiscated property did not interrupt the younger Despenser's attempts to obtain more lands by violence and fraud. One of his first actions after the civil war was to secure Gower for himself, over which the civil war had started in 1321.[8] It will be recalled that William de Braose VI was the last male Braose in the main line. He was impoverished, partly because his father had run into conflict with Edward I over the king's right to levy a fine on Braose's Welsh tenants in Gower. William's only son had died and he seems to have intended to bequeath his Welsh lordship to one of his co-heiresses, Alina, the wife of John Mowbray, though at different times he likewise negotiated with the earl of Hereford, also a descendant of the Braoses, and with Roger Mortimer of Wigmore, who were both anxious to purchase the lordship in Braose's own lifetime. In 1319 the younger Despenser had also been negotiating for its purchase. His intervention seems to have terrified the other contestants and Braose into finally making a charter granting the lordship to Alina, and, if Alina and her husband left no heirs, reserving the reversion to Hereford. Braose did this without a royal licence as he had some claim to do in the March. However, Edward also had some justification when he used this as a pretext to seize Gower and imprison Alina Mowbray in the Tower.[9] This sparked off in 1321 the ravaging of Despenser's lands and the civil war. After the rebels' defeat the king granted Gower to the younger Despenser by a royal charter dated 9 July 1322.

This grant of Gower, as soon became clear, formed part of one of the most dishonest and cynical of all these schemes of the Despensers. The idea was to force Gower upon the widow of Roger D'Amory in exchange for her much more valuable lordship of Usk and, then, to make William de Braose prosecute her for detaining his inheritance of Gower. Elizabeth D'Amory would thus lose both Usk and Gower. The last step would be to force William de Braose to resurrender Gower to the younger Despenser. The object of these tortuous proceedings was to assure Gower and Usk to Despenser in full inheritance and not by a mere royal grant that might one day be revoked by another sovereign.

We can now come to the details of these shoddy proceedings. We have Elizabeth D'Amory's own version of what was done to her, but there is no doubt that she was telling the truth.[10] Edward II clearly had as great a dislike for Elizabeth as he had fondness for her elder sister, Eleanor Despenser. Some time during the civil war, Elizabeth D'Amory was captured and put into Barking Abbey, where she learnt that her husband had died during the campaign. On 29 June 1322 she renounced Usk to the king in exchange for a promise of Gower. Force was used against her to make this renunciation, but the king promised to make up the difference between the £770 of the annual value of Usk and the £300 or so of Gower, by making her additional grants. He threatened that unless she consented 'she would never be allowed to hold any land in his kingdom of her inheritance'.[11] One of the royal envoys who imparted this news was William Clif, the chancery clerk whose corruption in his office on the Despensers' behalf had already been deplored in the 1321 indictment of them. The other envoy to Elizabeth was John Bousser, a justice of the King's Bench. The subsequent connection of these two officials with the activities of the Despensers will be cited again later on. The result was that on 10 July, the day after the king had formally granted Gower to Despenser, formal charters exchanging Usk for Gower and granting the same lordship of Gower to Elizabeth were drawn up.[12] In return for this surrender of Usk, Elizabeth was now allowed possession of her dower lands, including Clare, but contrary to the king's promise she was not restored to her jointure lands, except for the manor of Halghton in Oxfordshire. This she received on the same day, 3 November 1322, as the date of a final concord between her and the younger Despenser by which the latter gave her a solemn warranty for her title to Gower. Sadly depleted in her inheritance, she may have thought her troubles were over when she was invited to York to join the king for Christmas the next month. On her arrival, however, she found that the Despensers had not finished with her. She was detained and pressed to execute another quit-claim for Usk and all her inheritance in Wales as well as a further obligation by which 'sui oblige de mon corps et de mes terres' not to give any lands to anybody else. This happened two days after Christmas and, to lower her resistance, she was separated from her council, some of whom were imprisoned. Nevertheless, she managed to leave the court without sealing anything and only returned and complied with royal demands when Edward personally menaced her with the loss of everything and told her that 'otherwise she will hold nothing of him'.[13]

As has already been mentioned, soon afterwards the Despensers sought to recover Gower by bringing into play poor William de Braose, who seems to have been a tool in the hands of any strong man. Braose was now used to bring a writ of novel disseisin against Elizabeth for Gower which she had received from the king! But Braose won the case, as she complained, 'because the said Sir Hugh, by his lordship and through accroaching royal power, made the assize pass against me'.[14] Braose, from whom Winchester was meanwhile procuring the reversion of *all* his properties at his death, granted the newly recovered lordship to Winchester who regranted it to the younger Despenser.

Elizabeth had lost both Usk and Gower, but she was a lady of character and did not easily give in. No doubt her early life in Ireland, where her first husband, the earl of Ulster, had been done to death and, afterwards, the loss of her second husband in the civil war, had inured her to danger. She tried to invoke the warranty of Despenser for her right to Gower, but no sheriff would execute the writ of warranty for her over this matter. She petitioned in parliament but in vain. But, in May 1326, when Despenser was harassing her for further renunciations and promising her only paltry compensation, not half the value of Gower, she secretly, in the chapel adjoining her bedroom at Clare, executed a notarial act of protest recounting all that had been done to her.[15] Much of the evidence of her story comes from this protest, but it can be corroborated by charters and other deeds. It is a sign of Elizabeth's desperation, since this protestation was actually drawn up when the Despensers' regime was still in power and might have been used against her if its existence had been discovered.

Gower was not the only inheritance lost by the Braoses to the Despensers. If William de Braose was as clay in the hands of the regime, this was partly because in 1322 he was already a very sick man. More important still, his daughter Alina continued to be detained in prison after the execution of her husband, John Mowbray, as was Alina's son, John.[16] As is explained in a petition of Alina presented some time after the overthrow of Edward II, Braose was forced to surrender properties to Winchester in the hope of procuring her release. For example, he surrendered for this reason to the elder Despenser the manor of Wytham in Kent. The transaction took place in Winchester's chamber at Kennington and, as was to be expected, the indispensable John Bousser was again present.

Braose's own father, William de Braose V, had given the barony of Bramber in Sussex to trustees, William le Moigne and Richard Hakelut. His widow, Mary, had accepted these trustees as her own feoffees for her dower.[17] It was intended that they should regrant the barony to William de Braose VI for life and should grant him likewise Mary's dower portion after her death, with the remainder after his death to Alina and her husband, John Mowbray as already noted. After the execution of Mowbray in 1322 his widow, Alina, and his son, John, were kept in prison by the elder Despenser until 'by grave threats and fear of death' Alina surrendered the reversion of Bramber to Winchester. He entered the barony of Bramber after the death of Mary and William de Braose, presumably after May

1326. He also took over £256 12s. worth of Mary's goods and chattels which should have passed to the executors of her will.

The Despensers also attempted to despoil the widows of three of the greatest earls. One was Lancaster's widow, who was arrested with her mother, the countess of Lincoln, a few days after the battle of Boroughbridge.[18] The latter still remained in custody at York early in June and her guardian had strict instructions not to permit access to her by any suspect persons.[19] Her daughter, Alice of Lancaster, was also imprisoned at York. The two Despensers threw her into abject panic by telling her that she was the real cause of her husband's death and should be burnt for this. Alice was so terrorised that she agreed to accept everything that they might demand.[20] She surrendered to the king most of her lands, of which some went to the two Despensers, except for a modest compensation in the shape of properties worth 500 marks granted to her for life with reversion to the Despensers after her death.[21] The great Lacy lordship of Denbigh in North Wales went immediately to the elder Despenser.[22]

Another widow treated with unmerited harshness was Mary de St Pol, countess of Pembroke. Her husband had not been a Contrariant, though her friendship with the queen may have had something to do with her victimisation by the Despensers. A descendant of the unpopular half-brother of Henry III, Aymer de Valence, earl of Pembroke, had been a faithful and trusted servant of both Edward I and Edward II. He had fallen under the suspicion of the king and the Despensers for an uncertain reason and after the civil war was arrested at the end of the York parliament. He was forced to make an undertaking to be loyal to the king which looks very much like the submissions required of the Contrariants.[23] Perhaps his willingness to accept the exiling of the Despensers in August 1321 had left him under a cloud. However, he died suddenly in France in 1324. His widow's lands were an obvious target for the younger Despenser as her dower consisted of some of Pembroke's lands in South Wales. Her close connection with the French queen Isabella may also have earned her the hostility of the Despensers. She complained that the younger Despenser would not allow the escheator to return an inquest on Pembroke's lands because he coveted them.[24] The king's chancellor, Baldock, refused to hand over her dower until she produced original royal charters of title. She was obviously unable to do so in all cases, because in July 1325 the king granted Despenser Little Monmouth and its dependencies.[25] She had to give up Grantham and Stamford in Lincolnshire at this time though, in this case, a former owner, the earl, Warenne, received them.[26] Mary of St Pol later claimed, perhaps with some exaggeration, that the king also seized Pembroke's goods and chattels worth £20000 and only returned them for a quittance of royal debts owed to Pembroke, which amounted to appreciably more than the value of the goods.[27] Edward certainly possessed a splendid ship which had belonged to Pembroke. The result of these exactions was that she had insufficient means to pay Pembroke's debts.[28] As if this were not enough, the younger Despenser managed to buy a vast quantity of Pembroke's cattle and livestock for 1000 marks, a sum far below their real value.[29] She was forced to undersell them to pay for Pembroke's funeral. When she died fifty years later, the foundress (like another victim of the Despensers, Elizabeth D'Amory) of a Cambridge college, she still had not managed to clear her husband's debts.[30]

The narrative of the Despensers' dealings with the other Pembroke heirs is even more harrowing. Elizabeth Comyn, Pembroke's niece, only a teenager in the 1320s, was a prime target.[31] Originally they intended to bring her into their web of landholding by marrying her to the eldest son of the younger Hugh, yet another Hugh.[32] Before Pembroke's death she was already living at the elder Despenser's manor of Kennington, presumably as the future wife of the Despenser heir.[33] The Despensers deliberately delayed the settlement of the Pembroke will in order to give Elizabeth Comyn an unfair advantage. This prejudiced the claims of John Hastings, another of the co-heirs of Pembroke. Although he was married to Despenser's sister, Hastings had to execute an enormous recognisance of £4000 in Despenser's favour.[34] When Hastings died early in 1325 and the Despensers inevitably obtained the wardship of his young heir, Laurence, they decided to marry this boy to one of the younger Despenser's many daughters.[35] The favourites then procured an unfair division of the Pembroke inheritance giving Laurence Hastings and Elizabeth Comyn undue shares. Hastings' lands were expected to remain for many years in the wardship of the younger Despenser. Elizabeth Comyn's share was favoured in order that she could then be despoiled by the Despensers and their henchmen. Nothing more is heard of the marriage of Elizabeth Comyn to a Despenser. Instead, on 20 April 1325, they deprived Elizabeth of a part of her share in the inheritance by violence. Elizabeth had been kept first at Woking and then at Pirbright, both belonging to Winchester. She was threatened with injury and perpetual imprisonment,[36] until she executed a surrender of her properties giving Castle Goodrich in Herefordshire to the younger Despenser and Swanscomb in Kent and Painswick in Gloucestershire to the elder Despenser.[37] Painswick and Castle Goodrich were surrendered by a final concord before that indispensable royal justice, John Bousser, especially brought to her that same 20 April, and her acceptance of this enforced settlement was consolidated by a massive recognizance of £2000 before William Clif, the Despensers' usual clerical aide-de-camp. Even so, she was detained for a further six months.[38]

Nor were the Despensers content to leave untouched the inheritance of the Pembroke heir whom one would have expected them to favour, Winchester's own grandson, Laurence Hastings. When the younger Despenser obtained his wardship on 12 January 1325 he received goods on the Hastings estates worth £774 10s. 4½d.[39] By the time of his own death, only twenty months later, Despenser left on these properties goods worth, according to one inquisition, no more than £551 17s. 10½d., though an independent adding up of their value, as revealed by other inquisitions, shows only £474 19s. One of the executors later complained that 'the chattels which properly belonged to John...scarcely amounted to anything because everywhere they are ransacked' and still worse depredations were only averted by the executors.[40] Inquisitions also revealed that £375 of uncollected debts were due from the Hastings chief lordship of Abergavenny alone.[41] Whether this is an indication of the unco-operative nature of the estate officials and the tenantry or of the preoccupation of the Despensers with high

politics rather than estate management is an interesting
question.

The Despensers not only imprisoned their victims with
impunity but, as we have already shown, could call on the
active co-operation of royal justices, escheators and other royal
officials to enforce their wishes which was, no doubt, particularly terrifying to their opponents. Most of them only dared
petition against their ill treatment after the Despensers had
been executed. John de Sutton, most of whose estates were
derived from his wife, one of the co-heiresses of John Somery,
was detained in prison by the Despensers until he gave up
twelve properties including Dudley castle.[42] A mysterious gift
of £500 was also paid by Lucy Somery to the king.[43] One of the
beneficiaries out of this transaction was the favourite Despenser
retainer, Oliver Ingham, who received Shocklach castle and
the lordship of Malpas in Cheshire. After the surrender, Sutton
was handed over to Ingham as one of those standing surety for
the transaction. He kept Sutton in prison until the end of the
regime.[44] Ingham similarly detained William Grandison, the
heir to the manor of Lydiard Tregoze in Wiltshire, formerly
the possession of Henry Tyeys.[45] Grandison remained a prisoner
at Windsor castle until he had surrendered the estate. In other
cases the Despensers can be seen piecing together for themselves a manor which had become fragmented. They obtained
the controlling two-thirds interest in the manors of West
Horndon and Chiltenditch in Essex from the Contrariant,
Geoffrey de la Lee, on whom they also imposed a recognizance
of 500 marks.[46] They then proceeded to secure the remaining
one-third from Elizabeth Joce who held it as dower.[47] The
manor of Shalford in Surrey illustrates the same process. On
8 May 1323 Emma Mohaut granted to the younger Despenser
the reversion of her dower lands there, held through her first
marriage to Richard Fitz John.[48] About the same time Idonea,
wife of John Cromwell, who had rights of inheritance there,
released them to Despenser.[49] Finally the king granted to
Despenser Roger Clifford's reversionary interest which had
escheated to the crown on Roger's execution in 1322.[50] As it
happened, Despenser's fall preceded Emma Mohaut's death, so
that he never obtained full possession of the manor.

There are a number of indications that by late 1325 the Despensers were beginning to become apprehensive about the level of their extortions. Probably by now the Pope had heard of their scandalous seizures, for in May 1326 Edward received advice that he should treat his magnates better.[51] The most explicit evidence that the Despensers were developing cold feet was the mention in the protest by Elizabeth D'Amory in the same month, that now the two were offering her compensation 'in order to deceive the people'.[52] Paulinus of Cardiff, who had lost Walton Cardiff in Gloucestershire to them in May 1322, on 27 December 1325 received compensation in the form of the manor of Roehampton in the same county.[53] In the following summer, Margaret, widow of John Giffard of Brimpsfield, previously ejected from Weston Birt in Gloucestershire, was restored to her lands.[54]

The Despensers fell in October 1326 and this brought a deluge of petitions against them. For Elizabeth D'Amory the hoped-for 'future time when grace should be more openly dispensed and the law of the land be better maintained and common to all' had at last come.[55] In January 1327 the new regime of Mortimer and Isabella gave her back her lands, though other Despenser victims were not so fortunate. The countess of Pembroke did not recover hers until Edward III assumed personal control in 1330.

The judgement on the younger Despenser read out in dramatic and expressive medieval French at the termination of his trial on 24 November 1326 includes many of the cases which we have described.[56] It contains the charges of accroaching royal power, but the number of brutal crimes for which the younger Despenser was judged responsible puts his condemnation in a special class in comparison with the charges against other medieval royal favourites. Among them was the charge of robbing two Italian dromonds of goods worth £60 000 in the Channel to add to the other charge of piracy committed during his exile. Another was the torturing, by breaking her limbs, of Lady Baret, probably the widow of Stephen Baret of Swansea, so that she went out of her mind. We do not know to what end these injuries were perpetrated. The judge added, 'that this was against the order of Chivalry'. He was accused of bringing noblemen to their death, of depriving laymen of their lands and the queen of hers, of robbing bishops of their goods and depriving the church of its franchises. Among the episcopal victims, in addition to the obvious names of the bishops of Hereford, Lincoln and Norwich, is listed the bishop of Ely. It was with these charges ringing in his ears that Despenser went to the gallows.

9

The defeat in Scotland, 1322-3

Of all Edward's policies nothing affected the country more continuously than his wars. From his accession to 1323 England was at war with Scotland. Except for the final repelling of a Scottish invasion of Ireland in 1318, there was one long series of disasters. The Scots, led by their able leader Robert Bruce, retained the initiative most of the time. The English policy of trying to defend a chain of castles inside Scotland and on the frontier did not work, as the Scots gradually recaptured the key strongholds. They managed to organise raids deep into English territory and reduced the counties south of the border to abject terror and deep misery. The few English attempts to stage massive counter-invasions ended either in crushing military defeats, as happened at Bannockburn in 1314, or in frustrating failures brought about by the harassing tactics of the Scots and the lack of supplies for Edward's troops. After Edward finally concluded a prolonged truce with the Scots in 1323, he blundered later that year into a war with France that finally destroyed him.

Until 1322 Edward's warlike enterprises were hampered by a chronic shortage of money, though this was not the main cause of his military failures. Thereafter he was so rich that even enormous expenditures on war did not exhaust his large reserves, which at the time of his fall from power in late October 1326 still amounted to at least a year's revenue. But throughout the reign the heavy exactions of money for his wars were bitterly resented as it all seemed wasted in a series of defeats and failures.

The years 1315 and 1316 were a period of particular misery for the English population. For the first time in Edward's reign direct taxes were imposed two years in succession.[1] It was

E

typical of the brutal policy of Edward that this exceptional taxation was imposed during the worst period of famine ever experienced in medieval England.[2] This famine, together with resultant epidemics, may have killed in some parts of the country up to 10 per cent of the population and certainly encouraged the invasion of Ireland by the Scots. In spite of his exactions in these difficult times no Scottish campaign took place and Edward's military failure and indecision gave the Scots the courage to make more and more devastating raids further and further into the north of England itself. They would arrive in squadrons of fast-moving horsemen, plunder what they could, and drive back to Scotland such animals as they found. Often what could not be carried or herded back was destroyed, unless the locality bought itself immunity from the raid. Chroniclers and episcopal letters, as well as the starker evidence of the Subsidy Rolls, are repetitive in their tales of devastation and terror. Northumberland and Cumberland fared the worst. Durham, which was skilful in organising what amounted to a regular tribute to the Scots, fared least badly. Yorkshire did not suffer its first raid until 1313, but afterwards experienced them often.[3] Lancashire, which may until 1322 have been partly immune through Lancaster's possible collusion with the Scots, lost any immunity after his death and the raid of 1322 stretched as far south as Preston.

Dr Miller has reminded us that 'the simplicity of the economy made easier recovery from the destruction', but a comparison of the Subsidy Rolls before and after the period of raiding suggests that in 1336 the economic capacity of the northern counties was only a fraction of what it had been formerly.[4] The severity of the raiding altered the northern landscape. To give some warning against the coming of the Scots, even if there could be no protection, peel towers were erected. In some areas agriculture was abandoned. As usual in war, the population suffered from its defenders as well as its enemies. Officials exploited farmers' anxiety to evacuate their animals by charging their owners pasturage when moving the beasts or even fining the owners for trespassing.[5] War profiteering took the form of charging rent for refuge inside castles and putting troops on short rations, which caused a mutiny at Berwick in 1314.

During campaigns the king's Irish and Welsh troops brought exceptional looting and violence in their wake. Another group which seems to have profited spectacularly from the situation were some enterprising Yorkshire merchants who began to rise to great prominence at this time, most notably the De la Pole family of Hull.

The population was driven to make its own treaties with the Scots, technically a treasonable offence, but one which even the king on one occasion admitted was necessary. In 1314 John Halton, the unfortunate bishop of Carlisle, who was often driven from his episcopal residence by the Scots, made a treaty with a brother of Robert Bruce.[6] To deal with the same raid the men of Cumberland also came to an agreement with the Scots to pay a certain sum by Christmas. When they found that they could not meet the demand, they fled to other parts of the country taking with them what they could.[7] After the particularly terrible raid of this year people on the northern border were terrified when magnates were summoned to the next parliament as their absence left the northern March undefended.[8] In 1315, Andrew Harclay, later the hero of Boroughbridge, and at that time sheriff of Cumberland, assembled the remaining men of the county to try to organise them into some sort of local defence force, but this did not prevent the fall of Carlisle that year.[9] After one raid, the men of Cumberland in despair petitioned the king that, failing a royal truce, they should be allowed to make one of their own.[10] From Yorkshire there comes a remarkable incident when the king himself instructed the people of Ripon to pay the remainder of a ransom which they owed to the Scots to recover some men of the town who had been carried away as hostages.[11] Jean Scammell, who gives the best account of these raids and their social effects, rightly remarks that 'it is curious to see the king of England debt-collecting for his enemies and apparently indifferent to their correspondence with his subjects'.[12] The people of the north, in practice, became accustomed to acknowledging Bruce's title as king of Scotland some time before Edward countenanced it. This tendency for dual allegiance to develop went a long way in the middle years of Edward II's reign. Bruce's 'ransom' imposed on Cumberland in 1314 looks very

much like a simple tax assessment. He demanded a total of
£2202 11s. 5½d., based on a village-by-village estimate, and
actually received £1540 12s. 2¾d., as well as a pathetic series
of gifts of wine and fish for his brother, his agent and the agent's
servants.[13] We find William Melton, archbishop of York,
demanding that the assessment of the sum required by the Scots
for the protection of Ripon should be equally divided amongst
the population.[14] In Durham, which evolved a particularly
efficient way of assessing these levies, the contributions of the
clergy were collected like a normal subsidy.[15] Meanwhile
Edward did not even find it worthwhile to send out tax
assessors for the levy of royal taxes in Northumberland,
Cumberland and Westmorland.[16] The north of England was
rapidly becoming worthless to him as a source of revenue and
the Scots were moving their effective border slowly southwards.

The Bannockburn and Berwick campaigns of 1314 and 1319
had been parly undermined by the quarrels of Edward and his
magnates. In 1322 for the first time in his reign Edward was in
full political control, had enough money and could count on
the prestige of his recent victory over his domestic opponents.
And yet the campaign which followed was one of the worst
failures of the reign. He set out on this expedition with an army
free of men with whom he had bitter feuds, though it looks as
if some lesser Contrariants were released from gaol to partici-
pate. On the other hand the absence of many of his old military
companions, however fractious, left Edward with few experienced officers. One of the characteristics of the Contrariants as
a group had been that many of them had seen long war-service
in Scotland, some as far back as the siege of Caerlaverock in
1300. It was probably to fill this vacuum of leadership that
Edward created the victor of Boroughbridge, Sir Andrew
Harclay, earl of Carlisle, before the campaign.[17] His elevation
to an earldom must have seemed extraordinary to contemporaries. With the notorious exception of Gaveston, the direct
elevation of a mere knight to an earldom, with no claim to one
either by descent or marriage, or well-established status as a
major magnate, was entirely unprecedented.

Harclay came from a Cumberland knightly family of
modest landed fortune and his father, Sir Michael Harclay,

does not appear to have been a tenant-in-chief. Andrew's early career was similar to that of his father, who had also been sheriff of Cumberland and had faced the Scottish incursions of Edward I's reign. In 1313, possibly as the result of petitioning by the Commons, Harclay had succeeded Bishop Halton as keeper of Carlisle castle.[18] In 1315 he received the substantial reward of 1000 marks from Edward, ostensibly in return for handing over two relatively obscure Scottish prisoners, but also probably in reward for his vigorous defence of Carlisle the previous year during which he was taken prisoner by the Scots.[19] It is interesting to find him being given a pardon for supporting Lancaster in 1318, only four years before he brought about the earl's defeat.[20] He owed his remarkable success in the north to his energy, a characteristic observed by a number of chroniclers, and to the state of emergency in those parts. The unimportant and unprofitable shrievalty of Cumberland became a focus for Scottish incursions and English defence. In the counties along the northern border shrievalties and other administrative offices were repeatedly filled by barons and leading knights of higher rank than was usually the case in the rest of England. The Nevilles, Percys and Lucys are the most notable of these. They seem to have bitterly resented Harclay's sudden ascendancy and it was the representative of one of these families, Anthony Lucy, who later arrested him for alleged treason with the Scots and then, after his execution, obtained his lands.[21]

One chronicler maintains that Harclay had tried to persuade Edward to attack the Scots before the Contrariants had finally been defeated. Edward was certainly preparing for another Scottish invasion as early as February 1322, before the battle of Boroughbridge. As a subsequent letter of Edward to the earl of Richmond of 9 June 1322 clearly shows, Edward dreaded another Scottish invasion and the news that it was imminent threw him into great despondency.[22] The historian studying the records of the campaign, including the huge Wardrobe Book which survives, cannot fail to be surprised and impressed by the comprehensiveness and the speed with which Edward operated on that occasion. On the other hand, objective consideration of the plan of campaign, a major invasion and

long march through the east of Scotland, makes one wonder
what precisely Edward hoped to achieve. The danger that the
Scots would elude him and slip into England by another route,
as they had done in 1319, was surely an ever-present possibility.
The army which he took with him was described as 'heavy and
stately' and numbered apparently at least 22 000 men.[23] But
Edward I had taken a much larger army to suppress the last
Welsh rebellion of 1294–5 in a country where he had made
important military preparations in the form of road-, harbour-
and castle-building on previous campaigns. He had also the
control of the sea and therefore the means of supplying his army
and castles. None of these advantages was enjoyed by Edward
II and it is difficult to see what his precise aims and strategy
were. The most charitable assumption might be that he hoped
to provoke the Scots into fighting a full-scale battle and that he
felt sure of defeating them, though past experience could not
have justified any confidence of success. His generalship under
these circumstances may seem the height of futility.

Immediately after Boroughbridge Edward began to make
practical arrangements for the campaign. There was, as far as
we know, no attempt to secure a tax from the laity at the York
parliament of May 1322. Only the prelates granted on this
occasion an aid for the Scottish war.[24] Instead, the king
concentrated on squeezing out of his subjects as much military
service as possible. During the earlier part of the reign Edward,
in addition to the ordinary array, had already made attempts
to demand an additional service of one foot soldier per vill to
serve from 40 to 60 days. The *Brut* chronicle later blamed the
Despensers for this innovation, though it had been tried already
in 1316 and 1318.[25] In assembling men for the campaign in the
summer of 1322, Edward did not fail to leave this stone
unturned.[26] He also tried to ensure that the soldiers should not
be left starving in the Scottish countryside, as they had been on
their flight to England after the disaster of Bannockburn in
1314. In addition to making his own arrangements for
provisioning, he also demanded that the men coming to his
army should bring with them sixteen days' supply of food.[27]
Besides the normal array Edward made threatening demands
to certain counties and towns to send extra men. For instance

on 26 March he demanded 500 men clad in a uniform manner from Cornwall, 'the earls, barons and other men of the county not having hitherto rendered aid to the king against his enemies, any remissness on their part will entail severe penalties'.[28] The recent opposition of such prominent west-country Contrariants as Hugh Courtenay, the late earl of Hereford's son-in-law and Otto Bodrigan, an important Cornish landowner, was presumably rankling in his mind when this was written. In any case the reluctance of the men of Cornwall and Devon to contribute towards warfare against Scotland was a perennial feature of English history. The York parliament of May 1322 was supposed to have systematised these royal attempts to secure extra men into a grant of a foot soldier from every vill to serve for 40 days after the muster at the vill's expense.[29] Yet on 8 June Edward wrote once again to seventy-two towns to send extra infantry in addition to those granted by parliament.[30] By these means Edward gathered his large army.[31]

The volume of administration required to collect the massive supplies for the war was so great that John Killerby and nine other clerks of the chancery were paid special fees for writing letters of privy seal to the merchants who supplied stores.[32] Edward gave special instructions that these supplies were to be properly paid for.[33] The merchant community formed a group which the king could not easily bludgeon. He particularly needed their services in 1322 and consequently ensured that they should be properly treated. However, he also had the alternative of securing goods for the army from the countryside by purveyance. This was the royal method of taking a subject's goods for war. The value of the goods was supposed to be assessed at the current market price and usually no immediate payment took place. The owners were merely given tallies or other types of receipts. This was obviously capable of a variety of flagrant abuses, of which the most frequent was underpaying or allowing those who paid a bribe to keep their goods. Two recent studies have revealed distressingly well the effects of royal orders to purvey on a country already suffering from a severe agricultural depression.[34] By 1322 the country had to some degree recovered from the bad harvests of 1315–17, but there had been a severe cattle murrain in 1321 and the harvest of 1321–2 was again quite poor. It is significant that Edward found it necessary to import corn from Gascony and Ireland, both countries to which England was normally accustomed to export grain. As was to be expected, royal purveyances affected some parts of the country more than others. Wales, for instance, seems to have supplied little, while the corn-producing eastern counties were more frequently called upon. Dr Maddicott has traced these demands and enumerated them for the reign of Edward II. Lincolnshire and Essex were asked for supplies nine times, Norfolk and Suffolk eight times and Somerset, Dorset and Hertfordshire seven times. The worst feature of purveyance was that in practice it could be terribly disproportionate to people's real means. It was supposed to be evenly assessed, like the ordinary taxes on movables, but more often than not the purveyors did not bother to observe any strict rules. Contemporary poems give horrifying details of men selling their seed grain to pay purveyors since they had nothing else to offer, men losing their last animals and seeing their richer neighbours buying a royal protection against the purveyors, a protection which a poor person could not afford. The limitation of purveyance had formed an important part of the demands for better government formulated by Edward II's opponents. 'At the root of these attempts there may have been a constitutional complaint: that the king was in effect imposing taxation without parliamentary consent. But the impression remains that this was not the primary grievance. Concern with purveyance was probably not so much the product of reflections on the constitution, but rather of the position of the gentry and magnates as rentiers and of their possible fear of a peasant rising.'[35] The purveyances for the Scottish campaign of 1322 were among the largest of the whole reign. On that occasion the supplies controlled by the king's wardrobe alone were valued at £15467 3s. 6½d., acquired through both purveyance and purchase, though this does not include some separate amounts assembled by various royal agents. Unfortunately, as will be seen later, a part of these were wasted when ships were unable to reach the army to supply it and the goods were brought back to Newcastle and left to rot.[36] In 1326 Queen Isabella was anxious during her invasion to avoid this type of unpopular exaction and one chronicler thought it worth mentioning that she paid for the goods which she needed for her army.[37]

To augment his supplies of ready cash for the campaign, Edward wrote to the keepers of the rebel lands ordering them to send such money as they could find on the estates which were in their charge.[38] He attempted to obtain forced loans from some counties and some individuals. William Melton, archbishop of York, for instance, received a sarcastic demand for a loan 'so that the king's majesty may be honoured beyond the state that Thomas, late earl of Lancaster, lately held when the archbishop had treaty with him and granted him 2000 marks from himself and his clergy for the defence of his church and the marches of Scotland against the Scots'.[39] A large proportion of the supplies arrived at Newcastle-upon-Tyne before the king set out on his campaign, though some of the money which he was expecting did not. He left behind the Keeper of the Wardrobe, Roger Waltham, both to receive this money and to organise the sending-on of further supplies to the army after it had entered Scotland.[40] The collapse of the Scottish invasion was the outcome of unexpected events during the campaign and not of failure to raise sufficient supplies for it.

The long-feared invasion of Robert Bruce in fact materialised while these preparations were still proceeding. He crossed the border on 19 June and, taking advantage of the fact that the English forces were assembling in the east, moved down the west as far as Lancaster, where his two commanders Moray and Douglas, met him. Together they put Preston to flames.[41]

By 1 August the king had moved to Newcastle-upon-Tyne.[42] Two days later he sent scouts westwards to locate the Scots. By 6 August most of the troops had arrived and the Welsh and English troops were involved in fights with each other and with the citizens of Newcastle.[43]

It is impossible to calculate the size of Edward's army accurately at any particular date. As on all medieval campaigns some troops marauded or deserted. Some contingents were made up to their full strength relatively late, others speedily declined for unexplained reasons. The figures that follow do

not represent the army at its maximum concentration, because
information about this happens to be incomplete, but during
the actual campaign in late August and early September before
the return of the king to Newcastle-upon-Tyne on 10 September.[44] The figures that follow do not include the garrisons of
the various frontier fortresses.[45] Allowing for a certain degree
of fluctuation in numbers, there were present during the actual
campaign just under 300 knights, including earls, barons and
other bannerets, and about 950 other fully armoured and
equipped men-at-arms. The rest of the army numbered at
least 21 700. These included about 2100 hobelars, some of
whom may have been mounted.[46] The overwhelming majority
were made up of infantry of very diverse quality. The 3500
men brought by Harclay fairly late in August were presumably
first-rate troops.[47] So, probably, was the majority of the huge
body of Welsh foot, still numbering in late August at least some
6300 men. They consisted of the followers of the North Wales
leader, Gruffydd Llwyd, and his South Wales counterpart and
nephew, Rhys ap Gruffydd, as well as of contingents from the
Marcher lordships, including several newly confiscated ones.[48]
There was also a force of 200 Gascon crossbowmen and lance-
throwers who must have been highly prized as Edward continued to retain them in his service after the campaign was
over.[49] Most of these troops of high quality enumerated hitherto
do not appear to have suffered sizeable losses during the
campaign. The wastage was conspicuously greater among
arrayed contingents of infantry. Those shire levies which were
in the king's pay throughout the campaign suffered a loss of at
least 600 men between late July and late August.[50] One suspects
that the contingents that served at their own cost during the
first forty days must have melted more considerably, but some
7000 of these men were still present around 23 August actually
campaigning on Scottish soil.[51]

It was one of the larger English armies ever taken in that age
into Scotland. Its apparent deficiency in cavalry was a serious
weakness and represented a price paid by Edward for his
recent elimination of a large group of Contrariant aristocrats
and of their followers. Much of the infantry was presumably of
scant value for a campaign of this sort. But in appearance at

least it was a formidable force and the subsequent dismay at its failure to achieve anything was bound to be immense.

On 10 August Edward set out. On 18 August he was at Creighton, from where it was only a short distance to the coast, and part of his crucial strategy of supplying this enormous army by naval support could be put into effect. He moved on to Musselburgh near Edinburgh on 19 August. He was obviously already worried about supplies and used a servant of Henry de Beaumont to make a hazardous trip to Holy Island to hasten the arrival of much-needed stores. He moved on to Leith the next day and waited there for them, this time sending a chaplain with a detachment of 20 men to see if the provisions had arrived. They must have returned with an affirmative because the next day Edward was able to make an issue of stores to his men.

Possibly the ships which had brought the supplies also brought news of the impossibility of getting any more provisions through to the king, because he left Leith the next day, returned to Musselburgh and, retreating hastily, passed across Alcrum Moor in Roxburghshire on 30 August, to arrive at the border on 2 September. Edward had many services held in the next few months in thanksgiving for his safe return. As many of the chronicles point out 'he had achieved nothing...done nothing worth mentioning' save that six named Scottish prisoners were taken.

Drafts of letters which he sent to the bishops announcing his safe return into his own country[52] report his invasion and retreat in the unreal manner used by Napoleon in his correspondence with his wife during the tragic retreat from Moscow in 1812.[53] Edward simply stated that they had entered the country meeting no opposition, had reached Edinburgh and had returned by way of the Moor 'the better to harass our enemies but we found in our way neither man nor beast'. He added that he was resolved to winter in the Marches in order to discomfort the enemy. Finally he explained the otherwise curious failure of all the supplies to arrive. 'The Flemings had come to the aid of our enemies, the Scots, and put to sea with the navy just when our fleet was nearing Scotland, took ships with goods on them so that none dared to come to us.' Heavy

storms, which destroyed fourteen ships,[54] may have contributed
to preventing the remaining ships from leaving harbour. Since
other losses of ships on the campaign seem to have been small
(one ship was sunk at Skinburness, while a Colchester ship
sustained some small damage near Leith), it must have been
fear of the Flemish fleet which stopped English ships approach-
ing the king rather than actual losses.

Edward had expressed on a number of occasions the fear
that the Flemings would join in the war on the Scottish side
or take advantage of his absence in Scotland to attack him in
the rear, but somehow he had not taken the right measures to
avert what he had dreaded. There was plenty of warnings but
nothing effective was done. He had warned his naval commander before he set out of the danger from Flemish pirates and
their collusion with the Scots.[55] They had been causing problems while Edward was preparing for the campaign and he had
written to the count of Flanders in April expressing the hope
that he would prevent his men from aiding the Scots. In May
he had commissioned the men of the Cinque Ports to sail against
the Flemings, who were not only helping the Scots but murder-
ing people along the coast and preventing supplies from abroad,
intended for the war, from getting through.[56] In the same month
supplies from Ireland had to be delayed 'as the sea between the
land of Man and Ireland and Skymburnesse is infested by the
king's enemies with the intention of taking the victuals'.[57] The
death of the count of Flanders took place on 17 September
1322 and it is possible that the weakness of the government
there had given the pirates an even freer hand than usual.

Though Edward did not realise this at the time, his problems
were not yet over when he sent his summary account of the
campaign to the bishops on 17 September. The day after he
had recrossed the border, he had dismissed most of his troops
and kept with him only John Birmingham, earl of Louth,
Richard D'Amory, his steward of the household, Ralph
Neville, who was staying in northern England to help keep the
March and Hugh Despenser the Younger, who also sent away
most of his troops.[58] They were unaware that the Scots were
pursuing them and had sent out scouts to locate Edward with
the intention of capturing him.[59] Bruce crossed the border in the

west on 30 September while Edward was preparing for a parliament and trying to assemble another army to defend Norham against the Scots.[60] By 2 October Edward had clearly got wind of Scottish movements and intentions[61] and wrote to Andrew Harclay and eight others to meet him on Blakemore to repulse the Scots.[62] There is no evidence that Harclay received this letter in time to avert the catastrophe which now followed, though Edward later was indignant at Harclay's failure to appear. Failing to get Harclay's help, on 13 October the king ordered Pembroke, who was nearby, to join him the next day at Byland Abbey.[63] Henry de Beaumont and the earl of Richmond, who held lands nearby, had already rejoined him. It was just as well because the Scots were in hot pursuit and the king had no forces to match them. He fled from Byland to Rievaulx, and Richmond, who had been sent to reconnoitre between these two places, was suddenly attacked. He attempted to hold the pass against the Scots but could not. Many fled and the rest, notably the earl himself, were captured. The great French noble, Henry de Sully, together with a number of knights in his train, were also captured and later received rich gifts in recompense from the king, as did also a brave archer who had done outstanding service in covering the king's retreat.[64] The Bridlington chronicler, who may well have seen Edward just after this episode, when the king passed through his house on the way to York, states that Edward was with his half-brother, Kent, Hugh Despenser the Younger, John Cromwell and John Roos.[65] It was the prior of Bridlington himself who conducted them from Bridlington to Burstwick.[66] The Scots were still at the king's heels when he arrived at York on 18 October.[67] Four days later, baulked of their prey, they retreated into Scotland burning as they went.

The news of the king's narrow escape was greeted with tumult and horror in London.[68] To the national tragedy of the complete failure of the campaign was added yet another personal tragedy for Edward, since his mysterious bastard son, Adam, whom he had equipped with care and cost for the campaign, had died during it, perhaps a victim of the sickness which had struck the king's camp.[69]

Professor Michael Powicke has shown the significant part

played in the parliament which overthrew and publicly deposed Edward II in January 1327 by men who had fought in this disastrous campaign.[70] Most of the narrative sources mention enormous losses to troops through starvation and the campaign is singled out for its futility even more than the Bannockburn engagement, where at least the Scots had been brought to battle. The feeling was that the king had achieved nothing at great expense and loss of life.[71]

Although the campaign was disastrous, there is no reason to believe that the truce into which Edward entered the next May was acceptable to the English magnates. It represented for them admission of failure and an implicit threat to their claims to Scottish lands.[72] From Edward's point of view, however, the truce was a dire necessity. His original intention, at the end of the campaign, was to stay near the border to deal with the Scottish threat.[73] His near-capture may have unnerved him, but the treason and execution of Sir Andrew Harclay in January 1323 probably left him with no alternative but to come to some sort of terms with Robert Bruce. The more one looks at the state of northern England the clearer it becomes that Harclay was the most effective figure there in dealing with the Scots and that his earldom was a recognition of this as well as of his defeat of Lancaster (though without the victory of Boroughbridge, it is doubtful if Edward would have been generous enough to bestow it). His removal meant the abandonment of the north. The provision in the truce at Bishopsthorpe for a series of wardens to police the border was nothing more than a glossing over of the fact that the north had been sacrificed. Except for a brief period between 1332 and 1338, it would remain so most of the time for the rest of the Middle Ages, left to the mercy of the Scots, the king's overmighty subjects and its own devices.[74] The truce also made provision for referring disputes between the two kings to Westminster and for safeguarding shipping but these were only secondary policing measures. Edward gave as little as he could and Robert Bruce, whose ailing health also demanded some sort of break in hostilities, grasped as much as he could squeeze. Edward refused to accept Bruce's title and in the next year recalled to England from the ancestral lands in Brittany Edward Balliol, son of King John Balliol of Scotland.[75] He also completely broke the terms of the truce by despatching John Stratford to the papal court to prevent the Pope withdrawing the excommunication of the Scots.[76] The Pope acceded to this preposterous continuation of the excommunication but, at the same time, recognised Bruce as king. It is not to be wondered that in the face of such royal and papal duplicity the negotiations for a permanent peace at York in 1324 broke down. Instead in April 1326 Robert Bruce entered into an alliance with the king of France, an alliance of the utmost potential danger to Edward II.

The French war

Edward had scarcely recovered from his defeat and disgrace at the hands of the Scots when events in the English territories in France overtook him. The death of Philip V in January 1322 was probably decisive. A completely new group of advisers came to the fore in France with the new king, Charles IV. Henry de Sully, the former king's butler, fell from favour. This was a disaster for Edward. Sully's place in the new king's favour was taken by his uncle, Charles of Valois, who was notoriously anti-English.[1] Charles was a considerable military leader who had led the French invasion of Gascony in the 1294–8 war and who had seen the duchy pass back into English hands in 1303 with regret. He had attended his niece's coronation as Edward's queen in 1308 and been outraged at the favour shown by Edward to Gaveston. More decisive for his enmity towards Edward was probably his rivalry with Philip IV's financial adviser, Enguerran de Marigny. There were many personal incidents which bred this hatred, but one of the causes of enmity was that Marigny favoured friendship with England.[2] Charles brought about Marigny's fall and execution in 1315 and Edward's intervention could not save him. When Roger Mortimer of Wigmore escaped from the Tower in August 1323 and fled to France, Edward blamed Charles of Valois for complicity in the plot.[3] About this time, too, Edward's proposals for a marriage between young Prince Edward and one of Charles IV's daughters finally collapsed. A number of embassies had passed between England and France to treat for the marriage. Whether Edward genuinely wanted the match or merely used it to distract the French while he was fighting with the Scots it is difficult to say. He held up the proposals saying that he must have the advice of parliament which was to meet at Michaelmas 1323 and nothing eventually came of them. The realisation of the French that this marriage would not take place may well have contributed to the cooling of relations between the two countries. Edward's alternative marriage schemes were sure to increase French suspicions. In 1324 he was trying to arrange a marriage for his eldest son with an Aragonese princess. In 1325 there were proposals for a double marriage alliance through which Prince Edward and one of his sisters were to marry the two eldest children of the king of Castile. This state bordering on Gascony could be a potential ally against the king of France.

The background to the Gascon war of 1323–5 is a long and complicated one. A glance at the surviving mass of records supplies the most tangible way of appreciating this. By 1320 incessant negotiations about the precise obligations of the kings of England to the kings of France through French overlordship of Gascony had caused a crisis among the English royal clerks keeping the records. They had to compile, for easier reference, a calendar of documents concerning Gascon claims and French counter-claims.[4] When it was completed after a couple of years, late in 1322, this itself constituted a hefty record. The baffling complexity of this material may help to explain why, although historians, notably Yves Renouard, Pierre Chaplais and G. P. Cuttino, have completed editions of parts of the huge amount of evidence available as well as written several specialised studies, no general work parallel to Powicke's *Loss of Normandy* so far exists for Gascony.

To state the background briefly, the cause of strife ultimately lay as far back as the Treaty of Paris which Henry III had made with Louis IX in 1259. By this treaty Henry surrendered his claim to the lands lost by his father, King John, and by himself, that is Normandy, Anjou and Maine, Touraine and Poitou, but obtained acknowledgement of his title to Gascony, in return for which he was to do homage and fealty to the French king.[5] This last provision was of great importance in Edward II's reign, as Edward's refusal to leave the country to fulfil these feudal obligations was an important cause of his downfall, as we shall see later. In the Treaty of Paris very complicated

arrangements were made for the territories bordering on
Gascony, which were essential for the English defence of the
duchy but at that time were under the temporary control of
other French princes. One of these, the Agenais, which was to
be the cause of strife under Edward II, reverted to direct
English overlordship, in 1279. Because it formed a natural
gateway for the French invasions of the Bordelais, the French
were tempted to seek its recovery at the first opportunity. The
treaty had also given the king of France, as overlord of the
Plantagenets, the right to hear appeals from Gascony and the
number and importance of these appeals was also to give rise
to a great deal of ill-feeling. This ill-feeling spread to the subjects of the two monarchs and especially the seamen of the two
countries.

Enmities came to a head in 1293 when the men of the
Cinque Ports, not noted for their tolerance of even their sea-
going rivals at Yarmouth, defeated a Norman fleet off Brittany
and afterwards sacked La Rochelle in Poitou. Philip the Fair
demanded, in retribution, the surrender of the members of the
town council of Bayonne and the appearance of Edward I in
person to answer charges in Paris. He also had demanded the
surrender of Bordeaux and the Agenais. Edward was duped by
Philip into temporarily surrendering Bordeaux and Bayonne
with ten border towns in the Agenais and Saintonge in return
for a proposed marriage with Philip's sister, Margaret of France.
The temporary surrender was intended to reaffirm Philip's
position as overlord. The English officials had handed over these
territories before they realised that Philip had no intention of
returning them. To recover his lost lands Edward was forced
in 1294 to fight a full-scale war with the two chief harbours
of Gascony and the whole network of fortresses constructed by
him there to defend the frontiers already in Philip's hands.
Distracted by a Welsh rebellion, and later on by a Scottish
war, Edward could not go to Gascony in person. The French,
led by Charles of Valois and Robert of Artois, overran most of
the duchy. Only papal intervention brought about a treaty and
the betrothal of Edward I to Margaret, which was to provide
Edward II with his two much younger half-brothers and
ultimately enemies, Kent and Norfolk, as well as ultimately

lead to Edward's own marriage to Isabella, Philip's daughter. The treaty was made at Montreuil in June 1299. Philip, however, hung on to the duchy until his defeat by the Flemings at Courtrai in 1302. This made the English friendship important, so that Philip handed the duchy back to the English administration the next year. To sum up in Powicke's words, 'The status of Gascony has become involved in a network of juristic learning; the boundaries were not clearly fixed; old disputes had not been settled. In Edward II's reign all sorts of thorny difficulties survived to become still more complicated in the processes of Périgueux and the Agenais. The duty of the duke to take the oath of fealty as well as to do homage in person was disputed. The marriage between Edward II and Isabella of France raised the great problem of the French succession. The treaty of 1303 was but an incident, a breathing space in the interminable wrangle which the treaty of 1259 had produced.'[6] The newly discovered papers of one of the English ambassadors to the French court in 1323–5, William Weston, illustrate the mass of documentation and breadth of detailed knowledge which any clerk involved in attempting to vindicate English rights in Gascony was obliged to acquire.[7] In the event it was the brute force of Charles of Valois rather than negotiations of English ambassadors which settled the issue.

Edward II was, in fact, fortunate to have had peace in Gascony for as long as he did. Three major factors determined this. The first was that, however much certain pro-French noblemen in Gascony might find it advantageous to appeal over Edward's head to the king of France in their disputes, to the Gascon people, and especially the merchants, the English connection was a blessing and peace between England and France a necessity. This was because the duchy was dependent then, as the region is now, on its export of wine. Its chief market was England. This wine came not only, or even primarily, from the duchy itself but from the dominions of the king of France for which the Gascon ports, and especially Bordeaux, merely acted as the outlet. Conflict with France was disastrous for this trade. The Anglo-French war of 1294 had temporarily crippled the trade and when war broke out again in 1323 the imports of wine into England dropped by half in the year

1324–5.[8] This in turn caused an enormous drop in revenue for the king of England, as the duties on wine constituted his chief source of income from the duchy.

The groups in Gascony who depended for their living on peace between France and England had one exceptionally powerful supporter in the first seven years of Edward's reign. This was Pope Clement V.[9] He was an old friend of Edward I and had actually been an English royal clerk early in his career.[10] Bertrand de Got came from an ancient Gascon family. Before he even became archbishop of Bordeaux, he had acted as Edward's envoy to the Pope. After he himself became Pope, Clement remained deeply concerned with Gascon affairs. It has been estimated that one-quarter of the letters in his register concern Gascony. His involvement was in part due to his affection for Edward I, but was above all motivated by his predilection for his nephew, another Bertrand de Got, who was in the unfortunate position of having to serve two masters, the king of England and his overlord the king of France. The Pope and his nephew desired peace as much as did the desperate Gascon officials, whose horror at the idea of war with France is clear from the correspondence of this period. It was Clement who pushed through Edward II's fateful marriage with Philip the Fair's daughter, Isabella. When Edward was reduced to desperate financial straits and his barons had destroyed his chief source of credit, the Frescobaldi bankers, Clement filled the breach by first granting him the proceeds of the clerical tenth for several years and then making him a massive loan of 160000 florins in January 1313. His death on 26 May 1314 was a disaster for Edward.

Edward enjoyed one other advantage in the earlier part of his reign. His opponents, the last Capetian kings of France, inherited many problems similar to those of Edward himself, depleted treasuries and a reaction against the centralising policies of the monarchy. They also had additional problems which for long made a major war against the English over Gascony unthinkable. Louis X inherited the throne in 1314 just after his recently divorced first wife had died in prison and he faced a wave of rebellious provincial leagues. He inherited the Flemish opposition to French authority and in 1315 his campaign in Flanders failed completely through the ill-fortune of terrible weather. He died suddenly in 1316 leaving a serious succession problem, namely one daughter and a pregnant wife. His posthumous son, John I, died within a few days and his brother Philip V, who had been acting as regent, succeeded. At this time, however, the exclusion of women from the succession was not part of any settled custom and Louis' daughter had a strong claim. There were demonstrations by the nobility on her behalf in Champagne, Artois and Burgundy and most of the magnates refused to attend his coronation. But, as a reaction against his brother's regime, which had been much influenced by Charles of Valois, Philip was surrounded with advisers who were not hostile to England.

In these circumstances it is not surprising that Edward was able to act dilatorily in the discharge of his feudal obligations. He shared his father's dislike of doing homage for his French lands, managed to avoid doing so to Louis X and only did so to Philip V four years after the latter's accession. The success of various diplomatic missions to France during this time was probably due to the talent for diplomacy of Aymer de Valence, earl of Pembroke, who also had possessions in France and had personal connections with the French court. Two other French noblemen in considerable favour with both sides were the earl of Richmond, who was also a member of the ruling house of Brittany, and Henry de Sully, the holder of the high court office of butler to the king of France. Edward's own successive visits to the French court were not unsuccessful. An earlier visit to Philip IV in July 1313 had brought 'a remission of all penalties incurred by Edward II and his subjects in Gascony for offences against France'. The visit also brought Edward a hefty loan of 33 000 *li. tur* arranged through Antonio Pessagno of Genoa, a banker whose services both kings shared.[11]

It was not until Philip V had established himself in his realm, about 1320, that the French showed signs of asserting claims which were calculated to stir up trouble. In May 1319 Philip had allowed Edward the great favour of doing simple homage by proxy, but when Edward finally put in an appearance in France, at Amiens in 1320, to complete his recognition of

feudal obligations, the French made an unexpected demand
for an additional oath of personal fealty to the king of France
as well as submission for the French lands. Edward promptly
refused to make this without the advice of his councillors. He
claimed that no such thing had been required of him by Philip
IV when he had initially rendered homage for his territories
at the beginning of his rule. It was only the beginning of the
French pressure. It is significant that at about the same time
as the Gascon calendar was being drawn up in England, the
French royal officials were also drawing up a dossier, designed
to present precedents for an oath of personal fealty with which
they then confronted Edward at Amiens.[12]

Much of the time Edward could not be relied upon to behave
in Gascon matters as spontaneously in his real interests as he
had done at Amiens. The author of the *Vita* alleges that, to
save Gaveston, when the favourite was in the magnates'
custody in 1312, Edward was prepared to buy the aid of the
king of France and the pope 'by giving them Gascony in fee'.[13]
In 1321, at the height of the Despenser war in Glamorgan, the
messenger of the English seneschal of Gascony waited for three
weeks without obtaining a hearing from the king. Edward was
too preoccupied with the fate of his favourite's lands. In this
case, the fact that the seneschal's clerk was accompanied by
Edward's enemy, Adam Orleton, probably did not help, but
the case illustrates nicely how the affairs of the duchy were
being neglected because of Edward's difficulties in England.[14]
There are indications on this occasion that Despenser and his
clerk, Robert Baldock, did not want the king to be distracted
from dealing with the difficult situation in England. The
chronicler Geoffrey Baker tells the interesting tale that, after
Charles IV had succeeded his brother in January 1322, he
refrained from demanding homage from his English brother-
in-law while Edward was fighting the Scots.[15] The Scots at this
time were also not favoured by France as they were allied with
the Flemings and Henry de Sully actually accompanied Edward in the Scottish campaign of 1322 and fought most valiantly.
When Charles IV finally sent his notary, Andrew of Florence,
to England to demand homage, Despenser and Baldock kept
the news of his arrival from the king. At this point Charles

threatened him with forfeiture of the French lands unless he performed his feudal obligations.[16]

Edward had scarcely recovered from his near capture by the Scots at the end of his campaign in October 1322 when, in December, an *arrêt* of the parlement of Paris authorised the building of a *bastide*, a small fortress, at Saint Sardos.[17] This *arrêt* was an action more provocative to Edward than any demand for homage and it is difficult to believe that the decision to issue it was not made at the highest level, by the king of France himself. Charles had hoped that Edward would help him to defeat his Flemish adversaries. When their collaboration with the Scots led to Edward's resounding failure in Scotland, Charles gave up hope of using him. This meant that Edward lost his immunity from attack in Gascony. It was through a legal loophole that the erection of a *bastide* at Saint Sardos in the middle of the English territory of Agenais was possible. The ecclesiastical lord of Saint Sardos claimed dependency from an abbey which was directly subject to the king of France. Saint Sardos was thus in an anomalous position, but the political implications of building a fortress there were clear. Neither could the king of England countenance a French fortress in the middle of his lands, nor could the Gascon lords stomach the creation of a new town and commercial centre which would rob them of trade from which they drew handsome revenues.

It is impossible to say whether Edward's seneschal of Gascony, Ralph Basset of Drayton, took the initiative himself or if he was acting under a royal order when he decided on a dangerous line of action. He entered into a sworn agreement with the Gascon lord most affected and outraged by the building of the *bastide*, Raymond Bernard of Montpezat. The date for the erection of the *bastide* was fixed for Sunday, 16 October 1323, a day when armed resistance would be improper. Montpezat may not have broken the Sabbath but a few hours later he entered Saint Sardos with a gang of men, among whom were English royal officials, burned what was there to the ground and hanged the French royal official from the stake of claim which he had erected. The English seneschal of Gascony was in the vicinity while this was happening. News reached the

king of France on 1 November. Amaury, lord of Craon, who
had twice acted as seneschal of Guyenne for Edward, warned
Edward of the dangers resulting from this piece of gunboat
diplomacy. He wrote separately to Despenser begging him to
counsel Edward to placate the king of France. Either as the
result of such advice, or acting on his own initiative, Edward
attempted to do this. Five days after he had received the news
of what had happened, he ordered the constable of Bordeaux
to enquire into the outrage, and both the constable's official
superior, the seneschal Ralph Basset, and Edward himself
disclaimed all responsibility. But the French king established
his own commission and summoned Basset to answer charges.
The constable of Bordeaux wrote to the English government
that if he and Basset answered the king of France's summons
to appear before the commission they would not escape with
their lives. Basset, in his replies to the king of France, subsequently claimed that he could not appear because he was ill!
He attempted to redeem his legally inferior position by raising
a question similar to that which had caused the outbreak of
hostilities between Edward I and Philip the Fair. This was the
piracy and fighting at sea between French sailors and those of
the king of England's French subjects. Charles, having failed
to get hold of the seneschal and the constable of Bordeaux,
satisfied himself by imprisoning Edward's procurator at Paris.
The unfortunate man sent a pompous and outraged complaint
to Edward.

By February 1324 things had reached a serious pass. Charles
had moved towards Gascony over Christmas. His ostensible
motive at this stage was the wish to capture the miscreants who
had raided Saint Sardos rather than take the whole duchy; in
March the seneschal of Toulouse reminded Charles that his
commission was limited to seizing the lands of these miscreants.
Edward begged for a postponement of any seizure of the duchy
for his failure to appear to do homage and fealty. As his father
had done before when Gascony was on the point of being over-
run, he sent the most high-powered embassy possible, headed
by his brother Kent. Kent returned without success and when
he next left for Gascony later on in 1323, it was at the head of
an army to defend La Réole. Between 13 and 16 March

Edward's procurator delivered a formal complaint against the proposed seizure of Montpezat's castle and represented that Edward was bound to defend his own tenant-in-chief against his overlord. Conciliatory steps in July, like the removal from office of Ralph Basset and even the sending of Henry de Sully to France as Edward's special envoy,[18] could not dissuade Charles IV from going to war. A limited war could prove quite lucrative since it would enable Charles to impose some general taxes that he could secure only in wartime.

The French concentrated their efforts on the north-eastern region of Agenais. Charles of Valois, the French commander, arrived at Cahors ready for the offensive on 8 August.[19] He had already demanded the surrender of its capital, Agen, and its authorities duly notified Edmund, earl of Kent, the king's lieutenant in Gascony, of this demand. Kent had already antagonised the people of Agen. According to French sources he had aroused resentment by heavy levies of money and by abducting a young girl from the town.[20] Agen certainly made an early surrender, opening its gates to Charles on 15 August. Its commander was Oliver Ingham, a close associate of the Despensers. He failed to hold the town because the towns-people refused to support him.[21] Charles of Valois then moved on Port-Saint-Marie and his forces took the castles of Tonneins, Marmande, Sainte Foy and finally arrived at La Réole. There, somewhat foolishly, Edmund, earl of Kent, allowed himself to be boxed in. On 1 September the constable of Bordeaux in a panic wrote that the whole duchy was about to collapse.[22] In fact, although the Agenais and parts of the Gironde region including the castle of Gironde had been taken over, the whole duchy did not fall. The chief cities of Bordeaux and Bayonne remained in English hands, as did the lesser centres of Saint Émilion, Libourne, Bourg sur Mer and Condom. It is therefore unlikely that the English would have had to make a truce had not Kent's capture been imminent. For one thing the French were involved on two fronts. A revolt had taken place in Bruges in June 1323 and anarchy reigned in the county of Flanders which, sooner or later, was bound to demand French inter-vention.[23] Hence Kent was able to obtain a six-month truce after being besieged at La Réole for five weeks.

Kent would probably not have had to negotiate at all had he had any hope of swift reinforcements. There were excessive delays in England in despatching ships, troops and money. One has the impression that the royal government under-estimated the amount of help that was required. While Edward had plenty of money he was slow and niggardly in sending it to Gascony. As far as money was concerned, it was all the time a story of too little being sent and too late.[24]

The navy had originally been summoned by a royal letter of 28 July to be at Portsmouth on 27 August. Then on 18 August its arrival was postponed until 10 September. There was yet another postponement and finally only the western fleet was able to leave Falmouth on 22 October. It carried Nicholas Huggate, appointed as chief receiver in Gascony, who reached Bordeaux on 3 October bringing with him a mere £8000.[25] The Cinque Ports fleet which had set out from Ports-mouth slightly earlier, on 18 September, was blown by contrary winds into Falmouth, which it did not manage to leave until 4 October. It transported contingents led by eighty-three different leaders (ten of whom were former Contrariants), and also brought a further 14600 marks for delivery to Huggate. He only received this money in November.[26] Because of all these delays the authorities at Bordeaux disposed of very little while the French invasion of Agenais was pursuing its triumphant course. The constable of Bordeaux even lacked money to pay and feed his troops properly. When grain arrived it proved to be rotten and riots broke out at Bordeaux.[27]

The eastern fleet did not set out at all in 1324. News of a large enemy fleet assembling off Zealand made its stay in England essential to defend the coast. Another major expedition did not reach Bordeaux until May 1325, even though the admiral in charge of it, John Sturmy, had been appointed to his post as far back as 5 August 1324. This fleet did bring important reinforcements and Huggate received from it on 19 May £20441 18s. 8d.[28] By that time negotiations for peace were about to start at Paris and this money was largely spent on maintaining in Gascony an army that never had to fight again. Altogether, Edward had to spend on the war at least

£65 000 but he never used his ample financial resources to the best advantage.[29]

The autumn of 1323 was filled with rumour and alarm in England. The archbishop of Canterbury, the timorous Reynolds, felt vulnerable in Kent and produced a tale of a fleet of 180 German cogs and 60 French vessels assembled by the count of Hainault in Zealand.[30] This fleet, about which he warned the Chancellor, proved to be entirely fictitious. His cooler-headed prior, Henry Eastry of Christchurch, was trying to think of ways to prevent such constant scaremongering in Kent and tried to provide a system of reliable warnings.[31] In the south-west, ships which had set out for Gascony but been driven into Falmouth, found that they were laying at anchor alongside a fleet of foreign vessels. The leader of the fleet was questioned and, probably because of the unpleasant nature of this experience, the ships disappeared in the night.[32] A busy correspondent wrote to Despenser that there were 100 armed men aboard each ship. This was nothing more sinister than the annual Genoese fleet on its way to the Netherlands and carrying its customary complement of armed men to guard its valuable cargo.[33] In the state of fear and rumour in England, however, it raised the gravest fears. This particular Geonese scare was probably associated with the rumour that the Genoese, Antonio Pessagno, Edward's erstwhile financier, was assembling a fleet to sail against England with the aid of his brother, Manuel, the king of Portugal's Admiral.[34] In fact, neither a Franco-Hainaulter invasion from the east nor a Genoese–Portuguese assault from the south-west ever materialised.

The only alternative step open to Edward was to negotiate. He could not do so really effectively because he dared not leave the country either to do homage or fealty or to confer with the French king. Hugh Despenser, in a letter to Ralph Basset at the beginning of October 1323, wrote encouragingly that the king would come to France with an army after he had made a final peace treaty with the Scots on 18 November.[35] A treaty with the Scots never materialised, but it was fear of opposition in England which prevented Edward from going overseas. Pressure from the Despensers prevented him from going if the author of the *Vita* is to be believed. According to him both

Despensers, father and son, did not dare to go abroad nor, if the king crossed, to remain in England, because the nobles of the realm so hated them.[36]

As early as April 1324 it had been mooted that Isabella, Charles' sister, should act as an intermediary between her warring brother and husband.[37] She herself was in disgrace in England. Her lands had been seized on the pretext that they represented a particular danger at a time of harassment by the French. What was even more insulting, her servants were 'imprisoned', though this was thinly disguised by despatching them to religious houses throughout the country.[38] In July 1324, however, perhaps because there seemed no other way out of the diplomatic impasse, the Pope appealed to her to mediate. It may well have been from the Pope's appeal that Edward had the idea of sending her to France. There is a possibility that ever since their marriage he had held many of his difficulties in Gascony against her. According to the Bridlington chronicler he had married her 'in the hope of peace and of recovering the lands overseas occupied by the king of France as had been finally agreed between him and the king of France; but once the marriage had taken place, the French continued to occupy the lands in Gascony and elsewhere and hung onto them'.[39]

At the end of 1324, however, a further suggestion was made by ambassadors to the French court that the young Prince Edward, heir to the throne, should do homage for the English lands in France, having first been granted seisin of them by his father. There were obvious dangers for Edward in allowing his heir to visit an enemy country. The fact that the chief protagonist of the scheme was John Stratford, bishop of Winchester, who had recently incurred heavy royal displeasure by accepting papal provision to the see of Winchester, cannot have recommended the idea to Edward and his council. They rejected it, but arrangements began to send Isabella to France. She eventually departed on 9 March 1325.[40] The author of *Vita* wrote that 'The Queen departed very joyfully, happy with a twofold joy; pleased to visit her native land and her relatives, delighted to leave the company of some whom she did not like. Small wonder if she does not like Hugh, through whom her uncle perished, by whom she was deprived of her servants and all her rents; consequently she will not (so many think) return until Hugh Despenser is wholly removed from the king's side.'[41] Another source alleges that Despenser was encouraging the king to procure a divorce from her and that Thomas Dunheved had been sent to Rome for this purpose.[42] Dr Blackley has suggested that there is no reason to assume that Isabella wished to go to France because Roger Mortimer was there and has argued that there was as yet no close relationship between Isabella and Roger Mortimer.[43] This is probably correct. His notion that Isabella left the country entirely without an ulterior motive is not so easy to accept. Prior Eastry was obviously uneasy that she was departing in a dissatisfied mood; he wanted Isabella to be given back her lands and her French servants before she departed. He also showed his misgivings clearly when he urged his friend, Archbishop Reynolds, to avoid going with her, if possible.[44] Eastry was an exceptionally shrewd and well-informed man who took advantage of the visits of notables on pilgrimage to Canterbury or travelling between England and the continent to find out what was going on. Isabella herself passed through his abbey on her way to France and left her dogs in his charge.[45]

Once abroad, Isabella seems to have gone more slowly than the average ambassador about her important mission. She arrived before the middle of March 1325, but did not meet the king of France, her brother, until 30 May.[46] In spite of the apparent trust in her powers as ambassadress, Edward viewed her departure with suspicion from the outset. The king instructed the constable of Dover under the secret seal on 2 April 1325 to let no messenger from the queen or any other envoy pass freely or see anybody until he had first been conducted to the king.[47] Isabella, however, managed to achieve the purpose of her embassy fairly quickly, once she had met her brother, because Edward had received the terms of the projected treaty and drafted his reply to them by 13 June, when he issued letters patent agreeing to the terms evolved by Isabella and Charles. These terms were crushing for Edward, but whether anything better could have been expected given a more able or a more committed envoy than Isabella is doubtful. The king of France was provisionally given the right to nominate a seneschal in occupied Agenais, who would in turn appoint all royal officials. To prevent a recurrence of the military seizure of the main strongholds, which his father had suffered in 1294, Edward was allowed to maintain control of the castles and military administration. The constables of the castles were not, however, supposed to raise extra troops without the permission of the French seneschal. Edward was to do homage for the English lands in France at Beauvais on 15 August. Then he would be formally reinvested with them, excluding the Agenais. The title to this was to be submitted to judicial investigation. If the commission agreed that Edward had a valid title to it, he was to pay Charles an indemnity sufficient to defray the cost of the French army in the recent campaign. If Charles were awarded the territory, Edward would be spared paying the indemnity.[48]

On 1 June 1325 the date of Edward's homage was postponed until 29 August and even far into August Edward was holding meetings to obtain advice as to whether or not he should go. He pleaded illness and asked for his son to take his place at his investiture. Edward was waiting at Dover to cross when letters came from the king of France saying that the homage of his son would be accepted in place of his own.[49] Edward invested his son with the French lands and on 12 September, under the guardianship of Walter Stapeldon, bishop of Exeter, and Henry de Beaumont, the boy set out.[50] With this embassy Edward sent a message to Isabella demanding that, since the purpose of her embassy had been fulfilled, she should return but she ignored this request. On 24 September 1325 Prince Edward did homage for the lands and the dangerous impasse with France ended but only at the cost of letting an even more dangerous situation develop.

The opposition to royal tyranny, 1322–6

The king's reluctance to leave his kingdom to render homage to
the king of France is very understandable when one examines
the internal condition of the country at the time. Edward had
undoubtedly recruited a remarkably able judiciary whose
intelligence, wit and learning is amply attested in the earliest
surviving law reports, the Year Books. The best of these men,
William Herle, described as 'the greatest lawyer of his age',[1]
Geoffrey le Scrope and John Stonor continued their brilliant
legal careers under Edward III. Unfortunately there is no sign
that the ability of these men in court could halt the tide of
banditry, raiding, gang warfare and murder outside the courts,
which characterised both the countryside and the capital under
the Despenser regime. The lawlessness often had its basis in
the unending feud between the Despensers and the fugitive
followers of the dead earl of Lancaster. Neither side behaved
better than the other. For every good justice whom Edward
employed, he kept at court or used in the localities several men
who were nothing more than aristocratic criminals. The mis-
deeds of the Despensers themselves have already provided us
with a grim chapter. Edward favoured a number of other
lawless personalities. At the beginning of the reign Gilbert
Middleton, captor of the cardinals and Robert Ewer, who was
to lead two rebellions, were both favoured knights of Edward.
Malcolm Musard, terror of the small landowners in the Midlands, was also employed by him.[2] At the end of the reign
John Molyns of Stoke Poges, a member of the entourage of
Hugh Despenser, began his rise to influence at court. He then
used the chaos which accompanied Isabella's landing to
murder his wife's cousin and that man's only son, in order to

inherit his lands.[3] In Kent, Henry Valoignes' 'riotous assemblies' were disrupting a part of the country already endangered by invasion and full of rumour and unrest.[4] Valoignes so terrified Reynolds that the archbishop was afraid to move around his diocese.

One of the outstanding features of the English monarchy in the Middle Ages, which set it quite apart from the continental states, had been that it had made private war between great subjects illegal. Usually it had been able to enforce that prohibition. Under Edward II, however, the monarchy was effectively submerged by internal strife. This had begun with the murder of Gaveston, continued in the intermittent violence between Lancaster and Warenne, between Valence and Berkeley and between the Charlton and de la Pole families. Its high point was the ravaging of the estates of the two Despensers in the summer of 1321. However understandable the motives of the attackers, this was private war and also criminal brigandage on a horrifying scale inflicted by one group of aristocrats on the other.

After Boroughbridge, the violence which had been unleashed by the bitter civil war took a different turn. The Contrariants, formerly the pillars of the administration in many localities, were now hunted fugitives and their estates were open to plunder by their former tenants, neighbours, officials, and half the countryside as well, to judge by the returns to royal commissions. Even the great Lancastrian fortresses of Tutbury and Kenilworth and the Mortimer castle of Wigmore were despoiled. Jewels, money, plate, furniture, animals and grain were carried off in huge quantities. Often former officials who knew the location of these treasures were involved. Lancaster's receiver, Elias Stapelton, allegedly took the massive sum of £3000 from Tutbury castle as well as jewels worth £40. Some he gave to the prior of Coventry, who seems to have been an associate of the Despensers. The rest he kept for himself.[5] John Derley and Laurence Coterel, the latter being the member of a terrible gang whose fitting end under Edward III has been described elsewhere, seem to have started their career of crime at this time. Coterel specialised in robbing fugitive Contrariants even though members of his own family were of that party. He and Derley robbed those in flight from Boroughbridge of £20 worth of horses and armour. They also managed to lay hands on a quantity of silver plate. They were about to carry these off when a great army of Welsh troops with some English horse and foot arrived and robbed the robbers, as they claimed in one inquisition.[6]

A number of Contrariants, unable or unwilling to flee into exile, stayed and carried on guerilla activities against the Despensers and also involved large numbers of local sympathisers in their cause. Parts of the Welsh March formed a particularly troubled area. Roaming Contrariants carried off much game in the Forest of Dean. One of the chief culprits was its former chief forester and a Berkeley retainer, Walter Nasse.[7] As early as September 1322, when the Despensers were in the north with the king after the disastrous Scottish campaign, John Mautravers, William Whitfield with Nicholas and William, members of the Contrariant branch of the Percy family, attacked the earl of Winchester's manors in southern England and those of Winchester's knight, Ingemam Berenger. Thirty-one Somerset people and seventy-six Hampshire people were involved in this attack and one could give similar large figures from returns to inquisitions into other attacks on Despenser estates.[8] Another such occasion was in March 1323, when William Trussell, one of the most notable fugitives, who was to play an important part in the deposition of Edward II, together with his son and two members of the Zouche family, Ralph and Roger, attacked Winchester's Midland properties. On this occasion they failed to gain entrance to the earl's principal dwellings, but they did extensive damage to gates, windows and doors and carried off what stock they could find.[9] At an unknown date Winchester's estates in Worcestershire were attacked by followers of Mortimer. Malvern was their chief target.[10] One can trace similar attacks on much smaller people who may have been followers of the Despensers or who were simply attacked as loyal supporters of the regime. A Northamptonshire man, John Saint Mark, was the object of persecution by Sir Robert de Vere, younger son of the earl of Oxford and a man whose lawlessness continued to be notorious in the next reign. Saint Mark and his family dared not stay

F

in one place because Sir Robert had sworn to murder him. He complained that, although Sir Robert was supposed to be a fugitive after Boroughbridge, none of the justices dared indict him because of his menaces against them. His plaint tails off 'because there is no law in the land'.[11]

One sympathises with John Saint Mark because, whatever his offence against Sir Robert, the latter was a dangerous desperado who in later years lent his castles as hideouts in difficult times to the worst criminal gang of the day, the Folvilles of Ashby-Folville in Leicestershire.[12] Sometimes he joined these men on their ventures. The Zouches, whom we have already had cause to mention, also employed their years as Contrariants as part-time members of the same gang. Together, Folvilles and Zouches in January 1326 executed their greatest criminal coup of the reign. They murdered Sir Roger Belers, chief baron of the exchequer at Westminster, when he was riding to lunch with Henry, earl of Leicester. There was an ancient feud between the Folvilles and Bellers, who were neighbours. The Zouches' motive was probably political. Bellers had deserted the Lancastrian cause and had become one of the trusted and most used servants of the Despenser regime. Amongst his other responsibilities he had acted as a member of the commission sent to investigate the attack by the Zouches and Trussell on Winchester's Midland properties. Bellers' widow accused the murderers of his death but they could not be apprehended.

The Contrariants were also busy trying to whip up public opinion against the king by extolling their executed companions in arms as martyrs. One centre of these happenings was at Bristol. This was a particularly sensitive spot, as had been shown previously by the rising in Bristol over the tallage of 1316. The younger Despenser held the custody of the royal castle at Bristol as heir of its former Clare castellans and the hatred that he inspired was to be visited upon his father, executed in Bristol amidst popular rejoicings in October 1326. There was turmoil in Bristol in the summer of 1323; people were reported to be flocking to the body of Henry Montfort left hanging there, because it was believed to be producing miracles. The mayor of Bristol claimed in September 1323 that

Sir Reginald Montfort had come there and given a poor child two shillings to say that his sight had been cured through the intercession of the martyr. The mayor also alleged that another prominent Contrariant, William Clif, had also come and spread rumours of miracles until the authorities came to hear of this and he had to flee to sanctuary. An enquiry found that the mayor himself was implicated in spreading these rumours.[13] At the other end of the country William Melton, archbishop of York, had twice to remind his archdeacon that Lancaster was not a canonised saint and to tell him to stop the great crowds visiting the earl's grave at Pontefract, where people had actually been crushed to death in the throng.[14]

Edward and the Despensers were surrounded by a cloud of enmity and could never be certain from what quarter the next blow might come. Two of the potentially most serious conspiracies against the regime were due not to the Contrariants but to two men who had contributed to Edward's victory in 1322, Robert Ewer and Andrew Harclay. The news of the first conspiracy greeted Edward as he returned from the debacle of his Scottish campaign in the early autumn of 1322. The motives of its chief fomenter, Robert Ewer, remain a mystery. Ewer was a Hampshire knight of no great family, but he appears to have been brought up at court. He had been in considerable favour with the king, and was sufficiently disliked by the king's opponents at the beginning of the reign to figure amongst those whose removal the Ordainers demanded.[15] This attempt to get rid of him did not succeed and the king gave him custody of Odiham castle. He was clearly an unusually active soldier and the number of archers whom he kept in his service attracted notice. In 1320, for an unknown reason, Robert Ewer rose in revolt and threatened with death those who tried to capture him. The revolt was clearly against a person or persons closely connected with Edward because Ewer threatened them 'either in the presence or the absence of the king'.[16] It seems unlikely that the Despensers were meant because Ewer was pardoned and took a vigorous part in the civil war, fighting for the king in Gloucestershire and the Welsh March.[17] He was regarded as sufficiently trustworthy to be

responsible, with Earl Warenne, for conducting the Mortimers from Shrewsbury to the Tower after their surrender
in January 1322. He was then summoned to serve in the August
campaign in Scotland, where he had much useful military
experience, since he had been captured when serving there in
1315, perhaps on the same occasion that Andrew Harclay was
taken prisoner. However, he never served in Edward's last
Scottish campaign. He received a safe-conduct to come to the
king in August, but instead he used the king's absence in
Scotland to attack the estates of the earl of Winchester, who
had remained in England. There is a very interesting account
of the rebellion in the *Vita Edwardi*, whose author seems to
have known a good deal about Ewer and to have strongly
disapproved of him: 'So Robert le Ewer came to the earl of
Winchester's manors and carried off victuals and other neces-
saries as he liked. He also visited the manors of Henry Tyeys
and Warin de Lisle, granted by the king to the earl of Winchester after their condemnation. And there Sir Robert made
a great distribution to the poor in the name of alms for the
souls of the said barons. From this he profited little because
God has regard to the intention rather than the deed…When
the earl of Winchester heard that Robert had come to arrest
him he took refuge in Windsor castle and set a watch night and
day, until he should have collected a force sufficient to capture
Robert and his retinue.'[18] By the time that Winchester had done
so the king had returned to England and on 20 September he
ordered Ewer to hand over Odiham castle or have it taken
from him by force.[19] By 1 November the rebel had apparently
moved into Lancashire, for the sheriff of that county, Robert
Leyburn, was ordered to take him.[20] On 15 November the earl
of Kent with two knights was sent to Wales at the head of a
party to find him.[21] They were obviously unsuccessful and by
the end of the month Ewer was reputedly in Yorkshire, for
summonses were issued to find him there.[22] It looks as if he may
have been trying to reach the king. News of his eventual arrest
was received by the king on 15 December. By that stage Edward
does not seem to have valued it highly because he gave the
bearer of the good tidings only half a mark.[23] It is clear,
however, that the rebellion must have been a serious matter

at its height to have compelled Winchester to go into hiding at Windsor. To judge from royal mandates, Ewer had supporters, or at least was suspected of having them, in many counties in England. It is also clear from the *Vita* that he expected more help than he got and that, after coming north, he had returned to his home area and tried to flee the country.

At one point it was believed that Ewer was in Wales. This ominous rumour came at the same time as stirrings of trouble late in 1322, but in fact no serious rebellion materialised. Probably the presence of their most dangerous enemy, Sir Gruffydd Llwyd, with the king to Scotland gave some courage to a remnant of Marcher rebels. Oliver Ingham had reported this trouble in the March to the king and had challenged the imprisoned Mortimers about it.[24] They, needless to say, had denied all knowledge of subversion, but fear of their plotting may have caused Edward to reconsider his previous clemency. He decided to put the younger Mortimer to death and thus precipitated his escape. The king's long absence in the north also encouraged disturbing rumours in London, while the news of his near capture at Byland in October 1322 had caused panic in the city and alarmed Richard Swynnerton, the custodian of the Tower.[25] The king wrote to Swynnerton exhorting him to keep the fortress safe, but he seems to have developed doubts about Swynnerton's suitability for this post. As constable of the Tower he was in charge of a motley collection of former rebels, their wives, heirs, and other children. He was replaced by John Segrave, a cousin of the elder Despenser. Both constables were former Lancastrian retainers and members of their families had taken the earl's side in the civil war. Their switch of allegiance to the king illustrates the ability of retainers to adapt themselves to new circumstances and new masters. Their first loyalty was to their own future. It is a good illustration of how difficult Edward found it to obtain reliable servants of good standing, who were not in some way connected with his Contrariant opponents.

The year 1323 opened with a near disaster at another royal castle, Wallingford, where in January Maurice Berkeley nearly succeeded in escaping from custody. This was engineered by his followers from outside and the whole attempt may have been treated as a prelude to an attack on the earl of Winchester, who was in the area at the time.[26] It was also believed to be part of a nation-wide conspiracy on the part of the Contrariants still at large to seize some major castles. It was certainly the result of some very loose security at Wallingford. As in the case of the Tower of London, there was a great problem of finding gaolers who were not unduly indulgent to their political prisoners. At Wallingford, Maurice Berkeley prepared his attempt at escaping by actually inviting the constable of the castle to supper on the pretext of a visit by one of his esquires and some servants. During the dinner these men suddenly rose and demanded the keys to the castle! They must have carried concealed arms because they were able to threaten death to any who stood in their way. They let in another twenty men who stood ready at the castle gate. Had a boy not given the alarm in the town, Berkeley would certainly have escaped. Instead, Winchester and Kent arrived on the scene to aid the sheriff and townspeople. Berkeley and his rescuers surrendered after a few days' siege.[27] Berkeley died three years later while still imprisoned.

At the very time that Wallingford was under siege, in January 1323, intelligence reached the king of a much more serious rebellion. Andrew Harclay, whom the king had made earl of Carlisle only six months before, was rumoured to have conspired with the Scots.[28] On 8 January Edward wrote to Harclay to demand his appearance at court and to notify the king of any truces which he was making with Robert Bruce.[29] Harclay had already been responsible for making a number of local truces on the king's behalf, but in this case the summons was very sinister. He was to be charged with treason, though there is no certainty that this accusation was justified. Northern chroniclers offer a number of explanations for Harclay's presumed betrayal of his patron, Edward II. The most romantic was that he was in love with Robert Bruce's daughter.[30] Another was his hatred of the Despensers, whose jealousy of Harclay may have been an important cause of his downfall.[31] A further explanation was his estrangement from the king after the Byland episode when Edward had nearly been captured by the Scots.[32]

Edward, according to one source, believed that Harclay had not come to his aid as quickly as he might have done and was actually prepared to see his lord captured by the Scots. Harclay was not without enemies in the north who would have been very ready to feed the king's suspicions, justified or not. The most prominent was Anthony Lucy, lord of Penrith. Their enmity may have had its origins in their rival claims for the honour of Papcastle.[33] Harclay had high-handedly taken Lucy's lands into the king's hands in 1322 during the civil war, allegedly for treason, but he had to return them when it became clear that Lucy had never joined the rebel cause.[34] Harclay also obtained a pardon for Hugh Lowther, a Contrariant who had been sub-sheriff of Westmorland during the shrievalty of Roger Clifford, himself a leading Contrariant. Lowther, earlier on, had himself been responsible for disseising a member of the Lucy family from a property.[35] Anthony Lucy had his revenge when he took Harclay by surprise at Carlisle and arrested him. Lucy was shortly joined by members of the royal household who had been sent out from the king at York to deal with the traitor. Harclay was degraded from his title of earl, sentence was pronounced on him and he was hanged, drawn and quartered. His head was set on London Bridge and one of his quarters placed in a prominent place in Carlisle castle, the city which he had defended so strenuously against the Scots. It could be seen there for five years afterwards.

Harclay was a man of little wealth but with a considerable following. This is seen clearly from the list of his supporters in Cumberland assembled by the regime after his fall.[36] In this dangerous area, as in the March of Wales, it was not the wealth of a magnate which earned him reliable local support, as Lancaster learned to his cost, but his ability to provide good leadership against the Scots, which Harclay with his newly formed local militia had obviously tried to do. To some extent Harclay had supplanted his old lord, Roger Clifford, as the great power in those parts and his earldom had made him for a few months the most prominent figure in the dangerous vacuum of lordship in northern England. But this was something which his northern neighbours like the Lucys could not endure.

Harclay had journeyed to Scotland to conclude his allegedly treasonable truce on 3 January. Since Edward demanded his appearance at court only five days later it is possible that he had intelligence of the treason beforehand. If the charges against Harclay are true, it is amazing that he could have believed that Edward would accept the settlement which he and Bruce formulated. It must have smacked to the king of England of the Ordinances which he had recently so triumphantly repealed. It imposed on Edward a committee of twelve of whom six were to be chosen by Bruce and six by Harclay.[37] It included the provision that 'everything that has to be done for the common profit of both realms shall be negotiated, ordained and settled by this committee' and that if the king failed to consent, 'the twelve shall act according to their judgement for the common profit of the realm'. Assuming that all this is true, either Harclay had strong, secret backing for such a settlement, which is possible, or his sudden rise to an earldom had given him an illusion of power in the realm and made him lose touch with reality.

The price which Edward had to pay for the execution of Harclay was a truce with the Scots. Harclay's removal had deprived him of the only military force in the north capable of effectively dealing with the raids. It was Henry de Sully, a notable French magnate and butler of France, captured by the Scots at the Byland fight, who mediated to bring about a truce.[38] He must have been a man of ability and charm, for he managed to remain a favourite of Edward, who richly compensated him for his captivity, while also getting on well with Robert Bruce, who bitterly complained to him about Edward's deceitfulness. Through Sully a truce was arranged until Trinity 1323 to give time for negotiations for a more lasting peace. A Scottish embassy travelled to England for this purpose. Its leader, the earl of Moray, showed considerable courage in venturing into England since he had been the commander of Scottish raiders who had ravaged its countryside.[39] Several English hostages had to be sent in return into Scotland. They included Hugh, the eldest son of the younger Despenser and Despenser's nephew, Laurence Hastings, the descendant of one of the three main claimants for the Scottish crown in 1291.

Also sent as hostages were the heirs of the two great northern families of Percy and Wake.[40] In the event Moray returned unscathed and it was his colleague, the bishop of St Andrews, whose men were attacked.[41] However, a truce intended to last for thirteen years was concluded at the archbishop of York's palace at Bishopsthorpe on 30 May 1323. The agreement did nothing more than establish a cease-fire and make arrangements for preventing further hostilities on the border by ending the building of fortifications, establishing wardens to keep the peace in the northern March and giving protection to Scottish shipping as it passed along the English coast.

It also earned Edward a new enemy. Henry de Beaumont, a relative of the queen, had formerly been one of Edward's most loyal supporters. In a council meeting held after the truce, when Edward called on each member for an opinion, Beaumont 'with an excessive motion and irreverent mind' refused his counsel.[42] Edward ordered him to leave and Beaumont replied that 'it would please him more to be absent than present'. Beaumont, as earl of Buchan, in the right of his wife, had lost a great deal under the terms of the truce, which abrogated claims by Englishmen to Scottish lands, and there were many others among the northern lords like him. He retired to his considerable estates to be joined in his discontent by his brother, Louis, who held the great episcopal palatinate of Durham. Some months earlier, he too had been sarcastically rebuked by Edward for failing to defend the north properly against the Scots.[43] Henry de Beaumont was later outwardly reconciled to Edward and escorted Prince Edward to France in the summer of 1325.[44] Perhaps on this occasion he made some secret agreement with Queen Isabella and Mortimer who were already conspiring in France. In October 1326 he suddenly emerged as one of Isabella's adherents with a large northern army backed by the other great northern families of Wake and Percy. Edward's writ, and even the grasping hands of the Despensers, did not stretch effectively into the far north and enemies made there were highly dangerous to the regime.

Scarcely less dramatic than Henry de Beaumont's outburst in the council was the sudden flare-up of enmity between Edward

and one of his former favoured clerks. John Stratford, archdeacon of Lincoln, had been a most useful servant and had been
employed on the most important missions to the pope including
the one which procured the excommunication of the Scots and
inaugurated the proceedings against the Contrariant bishops
of Lincoln and of Bath and Wells.[45] When the bishop of
Winchester, Rigaud d'Asserio, died on 12 April 1323, Stratford,
then at the papal court, was commissioned to obtain the provision to the see of the king's favourite clerk, Robert Baldock,
keeper of the privy seal since 1320. Edward had made two
previous attempts to get a see for Baldock. He was specially
aggrieved therefore when Stratford obtained this second
wealthiest English bishopric for himself.[46] Baldock was promoted by Edward to the chancellorship in August 1323 and his
supplanter at Winchester was recalled to England to face the
king's wrath.

Stratford always claimed that his promotion to Winchester
was due entirely to the wishes of Pope John XXII. The Pope
felt particularly bound to protect Stratford as the papacy had
already intervened on behalf of other episcopal victims of
Edward, bishops Burghersh and Droxford. Fresh events in
England in August 1323 added Adam Orleton of Hereford to
the list of bishops who required the Pope's special help.[47]
Orleton, who had already incurred Edward's enmity in 1321-2
through his friendship with the Mortimers, again attracted the
king's suspicion when Roger Mortimer of Wigmore escaped
from the Tower of London on the most auspicious date of the
feast of St Peter in Chains, 1 August 1323.[48] A large number of
prominent Contrariants were detained at that time in the
Tower, including Roger's uncle, Roger Mortimer of Chirk,
the heir of John Mowbray, Bartholomew Burghersh and Giles
Badlesmere, as well as a host of less important men comprising
Thomas Gurney, John D'Eiville, John Fitz Simond, Hugh
Eland, Edmund Darel, John Vaux, John de la Beche, Walter
Selby, Geoffrey de la Mare, John Knoyt, John Page, Richard
Peshale and Henry Ashburn.[49] But Roger Mortimer of Wig-
more seems to have acted on his own. His situation was
particularly desperate since the king had decided to revoke
his earlier promise, made at Shrewsbury when Roger had

surrendered, to spare his life. To effect his escape, Mortimer managed to drug the constable of the Tower, John Segrave, and escaped with the gaoler with whom he was in league.

In spite of nearly losing his life through Mortimer's drugged potion, Segrave had to appear before the court of King's Bench where he was charged with collusion in the escape.[50] He denied the charge, but echoed what Maurice Berkeley's gaoler had no doubt also thought, 'that he could have kept Mortimer in deeper and closer imprisonment than he did'. Attempts to close all the ports could not be effective and Mortimer was undoubtedly on the continent before the king, who was in the north, knew of his escape. It was believed, not incorrectly, that several important Londoners were involved in his escape and the taverns of London were obviously humming with rumours, one taverner being imprisoned for being of Mortimer's party.[51] Six weeks after his escape Mortimer was sending messages back to England. There were rumours of risings in the Marches of Wales. Later in the year two of his agents were caught and a plot to kill the king and the Despensers was uncovered.[52] In the next year a commission of enquiry was sent into Wales where a group of disturbers of the peace were accused of supporting Mortimer.[53]

Edward used the findings of this special commission to bring Orleton before parliament in February 1324.[54] The bishop had refused to answer the justices at Hereford 'because he is the bishop of Hereford at the will of God and the supreme pontiff and…the substance of the aforesaid articles alleged against him is so serious that he ought not to answer here in court on the matters alleged against him, nor can he answer thereon without offence to God and Holy Church'. Charges were recited against Orleton in parliament. They consisted chiefly of accusations that members of his household retinue had aided Mortimer. Orleton again defended his right as an ecclesiastic to be judged by the ecclesiastical authorities and Archbishop Reynolds stepped in and asked for Orleton's custody. Orleton was brought before the chief legal prop of the regime, Chief Justice Hervey de Stanton, in the court of King's Bench. This provoked a dramatic intervention by the archbishops of Canterbury, York and Dublin. They marched into the court ceremonially,

processional crosses carried before them, and led Orleton out
of the court and symbolically from its jurisdiction. This prevented a head-on collision between the king and Pope John
XXII, patron of Orleton and defender of ecclesiastical jurisdiction and rights. Orleton apparently spent the remaining
years of the Despenser regime in poverty. His correspondence
and *Apologia*, issued to deny his part later on in the death of
Edward II, reveal a brave and hot-tempered man. An exponent
of fiery sermons, he was also sufficiently supple to flourish at
the papal court and sufficiently learned to borrow Hereford
cathedral's library's copy of Aquinas' *Summa* to read while on
his diplomatic duties there.[55] As events after 1327 were to show,
he was not irrevocably committed to Mortimer and the Despensers might have found it wiser to accommodate him to their
regime.

In the case of Stratford this is what happened, though, as
events in 1326 were to show, the reconciliation was superficial.
Edward made every effort to have Stratford's appointment as
bishop of Winchester revoked and brought him, too, before the
court of King's Bench.[56] He was not, however, imprisoned but
the king delayed the return of the temporalities of the see of
Winchester and levied a huge fine on him. Stratford may have
retrieved his position by the enormous recognizance which
he executed in favour of the younger Despenser in return for
interceding with Edward. Stratford's skill as a diplomat made
his continued employment in the royal service highly desirable
to the king and Stratford concealed his implacable hatred for
the regime. His proposal to send the young Prince Edward to
France to render homage for the French lands may have been
part of a deep-seated plot between him and Mortimer and
Isabella.[57] He certainly joined Isabella soon after her landing
in 1326.

About the same time as the prosecution of Orleton, plotting
of an altogether more exotic sort was proceeding in Coventry
and the extraordinary case which arose from it began in the
court of King's Bench in 1324.[58] A certain Robert, the lodger
of a Coventry 'magician', John of Nottingham, prosecuted
him for attempting to kill the Despensers by enchantment. The
story began when a group of Coventry people came to John

on 30 November 1323 and offered him a profitable commission. Their proposal, which was divulged after promises and security for discretion had been given on both sides, was a very remarkable one. They were incensed against the prior of Coventry for some undisclosed intervention in the city and against the Despensers who were maintaining him 'and they asked the master John if in return for a gift from them he would undertake by his necromancy and his arts to kill the king, the earl of Winchester, Sir Hugh le Despenser, the prior of Coventry and others they named. And he said yes and agreed. And thereupon they made a convenant with him that he should have twenty pounds sterling and his keep in any religious house he liked to choose in England'. They also offered Robert £15 for his assistance. Thus for £35 the people of Coventry hoped to achieve what the disunited force of half the nobility of England had failed to do, that is eliminate Edward and the Despensers. They hoped to throw in for good measure the prior of Coventry and half of his officials. The necromancer employed the time-honoured method of a wax figure of each proposed victim and the necromancy commenced on 7 December 1323 and proceeded for six months until the next May, the sorcery taking place in an old house in Shortley Park outside the city. They were ready to do a test on 27 April and chose the image of one of the less important victims, Richard of Sowe, 'by which they intended to test the others'. This Robert himself actually accomplished. On the instructions of the magician he drove a sharpened pin two inches deep into the image of Richard. An important reason for the choice of Richard was that it was more easy to check the results of the spell on him than its effects on other prominent personages far away. Robert was sent round to his house. 'He found the victim "screaming and crying harrou without being able to recognise anyone and so was out of his mind".' The unfortunate man remained in this state until 19 May when the magician instead drove the pin into his heart, whereupon the man, after four days died. Before they could apply their necromantic tactics to the next victim, the game was up and they were appealed. At this point Robert turned king's witness. The others charged were acquitted by a jury. A curious sidelight of this extraordinary case was that in

September 1323, shortly before this bewitching was alleged to have taken place, the younger Despenser received an answer to a letter which he had sent to the Pope.[59] The extraordinary coincidence of the reply makes it worth quoting. 'In answer to his complaint that he is threatened by magical and secret dealings the Pope recommends him to turn to God with his whole heart and make a good confession and such satisfaction as shall be enjoined. No other remedies are necessary beyond the general indult which the Pope grants him.'

While the Despensers terrorised the country, they lived themselves in a nightmare of fear. This clouded their judgement and drove them into disastrous decisions, such as sending Prince Edward to France instead of the king to render homage to Charles IV.

London

The assistance given by some Londoners to Roger Mortimer, which made possible his escape abroad in 1323, highlights one of Edward's most intractable problems. He could never be sure of the allegiance of the greatest city of his kingdom. The problem of London had faced all the English kings in the thirteenth century.[1] It was the rallying of London to the rebels that forced John to concede Magna Carta in June 1215. The Londoners saved Simon de Montfort from Henry III's forces in December 1263 and compelled the king to reach a compromise settlement with the Disinherited in 1267. Edward I, who had no use for autonomy in the capital cities of his kingdom and of his duchy of Gascony, tried to govern both London and Bordeaux through his own agents. The same man, Henry le Waleys, was used at different times in both these cities. In London direct rule by the king was imposed in 1285 and only the near revolution of 1297, when the Londoners again allied with the king's baronial opponents, ended what had been intended as a permanent abrogation of London's autonomy. Thereafter the city was perennially suspicious of royal intentions. The coherence of its ruling groups had been strengthened by the increase in the importance of the leading guilds. It had acquired a population so huge and clamorous, a small elite among its exceedingly wealthy and the great majority wretchedly insecure and poor, as to make it uncontrollable and permanently unreliable. Only a king's personal popularity or threats to deprive London by force of its liberties, could make it amenable to royal influence. Neither was a long-term possibility under Edward II. He feebly wavered between force and attempts to buy the support of the elected magistrates.

By 1307 the Londoners had not only strengthened their autonomous rights but had also developed a marked sensitivity to their preservation. True to form, the Londoners took the side of the baronial opposition from the very beginning of the reign and it is noteworthy that some of the most vivid tales of the unpopularity of Gaveston, his arrogant behaviour at the royal marriage banquet and other reports detrimental to the king, come from London chronicles. The citizens refused to accept Edward's candidate for the office of Common Serjeant in 1311, although there is evidence that they put a number of the magnates' creatures into city posts.[2] When the Ordainers obtained the exile of Gaveston and control of royal policy, the city obtained the revocation of Edward I's Carta Mercatoria of 1303, which had had the very unpopular effect of giving alien merchants special commercial rights in the city and other privileges. When the Ordainers were in arms and camped at Blackheath in the suburbs in July 1312 the Londoners flocked to join them. The reign was quite notable for the number of attacks on foreign merchants though this was generally a symptom of popular rather than patrician hatred. Rich foreign merchants were quite integrated with their native equals. At the very beginning of the reign, in 1309, two of Edward I's chief mercantile agents, the Frenchmen William Servat and William Trente, became aldermen of London in the same year as one of their fellow countrymen, Henry Nasard, became a citizen. The London merchant, Simon Swanland, kinsman of William Melton, archbishop of York, was on one occasion stated to have been a member of the 'company' of Antonio Pessagno, the king's Genoese banker and royal favourite.[3] Pessagno had close connections with a large number of the ruling merchants of London, but in 1313, after attitudes had hardened through city support for the Ordinances, Pessagno was refused admission as a freeman.[4]

This refusal to admit Pessagno to citizenship came at a time when the terrifying London mob was beginning to rear again its head, a thing it did once again with suddenness and terrible consequences in 1326. After the murder of Gaveston, when a reconciliation between the king and his magnates was possible, a group of the king's representatives including Pembroke, the elder Despenser and John Cromwell came on 20 September 1312 to parley with the city, which had assumed a position of such importance as to be treated as a separate entity.[5] They put various propositions to the mayor and aldermen at the Guild-hall, and in reply, the city representatives voiced complaints which, if they are true, suggest that Edward had been trying to impose some sort of martial law on the city. They alleged that the steward and marshal of the king's household had attached various citizens contrary to the terms of the city's charters. They complained of an extension of fortifications beyond the Tower on land which belonged to the city and protested against the wrongful imprisonment of two freemen charged with conspiring to open the city gates if Lancaster came. Finally, and most menacing, they demanded the removal of armed men from the city. While an apparently heated and unpleasant argument was going on inside the Guildhall, rumour passed through the crowd waiting outside that the king's men were going to imprison the mayor, John Gisors III, a member of one of the oldest city families. The crowd swelled into a mob and Gisors had to be produced as evidence of his safety. According to one chronicle, Pembroke, the elder Despenser and Cromwell scarcely escaped with their lives from the tumult. That night the Londoners attacked and destroyed the new fortifications near the Tower ward. To defend it, royal soldiers poured out of the Tower to cut off the Tower ward from the city, the better to deal with the attackers. The Londoners got the better of the affray and threw the king's men into Newgate. King and council were furious, claiming that the land was theirs and that the fortifications were necessary to protect the royal treasury. The mayor merely agreed to summon an enquiry.

Quite apart from outbreaks of violence occasioned by impor-tant political events, there was constant friction on the boundary between royal and civil rights. In 1312, shortly after the Guild-hall incident, when the Londoners went to present their choice of sheriffs at the exchequer, the royal treasurer and barons refused to accept the nomination of one who was not present in the city. An impasse was avoided when the acting sheriffs agreed to continue in office. A further dispute took place in 1317 as to whether the shrieval oath should be taken at the Guildhall or at the exchequer.[6]

The English defeat at Bannockburn in June 1314, which strengthened the hand of all Edward's opponents, brought benefits to the city. In 1315 royal writs curbed the hated power of steward and marshal. They also regulated prises, another major source of discontent. As repeatedly in the past, serious crimes recurred in London with apparent impunity. Especially shocking was the attack on William de Burgh's house on Thameside. This was particularly disturbing to the authorities since it took place when the king was actually holding his parliament at Westminster early in 1315. It occurred 'in manifest contempt of the king and to the terror of the king's people summoned to the king's parliament and to the serious loss of William de Burgh and in breach of the peace'.[7] De Burgh was, perhaps, the most notable attorney in the city. A gang, allegedly of several hundred men whose leaders were cooks, a taverner and several apprentices, entered de Burgh's house on the waterside and actually held it for fifteen weeks. They stole, gave away or spoiled his clothes and goods and, what was more serious, stole written bonds of statute merchant, letters of acquittance and various other business records in the house, altogether causing £500 worth of damage. They also imprisoned the attorney's four servants for three weeks. The motive behind it was a family feud over inheritance, but it is symbolic of the collapse of law and order in the city that a quarrel, which should have been fought in court, turned into a violent struggle which disrupted part of the city for nearly four months! It was this threat to public order, culminating in the murder the next year of a prominent fishmonger, John of Ely, which made the terrified city patricians amenable to Edward's attempt to ease his candidate, John Wengrave, into the mayoralty.[8] Wengrave was given a greatly enhanced authority since he also obtained the offices of recorder and coroner. Allied with a group of *nouveaux-riches* citizens, he was hated by the aldermen outside the charmed circle of Edward II's favour and by the populace at large. But after Wengrave's appointment as mayor, Edward was more conciliatory. In 1317 the vexed question of the free election of sheriffs and the

location of their oath-taking was decided in London's favour.[9]
In 1318 the king remitted a city debt of £1000 arising out of the
tallage of 1312, an arbitrary impost resisted by Londoners in a
series of conflicts from 1215 onwards. Eventually in 1319 the
government of the city passed out of the king's control when
Wengrave's rivals were able to collect enough evidence to
proscribe him for corruption. Their leader, Hamo Chigwell,
was elected mayor. The city also made very radical new demands about the election of aldermen. All this was made
however more palatable to the king by an offer of a loan of
2000 marks. In return London obtained a charter confirming
all its old liberties and adding some new ones. It has been
described as 'the highest peak of achievement that a popular
movement ever attained in medieval London'.[10] No wonder
that the French chronicler wrote at the end of his annals for
1320 that 'a good time was beginning'.[11]

In fact he was expressing this optimism prematurely. At that
very time Edward was instituting a means of depriving the
city of the rights so recently granted in the 'Constitutions' of
1319. On 20 November 1320 he proclaimed an eyre.[12] The idea
for such proceedings was variously attributed to the younger
Despenser and Bishop Stapeldon, whom a London mob later
murdered, partly for his alleged part in it. Its purpose, according to the earl of Hereford, one of the leaders of the opposition,
was 'to destroy the city'. The introduction of the eyre was one
of the complaints which Lancaster included in his petition after
the Sherburn meeting in June 1321. It was certainly an attempt
to beat the city into submission. It enabled Edward to institute
quo warranto proceedings questioning all the city liberties which
he obviously had deeply resented granting in 1319. The
merchants of Almain, both those of Cologne and the rest, also
had the validity of their charters queried during the eyre, even
though they had just given Edward a large sum of money for
their confirmation. Its main purpose was not however financial
and the fines from it scarcely yielded £200. It was the only
conceivable way, short of military occupation, left open to the
king to stamp out the growth of independence in the city.
Edward was alarmed by rumours that several Londoners had
entered into sworn confederacies to resist any royal intervention

in their city, to the great disturbance of the enforcement of law
and the discovery of truth. On the day of the opening of the
eyre he instructed the justices to enquire into these confederacies
at the start of their proceedings.[13] The royal justices were
extremely rough with those who appeared before them. As soon
as the proceedings opened on 14 January 1321, the city's
representative, William Denham, begged the justices to listen
to what he would have to say on behalf of the Commonalty of
London. When Hervey Stanton enquired to whom he was
addressing himself and he replied, 'To the justices', Stanton
pulled him up immediately for addressing the court before the
justices' commission had been read: 'You do not know whether
we are justices or not, and therefore wait until you know that
we are justices and then say what you will and we will hear
you.'[14] After the commission was read out Denham again
spoke. He reminded the justices that the Commonalty had the
right to send a messenger to the justices. The justices would
then inform the messenger, as the representative of the people,
whether they wished the Commonalty to be present and
whether the people might come and go at will and in safety.
Stanton overrode the right of the Commonalty to be summoned
by their own messenger. He maintained that 'they have had
ample warning to be here by the writ of the common summons
of the eyre, and therefore they need not be warned a second
time by other messengers. And as for their being able safely to
come in and go out etc. this is a thing that [implies] fear of the
people and disrespect to the king who has your life and limb
to guard, so what you say has no legal force.' In this atmosphere
of procedural squabbling and of the aggressive arrogance of the
royal agents the eyre began. Worse followed immediately.
The sheriffs failed to answer the summons to appear. At this
Geoffrey le Scrope demanded on behalf of the king that the
liberty of freely electing them be abrogated. At this point they
appeared and Stanton demanded that they give up their rods
of office. The mayor of London pleaded the city's right to elect
and remove mayors but, when called on to put this in writing,
Chigwell did not dare to stand up so decisively against royal
authority. The sheriffs handed Stanton their rods of office and
received them back as royal, not city, servants, and only after

the administration of an oath which said nothing of loyalty to
the city but swore loyalty 'to keep the counsel of the King and
the Justices'. After two days of further dispute between the
king's power and the city's rights, the justices invited all those
who wished to complain of city officials from the mayor down-
wards to submit their bills to the Chief Justice, Sir Ralph Beres-
ford. The horrified mayor and aldermen came before the
justices and claimed that complaints against officials belonged
to pleas of the crown and that pleas of the crown could only be
submitted in the liberty of London, through the mayor and
aldermen. The justices replied that 'enquiry ought not to be
made into their own deeds and trespasses by the mayor and
aldermen themselves'. Once again the city officials had to give
way. By this time they were thoroughly frightened and on the
same day handed a list of their claims of franchises and of
charters. Scrope, on behalf of the king, now replied that this
claim was made too late since it was the fourth day of the eyre
and that this was in contempt of the king since claims of
liberties were supposed to have been made on the first day.
He demanded, using this procedural point, that the liberties
of the city be taken into the king's hands. The justices did not
enforce this at once. It was not until 20 February that the king
used the pretext of the charges of conspiracy and complicity
in murder against a former mayor, John Gisors, which went
back to 1312, as an excuse to take the mayoralty into his own
hand.[15] The present mayor, Nicholas Farringdon, was deposed
and the mayoralty was suspended. Edward had won. The
liberties of the city were combed through clause by clause.
Shops and businesses were not allowed to open while the
justices were in session and this caused great hardship to those
legally uninvolved in the eyre, though the city had to bear some
of the costs of the proceedings as well as levy a huge sum of
money to finance its own legal defence.

The eyre had the effect of uniting all the disparate parties
in the city in a wave of ill-feeling against the king and the
justices. Wengrave refused to attend it. Hamo Chigwell and
Andrew Horn went to the king on 28 April to request the
restoration of the mayoralty, but it was only the total success of
the baronial devastation of Despensers' properties which made

Edward finally give way on 20 May. The justices were more sensitive to the change in political atmosphere against the king than Edward himself was. Although they were raging like lions before the Easter recess they returned like lambs after it, says a London record.[16] It was not until 4 July, however, when the rebel barons were almost at the gates of London, that Edward finally gave in and abandoned the eyre altogether.

One can imagine the warmth of the reception which the Londoners accorded to the earl of Hereford when he met them at Lancaster's Holborn house, just outside the city gates, on 29 July 1321.[17] He was the son of the man who had obtained the restoration of the city's liberties after the quarrel with Edward I in 1297. He was thus a well-chosen emissary. Hereford, backed by the Londoners, had demanded the exile of the Despensers. Some delaying tactics were all that Edward could offer before the arrival of the armed barons forced him to call the parliament which exiled the Despensers. The Despensers did not forget the hostile part that London had played against them, any more than London could forgive their part in organising the eyre of 1321, a part which Hereford had recalled to them when he met their representatives at Lancaster's Gate.

In October the ruling body reaffirmed Hamo Chigwell in the mayoralty 'to please the king', though Hamo's exact role throughout these years is a fascinating enigma.[18] When the first armed conflict broke out between the king and the barons at Leeds the city sent 500 men to Edward's aid against Badlesmere's castle.[19] The result was that the Londoners secured one concession. Edward agreed to investigate the complaint that the sheriffs had been illegally fined in the eyre against the city's charters.[20] This was in November 1321. The next month, however, when no further help was forthcoming against the Contrariants, the king wrote a furious letter to the city complaining that his enemies were being received there.[21] In January 1322 the citizens retorted by demanding the restoration of a free mayoralty, but they were unsuccessful. Hamo Chigwell remained royal warden rather than the city's mayor. He was obviously, temporarily at least, in the royal trust, because he was given special powers to arrest suspects in the city and after the victory at Boroughbridge was put in charge of rebel lands in London and was one of those to pass judgement on the Mortimers.

Edward's near capture at Byland in the Scottish campaign in October 1322 caused panic in London and the authorities feared that the city would pass out of control.[22] Between 1322 and 1326 the city was a tinder box waiting to be set alight and dangerous flickers accompanied every important political episode. When early in 1323 the prominent Contrariant, Maurice Berkeley, temporarily obtained control of Walling-ford castle where he was imprisoned, this was feared to be part of a wider attempt by Edward's enemies to take over a number of prominent fortresses including the Tower. London refused to send troops to retake Wallingford, claiming that it needed them to defend the city where the queen and her children were living. This unanswerable claim did not stop suspicion that the city had given assistance to Berkeley. After this episode the mayoralty was once again suspended and the careful Hamo Chigwell had to follow the court as a temporary prisoner. Other deeply significant signs of opposition included the report of miracles at the plaque presented by Lancaster to commemor-ate the Ordinances. This stood in St Paul's.[23] This veneration of Lancaster's memory may have caused the king to revive the proceedings against the bishop of London and the clergy of St Paul's which had been begun and abandoned with the eyre. The plaque was removed in 1323 and reappeared when London rose in the middle of October 1326 to support the invasion of Queen Isabella.

In 1323 the city refused to collect any longer the fines of the eyre which, they now openly claimed, was against the liberties of London. All opposition there was regarded with even more suspicion after the escape of Roger Mortimer from the Tower on 1 August. Ralph Bokton, a prominent merchant, was most directly responsible for arranging the escape, but John Gisors, fined in the eyre of 1321 and removed from his position of alderman after it, had given Mortimer the use of his Thameside warehouses.[24] It was probably as a reprisal as well as a defence measure that the king closed the city gates briefly in November 1323 on 'account of traitors and other evil men', once again disrupting London's trade.[25] At the beginning of the next year the prior of Bermondsey and some of his monks were suddenly charged with having hid Contrariants.[26] The next year, when a felon in Newgate gaol announced to the justices of gaol delivery that, if he was brought before the king, he would disclose Edward's enemies in the city, his word was thought sufficient to have all those whom he named arrested and put into Newgate prison.[27] From 1325 onwards the king was fortifying the Tower. By 1326 a small garrison of Flemish mercenaries was installed there.[28] As the regime was tottering to its fall belated but unavailing attempts were made to placate the Londoners. Four days after Isabella landed they were given permission to collect murage.[29] Their support was sought by pinning up outside the Guildhall statements justifying the king's foreign policy.[30] It is not surprising that within a few days of Isabella's landing on the east coast Edward and the Despensers thought it safest to leave London.[31] From the first days of October they were staying on manors to the west of the city. The total collapse of the king's hold on London was presumably not yet expected on 1 October when the sons of Roger Mortimer of Wigmore were brought from Odiham to the Tower.[32] Also the great bulk of the king's treasure was left at the Tower and in the exchequer at Westminster. Edward's conviction that he must not linger near London and must withdraw further to the west paralysed any possibility of organising resistance to Isabella in the south-east before her army had grown to an irresistible size. This was London's special contribution to Edward's downfall, though nothing could have saved him in any case.[33]

London rose in open revolt only in the middle of October. The houses of the stalwarts of the regime, the judges, the king's bankers, the Bardi and other foreign merchants favoured by Edward were pillaged. Hamo Chigwell joined a party of Londoners who rushed into the surrounding countryside to pillage the estates of the Despensers. In the city itself the Londoners succeeded in capturing and brutally slaughtering Bishop Stapeldon whom they blamed for the London eyre. While the Tower held out for several more days, London welcomed Isabella and was henceforth regarded as her most assured stronghold in the kingdom. The assembly that was to depose Edward was naturally summoned to Westminster and the pressure from Londoners assured that hardly anyone dared to defend the fallen king. The clever Hamo survived to be Isabella's mayor and then to serve her son in the same capacity and to die in his bed in 1332, one of the most enigmatic and successful figures of the period.

Queen Isabella's invasion and the end of the regime

As 1325 drew to a close the flagrant outrages of the disinherited rebels grew bolder, while, from abroad, rumours of an impending invasion by the queen hardened into certainty. The direction of the invasion, however, remained far from clear. Consecutive commissions against disturbers of the peace were issued without success. In one of these, issued in February 1326, Edward admitted that the problem of law and order was rapidly becoming more serious.[1] In his mind, when he issued this commission, were probably some particularly notorious outrages of the previous months. The most famous, and most recent, had been the murder in January 1326 of Robert Belers, chief baron of the exchequer.[2] But this was not the only attack on a prominent royal official. In July 1325 the deputy of Robert Sapy, keeper of Contrariant castles in the March of Wales, including St Briavels, was attacked in Gloucestershire while on his way to render his superior's accounts at the exchequer. His eyes were torn out, all his limbs were broken and his muniments and accounts were carried off.[3] About this time Edward started moving the imprisoned Contrariants about from castle to castle so that their whereabouts could be concealed. It is clear from this that he doubted his ability to defend the castles which were holding them. An outrage perpetrated in October 1325 may have added to his doubts. The constable of Conisborough castle in Yorkshire, one of the prisons for Contrariants, when auditing accounts in Conisborough church, was attacked and besieged in the church by a gang led by two members of the Vescy family and only emerged after some of his men had been injured.[4] In the same month of October 1325 the elder Mautravers made a sudden appearance at a fair in Dorset and wrought havoc.[5] At about the same time there was a series of attacks on royal manors in the Home Counties which must have underlined to Edward that it was no longer only his favourites who were the objects of hatred and abuse.[6]

Coastal districts were becoming particularly nervous because local disorder was accompanied by the fear of invasion from an unknown area. In January 1326 a general commission, covering all the most important ports, sought to control the passage of letters in and out of the country and communications with the rebels abroad.[7] This was, of course, entirely impossible to implement, as letters could be hidden in bales of cloth or false bottoms of barrels, and the king did not have a body of officials numerous, capable or loyal enough to carry out this order effectively. Consequently in March he was complaining that the rebels themselves were moving in and out of the country with impunity.[8] In May, although he had prohibited the import of letters prejudicial to him, two papal legates slipped into Dover with letters from the Pope to the younger Despenser.[9] The first letter enjoined the favourite to assist in the reconciliation of Edward and Isabella.[10] The other attempted to persuade him, 'instead of causing grievance to prelates and princes, to abstain from provoking enmities and to study to promote friendship'. Edward commanded the constable of Dover to imprison the papal legates and then himself galloped to Dover to interview them. A local, Kentish chronicle says that he threatened the legates with death if they published their commission which, in effect, expressed papal support for Queen Isabella. The legates fled without announcing their commission and Edward's ecclesiastical apologists, notably Hamo Hethe, bishop of Rochester, had to post letters in London churches denying that the papal envoys dared not approach the king and contradicting rumours that the queen and her son had been banished.[11] In the early summer of 1326 Edward was still maintaining that Isabella and her son would be treated with all honour if they returned obediently home.

Privately, their invasion was regarded as a constant threat. Edward's intelligence may have been hampered by the arrest in the spring of 1325 of a number of his spies in France and he was reduced to requesting Archbishop Reynolds to obtain information from his prior, Henry of Eastry at Canterbury, 'to whom a lot of people talk when coming and going'.[12] Happily we can use the same source of information for the rumours and unrest that were afflicting south-east England before Isabella's landing, because the 'Eastry Correspondence' survives voluminously in three different archives.[13] In fact all the alarums and excursions from Kent were false. The best intelligence which Edward received was from John English of Norwich, who charged the burgesses of Lynn with being in league with Mortimer and claimed that, pretending to be sympathetic to their cause, he had been retained by William Trussell to collect men to fight for the count of Hainault. The case was dismissed when English was found to have murdered a Lynn official and his accusation was probably discounted as being part of a feud between Lynn and Norwich, rival east coast ports.[14] In reality it came nearer the truth than any of the extraordinary stories produced by Reynolds or Eastry in their letters to each other.

The correspondence between Edward's archbishop, Walter Reynolds, and the prior of Christchurch, Canterbury, provides one of the best illustrations of the rumours which dominated people's minds at this time. Considering both their high office and the high favour in which they stood with the king, they seem surprisingly ill-informed, which is probably a reflection of the poor state of intelligence organised by the king himself.[15]

On 15 August 1325 Eastry wrote to Reynolds reporting a meeting between the king and magnates in which Edward had been advised that either he himself or his eldest son should go overseas to render homage for Gascony.[16] If we can believe Baker's chronicle, some of the bishops who are known to us as secretly participating in a conspiracy against Edward were advocating that his heir should be sent.[17] Knowledge of these divided counsels among the prelates may have added to the perplexities of Reynolds and Eastry. Ominously, in the same letter of 15 August 1325, Eastry added that in spite of much thought and advice, he had not yet decided what attitude to take in the quarrel between Edward and his wife. Reynolds was not likely to jump in where Eastry feared to tread, as we shall see. Some time before Christmas 1325 Reynolds must have expressed his fears to Eastry because, in his reply the prior sought to reassure Reynolds, adding, rather lamely, that the French were accustomed to terrorise their opponents with rumours without lifting a sword. He also reminded the archbishop that the Pope, who was trying to promote peace, stood in the way of war between the two countries.[18] By 12 March 1326 Eastry was writing on the presumption that Isabella would come back peacefully and that she and the king of France had acquiesced in papal proposals that would bring peace to the country, if only Edward would accept them.[19] We shall hear more of these proposals.

On 16 April[20] Eastry, replying to another nervous inquiry from Reynolds, reported that he had not been able to ascertain from visitors passing through Canterbury whether tales of a great army assembling in France were true. He tried to reassure the archbishop by pointing out that such an army would take a great deal of time to prepare and that there would, therefore, be warning. He doubted the ability of the poorer sections of the Kentish population, especially in the coastal areas, to cope with raiding by the French. Eastry seems to have had access to the most secret letters being carried through Canterbury to the king, because he claimed that he had seen a letter from the earl of Kent assuring Edward that he had not aligned himself with any foreign power and requesting permission to return to England. With this interesting dossier of very mixed views he closed his letter, advising Reynolds to receive the queen and her son well if they came. Such sage advice did not prevent Eastry from carefully soliciting the younger Despenser's help in relieving himself of the queen's hounds and huntsmen who had remained with him, as nonpaying guests, for several months.[21]

As has been already recorded, the two papal envoys slipped into the country in May 1326, bringing the papal proposals for a reconciliation between Isabella and Edward. The exclusion of the Despensers formed the main condition of such a reconciliation and Edward's gallop to Dover to prevent their publication was precipitated by his determination to suppress all knowledge of this. Eastry was convinced that if Edward did

not accept the papal message he would forfeit the support of
the Pope. Worse still, this would lead to intervention by the
king of France, which would mean that *confusio miserabilis
ubilibet pullulabit.* The Pope, who favoured the king of France,
would countenance this.

After Queen Isabella's invasion Eastry was at first carefully
avoiding any definite alignment with either side. On 28
September, four days after the queen's landing, he sent to
Edward the unhelpful proposal that three bishops should be
sent to treat with the invaders.[22] In a slightly later letter to
Reynolds, he exhorted him to maintain a neutral stance relying
only on the spiritual weapons of the church.[23] Throughout his
letters Eastry showed a constant preoccupation with saving
lives and preventing violence, thus striking a civilised contrast
with the brutality of actual events.

Abroad, Isabella had become the centre of a crowd of dissident
exiles and at some stage during her stay in France became the
mistress of the leader of them, Roger Mortimer. There is no
reason to doubt Murimuth's statement that this was the case
since he was, in the years 1327–30, a close confidant of Mortimer
and Isabella.[24] From the time that the king had sent Prince
Edward to France he had been writing to Isabella and demanding her return. The queen's refusal to come back, however,
only became public in November 1325 with the arrival back
at court of one of the young prince's guardians, Walter Stapeldon. He had fled out of fear for his life, and reported her liaison
with Mortimer's faction.[25] Isabella retorted by sending a
message to Bishop Stratford in January 1326 that she would
not return until the Despensers had been removed from court.[26]
The official French line was that Isabella had been expelled
from the country by her husband. This explanation is put
forward in the autobiography of Charles of Luxemburg, Holy
Roman Emperor and King of Bohemia.[27] He maintained that
the French invaded Aquitaine once more in reprisal for the
expulsion of Isabella and that, before he died, Charles of Valois,
had been responsible for promoting the engagement of the
young Prince Edward to the daughter of the count of Hainault,
who was Charles' own granddaughter. Charles of Bohemia is

a valuable informant here. He resided at the French royal court during these events in the 1320s, a young but very precocious boy, and he was himself a son-in-law of Charles de Valois.

Isabella went to the count of Hainault probably early in 1326. He was to be the main organiser of her invasion of England. There is no convincing reason to think that she was forced to leave France. All suggestions to this effect merely come from some imperfectly informed chroniclers. There is, for example, no evidence to support the suggestion that bribes from England led to a *volte face* in the French government's attitude. In December 1325 Charles IV made her a loan of 1000 *li par.*,[28] in spite of the repeated appeals of Edward in letters to Charles and to other French notables exhorting them to persuade Isabella to come home. It has also been suggested that the death of her uncle, Charles de Valois, in December 1325, may have weakened her position in France, but in reality his heir, Philip, was also her staunch adherent. Some time during her stay in France he and his closest supporters made an agreement to help her.[29] It is not difficult to see why. The probable reason lies in his schemes to secure the succession to the French crown. Charles IV had no sons and Philip of Valois was his nearest relative in direct male descent. In 1316 and 1322 daughters of the previous kings had been debarred from succeeding to the crown by their respective uncles and this series of virtual usurpations of the crown had established the presumption that no woman might be allowed to become the ruler of France. These *de facto* precedents did not mean that there had been any formal definition of the law of succession and, even if the inability of women to succeed was tacitly recognised, nothing was defined about their right to transmit a valid claim to their sons. As Isabella was the sister of the last three Capetian kings, while Philip de Valois was only their first cousin, Isabella's eldest son, Prince Edward, could be regarded as a strong claimant to succession after Charles IV.[30] Philip had therefore strong motives for reaching an agreement with her. One of the first things which Isabella did after overthrowing Edward II was to renounce her son's claim to the throne of France and we may hazard a guess that she did this in repayment of services rendered. The Valois clan had excellent reasons for encouraging her to leave France, where the royal crown was likely to be in issue, for England, where she would be distracted by the problems of ruling for her son.

As has been already noted, Philip de Valois was the uncle of the young Philippa of Hainault who was to become the bride of Prince Edward. The proceeds of her dowry would finance the invasion of England and her paternal uncle, John of Hainault, one of the most renowned warriors of his time, would provide an experienced and prestigious commander of the expedition. The count of Hainault was also the lord of Holland and Zealand and the invading force ultimately sailed from Dordrecht in Holland, using a little fleet of Dutch ships.

Four years earlier such action by the count of Hainault would have been inconceivable, as he was involved in a war with England's enemy, Flanders, but in 1323 he made peace with the Flemings, which gave him more freedom of action. In consequence, perhaps, of this, relations between his Dutch subjects and English sailors took a turn for the worse. After a series of fruitless negotiations in late May 1326, Edward ordered reprisals against the shipping and goods of the count's subjects.[31] To aid Isabella's expedition became a natural counter-move for William of Hainault. He was in a very strong position at this juncture. An agreement with Brabant had settled an old dispute about boundaries. He was an ally of France, one of his daughters had married Lewis of Bavaria, the emperor-elect, and another was the wife of the count of Juliers, a dangerous neighbour to the east of the Netherlands. Isabella carried the support of this alliance with her when she sailed to England.

Three months before she sailed an open war had recommenced between England and France. In the last days of June 1326 Edward ordered the seizure of all Frenchmen in his territories. Warfare restarted again on the borders of Gascony and on 16 August Charles decreed a fresh seizure of all Englishmen and of their goods in his dominions.[32]

In July the count of Hainault was starting to assemble ships to take his English protégés and an army of Hainaulters and Germans to England.[33] The expedition was very carefully planned. There is nothing to indicate that Edward had an early warning of these preparations. As we shall see, early in September he launched from his base at Porchester in Hampshire a raid into Normandy, which would suggest that he had no strong reason to think that an invasion would come from the east, from Holland.

Some time in the spring or summer of 1326 Edward was drawing up a complex scheme of defence against a possible invasion.[34] It is so elaborate as to suggest preparations for a French attack on a considerable scale and not merely against a landing by Queen Isabella. The earl of Winchester and Henry of Lancaster, earl of Leicester, were to act as colleagues in supervising the array in the central and northern Midlands. How unrealistic this was is shown by Henry's speedy adherence to Isabella after her landing, and by his capture of the treasure and military equipment of Winchester, his supposed partner in organising defence. In Kent, Archbishop Reynolds and Ralph Basset were to be responsible as supervisors, though we have already seen that Reynolds had no inclination for fighting. John and Stephen Cobham were to assist them, together with William Grey. In Surrey and Sussex, Ralph Basset and Robert Echingham were supervisors and Edward St John and John Erdington were to act under them. In Essex and Hertfordshire the king's elder half-brother, the earl of Norfolk, was to be the only supervisor, with Hamo Hethe, the bishop of Rochester, as his assistant. Norfolk was also put in charge of East Anglia. This was to prove the most crucial area of all and Norfolk was among the first to join Isabella, as was his assistant in this region, John Hotham, the bishop of Ely. The earl of Arundel, brother-in-law of the younger Despenser, was put in charge of Lincolnshire, with William Kyme and Ebulo Le Strange as assistant arrayers. As the latter was the husband of Alice Lacy, Lancaster's widow, who had suffered much at the hands of the Despensers, he could not have been a very reliable supporter of the regime. Earl Warenne was put in charge of Yorkshire and the northern parts, with Archbishop Melton, Henry Percy and Edmund Maulay as assistant. Percy turned out to be one of the leaders of the nothern army that came to Isabella's help. The Hampshire area was to be under the control of John St John and Ralph Camoys and the south-westerly

G

counties of Somerset, Dorset, Wiltshire under John Beaumont and Robert Fitz Payn. Hugh Courtenay, with Peter Ovedale, a retainer of the younger Despenser, and the bishop of Exeter were put in charge of arraying troops in Devon and Cornwall. All these magnates were to inform each other of news as they received it. The arraying was to be organised by the sheriffs on a hundred-to-hundred basis and the strongest troops were to be put in armour and organised in divisions of twenty. The notables of each county were to be consulted about the best way of finding wages for these men and when money could not otherwise be raised the sheriffs and escheators were ordered to provide it from the revenue of their offices.

A special role was assigned to Edward personally. 'And our lord the king himself' says the memorandum confidently, 'will make his way towards the March of Wales to rouse the good and loyal men of that land and will punish the traitors...' In fact this was one of the few parts of the plan which seemed to come to pass. A hasty postscript warned Louis de Beaumont to secure his town and castle of Durham because strangers were rumoured to intend to invade and secure the north.

Mention has already been made of the financing of a raid into Normandy, which probably took place during the first fortnight in September. The Canterbury chronicler confirms scattered references to it in official records.[35] According to his statement, at the beginning of September Edward sent a fleet of 300 ships to attack Normandy. He may be exaggerating the size of the expedition, but certainly at least 133 ships were assembled, manned by 4200 sailors. The force mustered for this raid numbered at least some 1600 men. The account of the paymaster of this army names John Felton, knight, as its leader. Something important was being attempted, though what it was remains mysterious. It is puzzling why the king should have launched this sudden attack on Normandy while the country was in reality being threatened by an invasion from Holland. The answer may well be that this expedition, which appears to have been driven back by the Normans, was sent to capture Edward, Prince of Wales. His presence there at the time of the raid is suggested by one piece of evidence. Early in the reign of Edward III a pardon was given to the same John Felton, a personal retainer of the younger Despenser, 'for hostilely entering the land of Normandy and committing depradations and burnings when we were in those parts'.[36] The 'we' in this context is the king, Edward III, and there is no other possible occasion when he could have been there as king or prince. It should also be noted that there is no mention in any known source of Edward's presence with Isabella when she landed in Suffolk on 24 September.

Isabella landed at Orwell in Suffolk with a small army of perhaps not more than some 1500 men, including 700 men-at-arms from Hainault.[37] They came in 10 fishing vessels.[38] Her crossing took one day and appears to have been virtually unobstructed, though one ship was captured at some stage. There is no mention in any known source of Dutch naval escorts for Isabella, but in view of Count William's elaborate naval preparations,[39] it is possible that she was screened by some Dutch vessels during the most crucial stages of her passage.

Be this as it may, it remains something of a mystery why the eastern English fleet did not try to destroy this modest expedition, which with its heavy load of armed men and horses could easily have been intercepted by swifter naval vessels. A key to what happened may perhaps be found in the personality of Robert Wateville who was in charge of the English royal fleet operating off the east coast. He had been a Contrariant and a follower of Bartholomew Badlesmere.[40] He had quickly procured a pardon after the civil war, but as a security for good behaviour he had to execute a recognizance for 100 marks in favour of the younger Despenser, whose retainer he now became. The recognizance was a reminder that he was not fully secure and an even sharper reminder was provided in 1325 by his recall from Gascony under arrest. It was reported to the king that he was trying to sell up his English properties.[41] Somehow he explained his way out of this dangerous situation. His considerable military reputation may have helped him. In the spring of 1326 he was back in high favour, and the royal chamber defrayed various expenses incurred during the celebration of Wateville's marriage on 19 May.[42] In September he was given the crucial job of guarding the eastern coast under the earl of Norfolk and commanding the ships there. Nothing more is known of the doings of this fleet.[43] Wateville, unlike his superior, Norfolk, who at once welcomed Isabella, rejoined the king and the chamber was paying his expenses while he was detained by illness in early October.[44] Yet at the end of October he reappeared as a member of Isabella's council at Bristol, one of the very few close followers of the Despensers to rise to a high position so early under the new regime.[45] This creates a strong presumption that he must have rendered some signal service to Isabella at the time of her landing or shortly afterwards. One chronicler tried to explain why Isabella was allowed to land unopposed by claiming that the English sailors refused to fight against her because they hated the Despensers.[46]

Isabella landed on a stretch of the Suffolk shore joining to the manor of Walton which belonged to Thomas, earl of Norfolk, the elder half-brother of Edward II, and the chief figure assigned to the defence of eastern England. Norfolk had a private grudge against the younger Despenser who had forced him to give up, at a ridiculous price, the lordship of Chepstow, a rich area lying between the Usk and the Wye, which nicely rounded off Despenser's estates.[47] He may also have been alienated from his half-brother, the king, by a temporary confiscation of his hereditary office of marshal because Norfolk had failed to send a representative to an eyre in Lancashire five years before.[48] With the queen came Edward's brother Kent. He had joined Isabella the year before, and one can reasonably suspect that Kent and Norfolk had been treasonably in touch with each other before the invasion. With her came also a mixed group of Contrariant exiles and of new enemies who had fallen foul of Edward fairly recently. Her companions, besides Mortimer and Kent, included also such Contrariant stalwarts as William Trussell and Thomas Roscelyn, but also more recent fugitives like John Cromwell and John Roos.[49] There is every reason to assume that Isabella landed on Norfolk's estates by careful prearrangement, for a number of her most important supporters managed to be soon on the spot to meet her. One was Bishop Burghersh, who came from nearby Lincoln, but Orleton, coming from the other side of the country, also managed it.[50] It was he who put Isabella's case to the assembled lords shortly after the landing. This was only the first of many rousing sermons which he delivered in her cause as the invaders pursued the king westwards. Isabella lodged the first night in Norfolk's castle. Chronicles say that victims of Despensers' plundering and relatives of Contrariants poured into her camp or joined her supporters. Within a few days she had an appreciable force and the risk that she could quickly be overwhelmed was over.

Edward and the Despensers were still in London. Isabella quickly despatched letters to the capital explaining her case and also sent copies to other towns.[51] Seeds of support had already been sown in London and probably intelligence of her movements was given to her supporters there by Gilbert Talbot, who had secretly come back to the city beforehand.[52] The king does not seem to have tried to send a further force against her. He had probably discovered by then, what we also know, that Richard Perrers, the sheriff of Essex and Hertford-shire, would not have helped him to raise a force. The men sent to deliver money for paying Perrers' troops returned with most of the cash.[53] Perrers was another of Edward's secret enemies. He was a tenant of Edward's cousin, the earl of Richmond, who had joined the rebel party abroad in 1325. He had also become a surety for his sister-in-law, Ela Perrers, who was found to have treasonable correspondence with the king's enemies abroad.[54] In spite of this Edward had restored the shrievalty to Perrers and he held this crucial position when the queen landed. He was one of the first to receive the reward of a land grant for his adherence to her cause and appears on the list of household knights of the new regime.[55]

Isabella moved from Walton to Bury St Edmunds where she seized a lucky windfall of 800 marks left on deposit at the abbey by Edward's chief justice, Hervey Stanton.[56] She paid her troops with this money, though this did not stop them further enriching themselves by pillaging Despenser lands as well as the properties of innocent landowners on their route of march. According to a subsequent petition from one of her marauding followers, she had proclaimed that all her supporters should take what they could from the possessions of her enemies. One quarter of all the plunder was supposed to go to Queen

Isabella, a second quarter to Mortimer and a third share to William Braiwode, 'sovereyn' of those who took the loot. The rest was later divided among the plunderers so that each of them received loot worth 2 marks.[57] Near Dunstable, Henry of Lancaster joined her. He brought a large contingent of Lancastrian retainers. He also brought war-horses and treasure belonging to none other than the earl of Winchester himself. Leicester had learnt that Winchester's retainer, John Vaux, was transporting these valuables to his master and that he was spending the night of 3 October at Leicester Abbey.[58] His informant was probably one of the monks, for Leicester was a Lancastrian house. Henry ambushed Vaux and captured everything.[59]

Isabella and Leicester together proceeded to Dunstable, where Isabella learnt that Edward had left London on 2 October.[60] The city was in a disturbed state and, although the ultimate outcome of this was to be an uproarious welcome for Isabella, she could at first not be sure and was nervous about any reaction there. A London chronicle says that her first letter to the city went unanswered 'for fear of the king', because the city authorities were afraid to act while he and the Despensers were still in the city.[61] The queen then sent another letter on 6 October, intended to appeal to the population at large.[62] She had this second letter sealed by the young Prince Edward and posted at Cheapside where it could be widely read. But it neither seemed wholly safe to enter London nor, as it soon turned out, was this a major priority. Instead she moved west to try to cut off her husband's escape.

Edward seems to have been trying to implement his strategic plan and move west to rouse the Welsh. After leaving London on 2 October and reaching Acton the same night he travelled via Wycombe and Wallingford to arrive at Gloucester on 10 October. Isabella followed in his wake. Some of the details about his resources of men and money during this stage of his withdrawal westwards have already been noted. He had apparently only relatively few followers left with him by the time he reached Gloucester. For a while reinforcements were still being sent after him. On 9 October the treasurer paid a contingent of 93 sailors from the king's own ships now lying

idle in the Thames and despatched them to Edward.[63] In view
of Edward's special delight in his royal vessels these may have
been particularly dependable men. Their further fate is
unknown. The same is true of some shire levies that mustered
at London and on the same day were furnished with money by
Chief Justice Geoffrey Scrope.[64] They too were sent westwards
after the king and vanish from further record, as do some other
levies paid by the sheriff of Wiltshire. They all presumably
soon disbanded or joined Isabella. On 11 October a substantial
force of Edward's followers mustered in Yorkshire, led by the
Earl Warenne. They received payments from the sheriff of that
county so that they might join the king.[65] At least one of them,
William Roos of Helmsley, who had served Edward most
loyally against the Contrariants and again in Gascony, changed
his mind about where his allegiance lay and proceeded to join
Isabella. He later received a debenture for the huge sum of 800
marks for obeying her summons to come to her at Hereford in
October.[66]

As has already been noted, on his flight westwards Edward
was accompanied by an exchequer official, John Langton, who
carried at least £29 000. The king was, therefore, never short of
money. From Gloucester Langton sent £10 000 by ship which
was duly delivered to Edward at Chepstow by 17 October,[67]
but by that time Edward's cause was past saving.

Edward presumably intended to use this money to pay his
Welsh supporters. As he fled westwards he sent summonses to
the Welsh lords, Gruffydd Llwyd in North Wales and Rhys ap
Gruffydd in the south.[68] Both had loyally served Edward
against the Contrariants in 1321–2. Why they failed to reach
the king remains a mystery. The writ to Rhys had been sent
out from Gloucester on 11 October and cannot have reached
him before a few days had elapsed. By the time Rhys was
marching eastwards, the king had moved on. He was at Tintern
on 14 October and at Chepstow on 16 October, where he took
to sea with the younger Despenser, leaving Winchester behind
to guard Bristol castle. They were never to meet again. At this
point Edward was deserted by his chief household official, the
steward, Thomas le Blount, and was left with only a few men.
A possible clue to the failure of Sir Gruffydd Llwyd to appear

lies in the reward later given to Robert Power, chamberlain
of North Wales, for his help 'at the time of the pursuit of Hugh
Despenser'.⁶⁹ It looks as if his contribution may have been to
contain Sir Gruffydd somewhere in North Wales. As for Rhys,
he certainly remained loyal to Edward, as we next hear of him
as a fugitive in Scotland.

When Isabella reached Gloucester she was joined by the
northern baronage led by Leicester's son-in-law, Thomas Wake,
Henry de Beaumont and Henry Percy.⁷⁰ This was the
most formidable military group left in England and their
junction with Isabella gave her overwhelming strength. She
could now safely venture on a siege of Bristol castle, though it
soon became clear that there was no need for that. Her movements were being reported to Edward who was sending out
spies,⁷¹ but this was the only thing that he could still do. At
Isabella's arrival at Bristol the garrison refused to stand by
Winchester and he was forced to surrender on 26 October. The
next day he was tried by a court of chivalry over which William
Trussell presided. The denunciation was read out in French
and he was sentenced to death under martial law, 'damned
without reply'. The commission specified that against the law
of the land, usurping royal power, Winchester counselled the
king to set aside the laws of the land and execute Thomas of
Lancaster without just cause. It accused him of robbery and
claimed that for his cruel depredations the whole land was
demanding vengeance against him. They also accused him of
depriving the church of its rights. The sentence was that he
should be drawn 'for treason, and hanged for robbery, decapitated for his crimes against the church and your head taken to
Winchester where you were earl against law and reason'. The
final indignity was that because he had broken the laws of
chivalry he should be executed in a robe bearing his coat of
arms but reversed so that the arms would be discarded for
ever.⁷² One source makes the remarkable claim that Isabella
tried to save him.⁷³ Until the last moment Edward tried to
remain in touch with Winchester through messengers.⁷⁴

Legend and rumour follow Edward's travels in Wales. On
21 October, still well supplied with money, he had set sail
again from there in an attempt to flee abroad. On board ship

he offered money to Despenser's confessor who gave prayers to
Saint Anne for a fair wind.[75] Saint Anne proved unhelpful and
the ships were driven into Cardiff where they remained until
27 October. That day Edward and Despenser set out for
Caerphilly but, probably from fear of being blockaded and
captured there, they left the castle in the charge of Hugh's
eldest son, a teenager who with John Felton led a remarkable
defence of the fortress.[76] Here Edward abandoned his records,
notably the last chamber book recording daily expenditure.
The last payments recorded in it occurred at Caerphilly on
31 October.[77] The book was presumably captured in the castle
and taken to Westminster for auditing.

We can gauge a little of the fugitives' state of mind at this
time. They can only be described as living in a cloud-cuckoo
land. The story of Bogo de Knoville is particularly instructive.
He had been a Contrariant and had been pardoned in December 1325, on entering into a recognizance for 1000 marks.[78]
On 10 October 1326, when the king was already in flight, *half*
of this fine was pardoned.[79] On 20 October, when Edward was
in Wales and the queen in hot pursuit, Knoville and two others
were commissioned to seize the estates of Henry of Lancaster
in West Wales.[80] At this point Knoville led the only force still
left to Edward. Knoville's loyalty was still in the balance on
29 October when he was remitted the 500 marks remaining on
his fine – but the Patent Roll bears the memorandum that the
letter of pardon was handed over to Hugh Despenser to keep –
he was to deliver it to Bogo 'if he had borne himself well to the
king and his party'.[81] This was three days after Bristol had
fallen. Ruinous mean-mindedness is clearly an understatement
when applied to this sort of behaviour. Not surprisingly, soon
afterwards Bogo is found deserting to the queen's side.

From Caerphilly Edward moved west. He was at the Cister-
cian abbey of Margam on 3 and 4 November and at the other
Cistercian abbey of Neath from 5 to 10 November. Thereafter
he disappears from view, but appears again on 16 November,
betrayed, some say still near Neath, some say near Llantrisant.
The younger Despenser, Baldock, and the loyal knight of
Despenser, Simon of Reading, were taken together with Thomas
Wyther, John Beck, John Blunt, John Smale and Richard

Holden.[82] The captors represented various branches of the
opposition party – two men with important interests in Wales,
Henry of Leicester, brother of the dead Thomas of Lancaster,
and himself a Marcher lord, and Rhys ap Howel from an old
Marcher official family with generations of service to the earls
of Hereford and also an associate of Mortimer. With them was
John of Hainault the redoubtable leader of Isabella's troops,
Henry Leyburne from an old and turbulent Kentish family,
and Robert Stangrave. Leicester took Edward to his castle of
Monmouth, where on 20 November Orleton and Leicester
took away his great seal.[83] From Monmouth Edward was taken
to the royal castle of Kenilworth, where he remained in the
charge of Leicester.

Leyburne and Stangrave took the younger Despenser, Baldock
and Simon of Reading to Hereford, which had already wit-
nessed the hurried execution of Arundel, Despenser's brother-
in-law. The queen wanted to take the younger Despenser to
London, but he had apparently refused food and drink since
his capture and was too feeble.[84] As it was, his death in Hereford can have been hardly worse than anything which awaited
him in London. Outside Hereford he was dismounted from his
horse with Reading and Baldock, stripped and dressed in
reversed arms. A crown of nettles was placed on Despenser's
head. Verses of scripture denouncing arrogance and evil were
scrawled on his skin by people who were obviously finding it
difficult to express with sufficient vehemence their hatred of
him. In this way he rode into town, his marshal, Simon of
Reading being forced to parade in front of him, his standard
reversed. Simon of Reading was included in the punishment
meted out to his master because he had in some way insulted
Isabella. People flocked from the surrounding countryside and,
to the noise of trumpets and appalling din created by the
hostile crowd, judgement was pronounced on him and he
suffered the full horrors of a traitor's death – with the further
refinement of being drawn by four horses rather than two and
being hanged from an exceptionally high gallows fifty feet up.
He survived both these ordeals. He was dragged down still
conscious to have his intestines cut out and burned before

his eyes and to be put out of his misery by decapitation. This was the barbaric ritual meted out to unsuccessful tyrants and rebels. Simon of Reading was hanged from a lower gallows. Baldock was rescued, as a cleric, by Orleton, who had good reason to guard clerical privileges since his own life had undoubtedly been saved by them. He removed Baldock to his London house where the man was discovered by a London mob. It threw him into Newgate where, say many chroniclers, he died in torment.

Meanwhile, in and around London, there was an orgy of rioting, murder and looting. The city rose against Edward on 15 October when Isabella had reached Wallingford.[85] The Tower, however, held out and John Weston did not surrender it with its titular custodian, John of Eltham, and with all its prisoners to John Gisors and Isabella until 17 November.[86] It was against this background of a besieged Tower that mob violence broke loose in London. As we have mentioned, the city had not responded to Isabella's first letter. The mayor, Hamo Chigwell, was in a quandary. He had been one of the men who had pronounced the death sentence on the leader of the invaders, Roger Mortimer, but he also had much reason to hate the Despensers and had been grossly maltreated by Edward II. Another hesitant notable was Walter Reynolds, the archbishop of Canterbury. He had originally issued a papal excommunication against the invaders, adjusting a text originally manufactured for banning the Scottish invaders.[87] Eventually, it was probably the ferocious murder of Bishop Stapeldon which persuaded Reynolds to jump onto the queen's bandwagon before it was too late. Stapeldon had been left by Edward as guardian of the city. As he rode through the streets he was dragged from his horse and butchered.[88] A frenzied mob remembered him as a royal treasurer and held him responsible for the hated eyre of 1321. Reynolds himself only escaped from the city by appropriating the horses of the bishop of Rochester, Hamo Hethe, who, although an old man, had to escape on foot. Others closely connected with the regime were also attacked. Arnold de Hispania, a Spanish merchant whom the city held responsible for a recent new tax on wine, was murdered. The house of the Bardi, bankers to Edward II, was looted and they themselves were too terrified to emerge from hiding.[89] This was very embarrassing to Isabella's government which was as anxious to use the services of these bankers as the previous regime had been. Later Isabella assisted the Bardi by purchasing the looted premises for £700.[90] Significantly this leading Florentine firm showed no desire to own property in the city again. Geoffrey Scrope's house was also plundered, though he himself lived to serve the new regime very well.

Outside the city, the progress of Isabella's adherents through the country was marked by wholesale plunder of the estates of their opponents. One Berkshire property belonging to Winchester was plundered of 95 per cent of the value of its goods.[91] Further from London the proportion was smaller – in Gloucestershire over £800 was carried off from Despenser estates, or 76 per cent of their value.[92] The sum of £1800 belonging to the elder Despenser was carried off from Leicester abbey and never seen again.[93] The very leaders of Isabella's army led the plundering as well. Some of the northern barons did so on a huge scale and the Hainaulters were also held particularly blameworthy. But the most notorious were Edward's two half-brothers, Kent and Norfolk. They plundered not only along their line of march but sent agents far and wide to search for suitable booty. Kent and Norfolk, in spite of their rank, had later to receive a special pardon for their agents who had looted the property of Arundel and Despenser on twenty-three of their estates dispersed over huge areas of country.[94] Such disorder was not easily brought under control and persisted for several months. The large number of subsequent commissions to hear and determine cases of robbery and violence and the hundreds of pardons for homicides committed before Edward III's coronation fully confirm the terrifying descriptions of chroniclers. The danger was that the political chaos might give occasion to popular revolts, as happened at Bury St Edmunds and St Albans.[95] Any failure of government could at any moment let loose a terrible flood of anarchy and banditry.

14

Edward II's deposition and ultimate fate

Queen Isabella and her party had arrived in England with
the removal of the Despensers as their publicly proclaimed
programme and not the deposition of the king. Deposition was,
as Bertie Wilkinson rightly expresses it, 'a tremendous step'.[1]
The execution of Lancaster and of the rest of the Contrariants
had made political murder or execution for treason (whichever
way you happen to view it) into one of the most terrifying and,
for many notables, inadmissible recent innovations. How much
more terrifying, to the point of seeming at first almost unthinkable, would be the deposition of a king, especially as this might
ultimately involve his death as well.

These unique difficulties made the new rulers very hesitant
about how they might best proceed. The delay in holding
parliament presumably arose in part from these uncertainties.
Originally summoned to meet on 14 December, it was then
postponed until after the Christmas festivities, while the *de
facto* rulers dealt with the embarrassing question of the *de iure*
ruler. The problems which had to be faced were, firstly, the
personal ones of how readily their supporters, including the
young Prince Edward, would countenance the removal of the
king. The second question was the more academic one of how a
veneer of legitimacy could be laid over an act which was
undoubtedly illegal. This was largely a question of 'staging'.
As we shall see, the regime carried this out with aplomb and
the proceedings for deposing Edward II were extraordinarily
well orchestrated although exactly by whom we shall never
know.[2]

If Edward were to be deposed that required some public
proceedings resembling a formal legal trial at which Edward's

presence would normally be expected. Here lay precisely one of
the chief dangers to the new regime. Dare the new rulers produce him and allow him the opportunity to speak? Dare they
produce him before his son and risk a public reconciliation
which might place them in an impossible situation, and before
the prelates among whom he had some staunch supporters led
by William Melton archbishop of York? For all these reasons
they probably decided to avoid at all costs bringing Edward
before the Westminster assembly. Their tactics had to remain
very flexible as they nervously felt their way, step by step, and
hence arose the peculiarly tortuous and confused nature of the
proceedings that followed. According to all the known evidence,
Edward may really have played into their hands by apparently
refusing to appear before the assembly at Westminster, but all
our sources reflect only what the government allowed to be
known and this may not be the whole truth about Edward's
attitude.

Mortimer and Isabella did have certain factors in their
favour, quite apart from the overwhelming success of their
military campaign, or rather progress, through the country.
The Pope definitively bestowed his blessing by despatching
papal legates.[3] The Hainaulters were still at hand in the
queen's service and did not depart until the deposition proceedings were over, leaving for home only in March 1327.[4]
Last, but not least, they had taken over the royal treasury, and
the reserves in the Tower of London and at Westminster alone
totalled over £60 000.[5]

The assembly for deposing the king was summoned, completely illegally, in the name of the Prince of Wales. He was
acting as Keeper of the Realm on the pretext that the king was
abroad although, as we have seen, Edward II's travels had taken
him no further than West Glamorgan. The assembly met for
the first time on 7 January. We have no record of the first day's
proceedings. Since bishops Orleton and Stratford seem to have
departed immediately for Kenilworth to speak with the king,[6]
it may have been now that Melton demanded Edward's
appearance before the assembly.[7] The visit of Orleton and
Stratford to Kenilworth did not result in any such appearance
by the king at Westminster and was probably never seriously

intended to do so. The two prelates were apparently the least likely people to persuade Edward into anything. His continued absence, however, further invalidated the subsequent 'parliamentary' proceedings. The new regime attempted to conceal this persistent illegality behind a show of popular support. Oaths of adherence to the new regime and noisy public acclamations became the order of the day. There was even, at a later stage in the proceedings, the extraordinary proposal that the whole population should be required to take an oath of allegiance to the regime. This oath was to be administered by sheriffs through the county courts.[8]

Our most detailed source for the early part of the parliament is the Lanercost chronicle. This reflects the views of a monk living in a faraway northern house, although a man who was clearly well informed. After reporting that Orleton and Stratford had been despatched to Kenilworth to speak to the king, the chronicler does not actually say that they were despatched to bring Edward with them, but remarks that their purpose was to discuss what should be done about the crown. This itself, however, implies that the possibility of deposition was now being considered. The Lanercost chronicle states that Edward reviled them. As has already been noted, the effect of Edward's failure to appear, although it made things far easier for the regime, also made the assembly invalid as a 'parliament' held against the king's wishes in his absence. This was not a lawful assembly and several contemporary narratives show their awareness of this by using terms other than 'parliament' to describe it.[9]

The assembly adjourned during the two bishops' absence and resumed on 13 January. Isabella and Prince Edward were present and the proceedings were conducted by Mortimer.[10] He stated that the magnates had decided at some earlier meeting of an unspecified assembly that Edward should be deposed. He carefully removed responsibility from his own shoulders by saying that this was their decision. The reasons given amounted to a summary of the queen's proclamation at Wallingford of 15 October 1326. This was the first full-scale justification of Isabella's invasion issued after her arrival in England. One of the known texts of this proclamation is preserved in a manuscript closely connected with Bishop Stratford,[11] and it is very possible that he had shared in its drafting. The 'articles' presented against Edward on 13 January stated that he should not have rule over the kingdom of his ancestors because he was insufficient, a destroyer of the church and of the peers of the realm, an infractor of his Coronation Oath and a follower of evil counsel.[12] For the first time, however, the proposal was made publicly to replace him by his eldest son, Edward. Thomas Wake, Leicester's son-in-law, in what was obviously a well-rehearsed piece of showmanship, broke in with the statement that 'as far as he was concerned the old king should never again rule'. This cry was taken up by those present.[13] Orleton then delivered a rousing sermon on the theme that 'where there is no true ruler the people will be destroyed'. As part of the sermon, he also announced the decision of the magnates to go to Kenilworth and told the assembly what would be announced to Edward there.

There may have been some opposition, as these proceedings were not regarded by Mortimer as sufficient 'audience' or support for his next step, and that afternoon he led a deputation to the Guildhall to present the decision of the magnates to the city of London.[14] With London behind him the greatest magnates dared not oppose him. The Londoners had been responsible for his own escape and preservation in 1323 and they were particularly hostile to the old king. Mortimer staged his performance impressively. This was presumably less for the benefit of the citizens than to overawe his opponents among the bishops. One source specifically named the bishops among those present, while including the magnates only under the generic heading of 'the great company there'.[15] This was indubitably because it was the support of the bishops at this stage which was so crucial and which hung so much in the balance, as the *Historia Roffensis* shows. Mortimer swore to maintain the queen's cause and to uphold the liberties of the city. After the bishops had taken the oath the sheriff of London recited it in French to those assembled and many Londoners also joined in taking it.

Neither Orleton nor Stratford are named as having been at the Guildhall and it is likely that they had again left for

Kenilworth or were preparing to do so, but the chronology of these journeys is confused and controversial. What happened at Kenilworth is, at any rate, clear enough. A curiously composed group accompanied them to meet the king. Led by William Trussell, it comprised 4 barons, 2 justices, an abbot, a prior, 2 Dominicans, 2 Carmelites, 2 barons of the Cinque Ports, 4 knights, 3 Londoners and the representatives of towns. The Friars Minor were originally to have been included in the delegation, but were removed at the request of the queen who respected Edward's partiality for the order.[16] No Welshmen were present. Also firm supporters of the king and enemies of Mortimer, they were summoned to the parliament of January 1327, but these representatives of the Principality refused to attend.[17] The Kenilworth delegation was a partisan body whose purpose was to show to Edward how much his removal was popularly desired.

Orleton acted as spokesman. He told Edward that his rule was evil and intolerable, that he was led by wicked councillors and traitors, that he had destroyed peers of the realm and dissipated his father's lands 'whence it pleased the prelates and peers of his kingdom that his son should be substituted for him if he should give his assent'. Edward first refused and then gave in.[18] It was clearly a very emotional scene. William Trussell then led the others in renouncing his homage to Edward II. It was deposition with the consent of prelates and peers. Orleton had mentioned no other authority and Trussell declared himself the spokesman for the prelates, earls and barons and the others named in my procuracy.[19] No reference was made to the Commons' consent at this stage since they had never done homage to the king and could not therefore renounce it.

After the delegation returned from London, it was Stratford's turn to preach on the text 'my head pains me'.[20] The sermon is very interesting because, for the first time, the assent of the people was now required. Stratford stated that it had been decided by the unanimous assent of the peers that the king's eldest son should rule in his place if the people would be party to it. Thomas Wake again broke in, raised his arms and shook his hands asking theatrically whether the peole would consent to this ordinance. He received the desired and expected acclamation. It is interesting that the assent of the peers and prelates was felt to have constituted an ordinance. Then Archbishop Reynolds underlined the popular approval of the proceedings by taking as the text of his sermon 'the voice of the people is the voice of God'. Part of his text is preserved to us and runs as follows:

> Dear friends, you know well that you have long been afflicted with many oppressions committed by the king and his ministers. You have fervently acclaimed the proceedings here because you desire redress. Your voice has been clearly heard here, for Edward has been deprived of the government of the kingdom and his son made king as you have unanimously consented. This is because of the inadequacy of the former king and his offences against his kingdom and the church. It has been done with the advice of the wise men of the kingdom.

The sermon was greeted by a popular cry of 'let it be done, let it be done' and by a universal show of hands.[21] The Lichfield chronicler believed that it was the acceptance of this 'proposal' made by the Archbishop Reynolds to the people which actually deposed Edward II. 'In that Council', as he scrupulously called it, 'to the persistent cry by the whole people that he should be removed, Edward was deposed by Walter, archbishop of Canterbury, pronouncing some articles with everybody's consent.'[22]

In Bertie Wilkinson's words, 'the precedent of 1327 was not a precedent for "parliamentary" deposition; it was not even a precedent for deposition by the parliamentary "estates". It was a precedent for deposition by the magnates with the co-operation, agreement and acclamation of the people.'[23] Edward's own tyrannical regime was replaced by a government which was entirely illegal but was adept at manipulating skilfully the traditional instruments of government.

By the summer of 1327, and certainly by 5 July, Edward II had been removed from the custody of the earl of Leicester at Kenilworth and incarcerated at Berkeley castle in Gloucestershire.[24] To judge from the provisions bought for him, Edward was well fed there and the castle lay in the most beautiful wooded surroundings with a distant view of the Bristol Channel. It was not, however, the safest of fortresses.

It was a relatively small castle owned by the Berkeleys since the twelfth century. They were not popular beyond the immediate locality and particularly not in Bristol. The proximity of the Channel made a sea rescue an ever-present danger. The choice of this west-country prison for the king was probably determined by the unreliability of the northern lords and the danger of a Scottish rescue bid led by Edward's old friend the earl of Mar. This made a strong northern fortress impracticable. The volatile nature of London's support and the disturbed nature of the capital probably made the Tower an unacceptable alternative. However, the choice remains a puzzling one. In the event it did, indeed, prove insecure. On 9 July 1327 Edward was rescued by a group of desperadoes led by his former confessor and ambassador to the papal court, Thomas Dunheved.[25] A letter from John Walwayn, referring to this attempt to free the king, still survives and has been the object of close study by Tanquerey and by Tout.[26] One interesting point about this letter is that it nowhere states that the king had been recaptured. The letter is, in fact, a demand for additional powers to arrest certain of the conspirators who had so far escaped Walwayn's net. This point is pertinent when considering other evidence which we shall be presenting later. In the Lincoln parliament it was announced that Edward had died at Berkeley castle on 21 September and a funeral service was held for him after the lapse of several months, just before Christmas 1327. Subsequently a fine tomb was erected in the church of Gloucester Abbey.

If we separate contemporary evidence about his fate from the legend which has accrued around it, we are certainly left with more mystery than certainty. The legend was that Edward II was ill-treated, dragged about the countryside and then brutally murdered. This picture does not derive from contemporary evidence. As Tout says, 'the exact manner of the king's death comes later'. It can be found in Higden's *Polychronicon*. The source closest to Mortimer and Isabella that we know, the chronicler Adam Murimuth, writing from the safety of Edward III's reign, stated in his usual oblique way that the king was 'commonly said' to have been murdered as a precaution by the orders of Sir John Mautravers and Sir Thomas

Gurney.[27] Murimuth was presumably in a position to know more than his cautious 'commonly said' would suggest, since he had been favoured by the regime of Mortimer and Isabella and given custody of the temporalities of the murdered bishop of Exeter, Stapeldon. The only point which Murimuth makes about the king's imprisonment is that he was moved around from place to place, including Corfe, before being taken back to Berkeley. This may be the origin of the legend of Edward being dragged around the country, forced to shave with muddy water, etc. More explicit record sources amplify evidence about attempts to release Edward at this time. One attempt was organised from Buckinghamshire. It failed and the conspirators were rounded up. There was an interesting Welsh attempt, said, not surprisingly, to have been organised from just over the Bristol Channel by Edward's old follower in South Wales, Sir Rhys ap Gruffydd, 'with the assent of certain of the great men of England'. According to the tale which came out after the downfall of Mortimer, the plot was revealed by Mortimer's lieutenant in North Wales, the English burgess, William Shalford. This alleged attempted rescue took place very shortly before the official date of Edward's death (21 September), because Shalford was supposed to have sent the letter to Mortimer on 14 September. Shalford was acquitted of any complicity in a plot to murder Edward II when he was brought to trial during Edward III's reign. His acquittal was on a technicality, but Edward III continued to employ him, so we may presume his innocence.

At the reputed time of the murder, that is on 21 September, Edward III was at Lincoln awaiting the parliament while Mortimer was at Abergavenny. The heart was removed from the body alleged to be that of Edward II and placed in a silver vase. Queen Isabella later had it buried in her own coffin. It is also worth mentioning that she was buried in her wedding dress.[28] She certainly displayed here grave remorse and the incident of the heart suggests that she accepted the heart as being that of her husband. The king's body was displayed publicly to the assembled ecclesiastics and knights of the region, although Murimuth tells us their view of it was a very distant one. The legend that Edward was laid out naked and appeared unscratched is hardly supported by the evidence that his heart had been removed. This again is part of the legend. The king was probably laid out in state and viewed from a respectful distance by worthies filing past. When it came to the funeral at Gloucester Abbey on 21 December the crowds were kept at a distance by heavy oak barriers, especially constructed for the purpose.[29]

Such is the contemporary evidence about Edward II's end. How far can later sources be trusted? Tout placed particular reliance on the English translation by John Trevisa of Higden's *Polychronicon*, which accepted the legendary version of Edward II's murder. Tout's reliance on Trevisa's translation was based on his belief that it was a valuable local source, since Trevisa was vicar of Berkeley and was writing during the lifetime of the son of Thomas Berkeley, custodian of the castle at the time of the murder. 'The translator would not have lightly adopted such a suggestion [the murder] against the honour of his patron's father.'[30] Very strong objections can be offered to this statement by Tout. It was harmless for Trevisa to state this since it was well known that Berkeley was away from the castle at the time of the murder (substantiated by record sources which Tout himself cited) and Berkeley was acquitted in the most public place possible, parliament, of any complicity in the murder, in 1330–1. What is far more interesting is that in the course of his interrogation, Berkeley claimed that he did not know until the present parliament that the king was dead.[31] This is at first sight a most surprising statement, until one considers another piece of evidence, the mysterious 'confession' of Edward II, which came to light in the nineteenth century and which was dismissed by Tout, although Tanquerey viewed it more dispassionately. This was a long letter found in the binding of a cartulary of the bishopric of Maguelonne preserved among the departmental archives of Hérault. It was discovered by an archivist called Germain. He told an English visitor that he was convinced of its authenticity, 'but modestly declared that he did not pretend to impose his own convictions on others'. He limits himself to asking for 'a revision of the process on this period of history'. The first English report of the letter appeared in the local history transactions of Newcastle-upon-

Tyne and is cited by Bishop Stubbs[32] who, however, refused to take it seriously. The letter may be translated as follows:

In the name of God, Amen. These things which I have heard from the confession of your father, I have written down with my own hand and for this reason I have taken care to communicate them to your lordship. First of all he said that, feeling that England was in insurrection against him because of the menace from your mother, he departed from his followers in the castle of the Earl Marshal by the sea which is called Gesota [Usk]. Later, driven by fear, he went on board a vessel together with Lord Hugh Despenser, the earl of Arundele and a few others and landed in Glamorgan on the coast and there was captured together with the said Lord Hugh and Master Robert de Baldoli [Baldock] and they were taken by Lord Henry de Longo Castello [Lancaster] and they led him to Chilongurda [Kenilworth] castle and others were taken elsewhere to other places and there, many people demanding it, he lost his crown. Subsequently you were crowned at the feast of Candelmas next. Finally they sent him to the castle of Berchele [Berkeley]. Later the attendant who guarded him, after a time, said to your father, 'Sire, Lord Thomas de Gornay and Lord Simon d'Esberfoıt [Beresford] knights have come to kill you. If it pleases you I shall give you my clothes so that you can escape more easily.' Then, dressed in these clothes, he came out of prison by night and managed to reach the last door without resistance because he was not recognised. He found the porter sleeping and he straight away killed him. Once he had taken the keys of the door, he opened it and left together with the man who had guarded him. The said knights, who had come to kill him, seeing that he had escaped, and fearing the queen's anger, for fear of their lives decided to put the porter in a chest, having first cut out the heart. The heart and the body of the said porter they presented to the wicked queen as if it were the body of your father and the body of the porter was buried in Glocestart [Gloucester] as the body of the king. After he had escaped the prison of the aforesaid castle he was received at Corf [Corfe] castle together with his companion, who had guarded him in prison, by Lord Thomas, castellan of the said castle without the knowledge of Lord John Maltraverse, the lord of the said Thomas, in which castle he remained secretly for a year and a half. Later on, hearing that the earl of Kent, who had maintained that he was alive, had been beheaded, he embarked on a ship with his aforesaid custodian and by the will and counsel of the said Thomas, who had received him, had crossed to Ireland where he remained eight months. Afterwards, because he was afraid that he might be recognised there, donning the habit of a hermit, he returned to England and came to the port of Sandvic and in the same habit he crossed the sea to Sclusa [Sluis], travelled to Normandy and, from Normandy, as many do crossing 'per Linguam Accitanam', he came to Avignon, where he gave a florin to a papal servant and sent by the same servant, a note to Pope

John. The pope summoned him and kept him secretly and honourably, for more than fifteen days. Finally, after various deliberations covering a wide range of subjects, after receiving permission to depart [licencia] he went to Paris, from Paris to Brabant and from Brabant to Cologne to see the Three Kings and offer his devotions. After leaving Cologne, he crossed Germany and reached Milan in Lombardy and in Milan he entered a certain hermitage of the castle Milasci where he remained for two and a half years. Because this castle became involved in a war he moved to the castle of Cecinia in another hermitage in the diocese of Pavia in Lombardy. And he remained in this last hermitage for two years or thereabouts, remaining confined and carrying out prayers and penitence for us and other sinners. In testimony of these things I have appended a seal for your lordship's consideration. Your devoted servant and notary to the lord pope, Manuel de Flisco [Fieschi].[33]

The cartulary can be dated to 1368 and attributed to Gaucelin de Deaux, bishop of Maguelonne. Its resting place is not so strange when one recalls that Gaucelin was treasurer to Pope Urban V and, like the writer of the letter, a high papal official.[34] Fieschi, who was treated as unimportant by previous authorities, was a veteran senior clerk of Pope John XXII. Manuel was certainly as little likely to have wished to wrong his patron John XXII by accusing him of harbouring pretenders as the vicar of Berkeley was of wrongfully doing evil to the reputation of his patron Thomas Berkeley. It is important to note that Manuel Fieschi was also a canon of York and archdeacon of Nottingham and possibly, if he ever resided, even previously acquainted with Edward II as well as with Edward III to whom the letter is addressed. If he had never actually met the king previously he would certainly, as an official in such a high position, have known enough about the court to have identified a complete trickster and would also have known Edward III well enough not to bother him with fraudulent outpourings. It is very difficult to think why Fieschi himself, as an alternative explanation, should have manufactured such a letter. While we do not know if a copy of the letter ever reached the king, Fieschi apparently considered it essential to tell Edward III that his father had not been murdered and he called the hermit 'your father' without exhibiting any doubt about the man's identity. An interesting postscript to the evidence in the letter, which said that the hermit visited the pope, is the statement in some sources that the earl of Kent was receiving papal encouragement in his attempt to find his brother. It was, of course, after visiting Corfe, where the hermit had once been, that Kent was captured during a search for his brother.[35]

One is very impressed by the detailed placename knowledge and interesting circumstantial evidence surrounding this Italian hermit. However, Tout dismissed the letter with great energy. 'It is a remarkable document, so specious and detailed and bearing none of those marks by which the gross medieval forgery can be generally detected. Yet who can believe it true? Who shall decide how it arose? Was it simply a fairy tale? Was it the real confession of a madman? Was it a cunning effort of some French enemies to discredit the conqueror of Crécy? Or was it an intelligent attempt to exact hush money from a famous king whose beginnings had been based upon his father's murder and his mother's adultery?'[36] These rhetorical suggestions are the more groundless when we recall that Fieschi was a high papal official and not, as Tout put it, a mere 'Italian priest'.

Nobody was ever convicted of the king's murder. Berkeley, as we have already mentioned, was acquitted. Shalford, as we have already seen, was acquitted on a technicality and later employed by Edward III. Mautravers fled abroad, but offered in 1345 to stand trial and to purge himself by oath that he had not killed the king. Edward III refused to allow any trial, but later took Mautravers into his service and favoured him with land grants. The greatest mystery attaches to Gurney, who was murdered in or off the coast of Gascony when being brought back from Italy in the custody of royal agents. He may have known too much, but what he knew is something we can only surmise.

Epilogue:
The regime of Mortimer and Isabella

The epilogue to a book about Edward II and the Despensers is not the place to attempt a detailed study of the regime which overthrew them. Some introduction to the early years of Edward III's reign is, however, necessary to contrast it with what went before. It illustrates strikingly what a dangerous legacy Edward II left, since he had inured the country to tyrannical regimes and demoralised his leading subjects into condoning illegitimate and unstable ones.

It would take a more detailed narrative to unravel who precisely ruled England from October 1326 to October 1330, when Mortimer and Isabella were overthrown by the young King Edward III. Whether Mortimer or Isabella had the last word on any issue is, in any case, an intriguing rather than an important question. Different chroniclers attribute more greed to one and more incompetence to the other, but in the eyes of outsiders they remained united and seemed to bear joint responsibility. There was no institutional basis to Mortimer's control of the country. The arrangement was that the young king should be surrounded by a council of 4 prelates, 4 earls and 6 barons, headed by Henry of Lancaster.[1] Mortimer was not a member of this council. In practice, however, he stood above it and was treated as a member of the royal family, receiving livery as part of it just as Despenser had done.[2] He assumed ever increasing power and wealth, but 1328 appears to have been the decisive year here rather than 1327. It was in this year that he organised his ostentatious Round Table celebrations at Bedford.[3] He also married off two of his daughters to the heirs to the earldoms of Norfolk and Pembroke.[4] This year, too, in June he became the greatest figure in the west of the country as Justice of Wales, with additional powers to appoint and dismiss officials. In September he obtained a formal grant of Arundel's lands in the northern March and Thomas of Lancaster's former lordship of Denbigh.[5] At the end of the year he became earl of March during the Salisbury parliament. Mortimer was warned of the dangers of too ostentatiously flaunting his new power and wealth. One of his sons mockingly bestowed on him the title of 'King of Folly' but, as one of the chroniclers says, '*in magnificentia perduravit*'.[6]

The open-handedness and splendour of the new regime were in marked contrast to the miserly behaviour of Edward II and Despenser. Besides Mortimer, Isabella the queen mother and the two brothers of Edward II, Kent and Norfolk received large grants. Sporting of wealth and greed for lands after the lean years of exile were characteristic of Isabella. Before she had voluntarily exiled herself in France she had possessed the quite considerable annual endowment of £4500 a year. It was now increased to an annual 20000 marks.[7] This included a lion's share of the property of the younger Despenser, comprising Glamorgan and some of his most valuable Gloucestershire estates. Isabella also received the Chamber estates of Edward II, including the exceptionally valuable lordship of Burstwick in Holderness, appreciated at £800 but worth more than that.[8] All the movables on the Despenser and Arundel estates were granted to the rapacious Kent.[9] Faithful supporters like Trussell, Beaumont and Wake received shares of the spoils in the form of various manors. The queen's lady friends, the countess of Pembroke and Joan de Warenne, also benefited, as did all manner of menial servants who had been loyal to the queen during her exile or who had cared for her children.

The new regime also displayed greater generosity to some of the former Despenserians than might have been expected. Tout was fascinated that Mortimer and Isabella took over the central civil service of their predecessors.[10] What is more fascinating is that they took over some royal servants who had been extraordinarily close to Edward II. A striking example is Richard Potesgrave, the old king's chaplain and confessor, who was put in charge of the burial arrangements of his old master and favoured with land grants.[11] Despenserians like Ingemam

Berenger, John Inge, William Anne, and Richard Baldock were all pardoned, as were all those who took part in the long drawn-out resistance of Caerphilly. The only truly recalcitrant opponents of Mortimer and Isabella were former Welsh favourites like Rhys ap Gruffydd, who fled to Scotland, as did one of Edward II's closest friends, Donald earl of Mar.

The new regime inherited huge financial assets. The reserves accumulated in the treasuries of Westminster and the Tower of London amounted on 17 November 1326 to £61 921 4s. 9½d.[12] Considerable stores of cash and silver plate were also found on the properties of Arundel and the Despensers. Much of this was appropriated, licitly or otherwise, by Queen Isabella's followers or simply vanished. Mortimer's Round Table celebrations were believed to have been paid for out of Despenser's treasure which should, of course, have gone to the young king. However, £1748 10s. 11¼d. of Arundel's money was delivered into the king's wardrobe late in 1326, as was £867 19s. 11d. belonging to the younger Despenser and £200 of other 'windfalls'.[13] Despenser's plate, valued at £124 2s. 7d. was deposited in the treasury at Westminster.[14] The long delayed surrender of Caerphilly produced yet another huge treasure, amounting to at least £13 295, which reached the wardrobe on 26 June 1327,[15] just in time to help in financing the war against the Scots. It all adds up to the grand total of £78 156 18s. 2¾d. This still does not include everything as we have no record of the sums paid into the king's chamber and nothing is known for certain about the ultimate fate of the large store of money kept by Edward II during the last days before his capture.

One of the most notable features of the rule of Isabella and Mortimer is the speed with which they dissipated these huge reserves. When, on 27 March, Bishop Adam Orleton handed over the office of treasurer to his successor, Bishop Henry Burghersh, only £12 031 2s. 8d. was left in the treasuries at Westminster and in the Tower,[16] representing a decline of £49 890 2s. 1½d. in slightly more than four months. Unspecified amounts were withdrawn from the store in the Tower on 17 December 1326 and a further £31 000 was removed in February 1327.[17]

This running down of reserves was to some extent inevitable. The new regime was suffering from a permanent fall in its regular income from land. The new rulers had to restore to the erstwhile Contrariants, or their relatives, most of the estates confiscated in 1321–2. As has already been noted, the newly seized properties of Arundel and the Despensers were mostly distributed among the leading supporters of the new regime and valuable royal properties were given away as well.

By its generosity and mercy to its lesser enemies the regime showed that it had learnt the lesson which Edward II and the Despensers had never grasped, namely that followers and military support were more important than cash. This was as well because on the very night of the young king's coronation, on 1 February 1327, the Scots invaded and laid siege to Norham castle. It was indubitably the right moment from the Scottish point of view for such an attack, while an illegitimate regime headed by a woman was guiding the realm for a boy. Robert Bruce had to snatch at any advantage that came his way. He was ill with leprosy and his heir, too, was a young boy. Like Mortimer and Isabella, who were under pressure from the northern lords, he had his own warlike followers to appease. The statement in the deposition parliament that Edward II had failed as a king by losing Scotland must have sounded very much like a declaration of war to Robert Bruce when it came to his ears.

By chance more than military preparedness the attack on Norham failed,[18] but the English regime was not yet ready to fight the Scots. One reason was indubitably that the country had not sufficiently recovered from the civil war to proceed straight away to hostilities with Scotland. In fact, in February Caerphilly castle was still held by friends of the younger Despenser and did not fall until March.[19] In addition, the Hainaulters had gone home and had to be recalled. The tergiversations of the Scots and the English in the spring and summer in truce-making and truce-breaking have been well reconstructed by Stones.[20] Both sides were really content to wait until the real 'campaigning season' in the summer. In March Mortimer and Isabella obtained a truce. On 5 April, however, scarcely a month after the truce was concluded, writs went out ordering military preparations. On 20 April the general summons of array followed.

At this point, very unwisely as it turned out, the government also bethought itself of the desirability of getting reinforcements from abroad. The followers of John of Hainault had formed a valuable element in the army of invasion of Isabella and Mortimer though even on that occasion they became a heavy financial liability.[21] They had finally left England on 10 March 1327. At that date £13491 18s. 5d. was still due to them, over and above the unspecified advances received by them previously and the considerable amount of loot amassed by them on their progress through England. The outstanding debt included £7380 2s. 3d. due for their horses lost during the campaign or left behind in England on their return home.

It is not surprising that John of Hainault responded with alacrity to the summons to return to England for the Scottish war. According to the Leicester chronicler, he brought this time 2000 men and they stayed in England from 8 May to 8 September 1327. They were reputed to have killed in an affray at York some 300 men drawn from among the English shire levies. The same chronicler attributes the unwillingness of the English army to fight the Scots at Stanhope Park to the hatred felt towards these Hainault mercenaries.[22] The enormous sum of £41304 fell due to them for this second campaign. The compensation for horses alone amounted to £21482 5s. 6d. This was a case of gross profiteering, as the Hainaulters preferred in most cases to leave their horses behind in England, selling them to the king at exorbitant prices. When 407 of these animals were resold by royal officials to various magnates they fetched only £920. Earl Warenne who presumably bought only reasonably fit beasts, paid £3 per horse.[23]

The Scottish war was popular. There was probably considerable trust in Mortimer, who had been a very successful campaigner against Edward Bruce in Ireland. Murimuth says that there were more volunteers than conscripts, undoubtedly an exaggeration, but borne out by other references to numerous northerners joining the king's standard.[24] One such group was massacred by the Scots.[25] As Prince has shown, it is impossible to give any account of the size of the army because no 'payroll' survives.[26] The campaign did not start well for the English side. Delays in assembling and provisioning a fleet brought abortive attempts by the English to make another truce. But the Scots were now ready and invaded on 15 June. They employed their usual strategy of arriving in a number of columns which by-passed the English forces. The leaders were the earls of Moray and Douglas and the earl of Mar, the friend of Edward II.[27]

The first evidence which the English army had of the presence of their opponents was the fires which the Scots left in the wake of their devastation of northern England.[28] English military intelligence during the campaign was poor and the English had great difficulty in making contact with the enemy.[29] On 26 June, however, the English leaders were sufficiently aware of the difficulties to summon reinforcements.[30] They moved extraordinarily slowly towards Durham and marched into the city on 14 July.[31] It is clear that they had no idea in which direction to proceed. The *Scalacronica*, whose author subsequently became an experienced campaigner against the Scots, later said that 'none of them dared go forth so grievously were they demoralised'.[32] However, on 18 July, they set out again from Durham in the direction of the fires in an attempt to cut off the Scottish retreat.[33] Those who had arrayed the forces for the campaign had had the right idea in demanding that those summoned should bring good, sturdy, fast horses.[34] The order seems to have been of no avail on this occasion and the English army was slow and cumbersome. As a Scottish *Brut* chronicle put it, 'fra place to place so sped they past, the Englishmen could not follow fast'.[35] The Scots exhausted the much larger English army, which could not even catch a glimpse of them. It was only on 31 July, when they had been campaigning for weeks, that Thomas Rokeby brought definite intelligence of the precise Scottish position on the river Wear some nine miles away from the English army. He had been captured but such was the assurance of the Scots that they freed him to reveal their position to the English.[36] The Scots were playing with the English like a cat with a mouse. The English force-marched after the Scots until they came to the bishop of Durham's hunting park of Stanhope. The young king seems to have been inclined to attack them but was 'traitorously counselled' against it, says one chronicler.[37] The only feat of arms was done by Douglas who, with 200 men, made a dare-devil attack on the English camp on the night of 4 August, killed many and brought down the king's tent ignominiously over his head by cutting the guy-ropes.[38] The bravery of the king's household troops may have prevented the disgrace of Edward's capture. It was not surprising that the young Edward III finished the campaign in tears and with recriminations against his elders and betters.[39] The Scots escaped without serious casualties from the raid and, as a final affront, simply disappeared two days later back over the border. They later returned with Bruce himself to ravage Northumberland and to besiege the main castles of Norham, Alnwick and Warkworth.

There was little that the regime could do, apart from leaving behind, on 12 September, Henry Percy as warden of the March.[40] They had little choice but to make a truce because, as will be seen later on, very little of Edward II's vast treasure was left. A week later, at the Lincoln parliament, the government had to ask for a clerical grant, alleging misleadingly that the treasure of the Despensers and other traitors had been used up in the Scottish war. The Leicester chronicler expressed his doubt as to the fate of all the money, which he shrewdly claimed had been swallowed up by 'new traitors'.[41] In fact, military obligations to the Hainaulters had been one of the chief factors in eating up the huge treasure of Edward II. As the Leicestershire chronicle said, they had returned home with immense amounts of gold and silver.[42] The mention of gold seems correct as the store of £3122 in gold coins kept by the exchequer on 27 March 1327 dwindled to almost nothing by the next stocktaking on 2 July 1328.[43] Altogether John of Hainault received between 11 May 1327 and 1 March 1328 at least £32 722 10s., apart from his annual fee of 1000 marks out of the customs. A stream of royal mandates insisted on the urgency of satisfying him. Because of this, there was a revival of large-scale borrowing from bankers and one payment of £4000 in August 1327 could only be procured by pledging royal jewels.[44]

In its first months the new regime had not needed to borrow

much money and had used professional financiers mainly for certain specialised purposes like transfers of money to foreign countries, purchases of luxuries abroad or short-term, small credit transactions. The Peruzzi of Florence virtually ceased to be used as they had been too closely connected with the Despensers.[45] The other principal Florentine firm, the Bardi, had strong incentives to remain in royal service. They wanted to recover debts due to them from the fallen regime of Edward II, totalling nearly £4000.[46] The great bulk of this debt arose out of advances made by the Bardi to Queen Isabella during her stay in France. They appear to have been made on Edward's orders, but Isabella accepted a special responsibility for their repayment in the first months of her rule.[47] This special connection with Isabella may have smoothed the way for the re-entry of the Bardi into royal service. After the sacking of their house in the City of London in October 1326 the Bardi did not wish to own any more property there and preferred henceforth to rent houses belonging to native Londoners. The new royal government was willing to oblige them by buying their London house for the large sum of £700.[48]

The renewal of the Scottish war, and the resultant new debts of John of Hainault, compelled the government to borrow more frequently. In the summer of 1327 the Bardi provided for this purpose £3233 6s. 8d., including £900 paid to John of Hainault at Paris, where he went as one of the king's envoys.[49] Edward's wedding at York in January 1328 occasioned large additional expenditure. The Bardi alone spent £2417 10s. 3d. on jewels and other precious objects furnished for this occasion.[50] The exchequer ceased to be able to provide the wardrobe with a sufficient flow of ready money and regular borrowing from bankers to finance the king's household became a necessity. The brothers Richard and William de la Pole met this need. They were willing to serve every regime in turn.[51] Earlier on, in 1327 Richard had become the king's butler. Their first loan to the household appears to have been made on 3 December 1327 and amounted to £1200.[52] This was the forerunner of a series of advances. They lent a further £1666 15s. 4d. by late May 1328.[53] The wardrobe could not manage any longer without such loans. The exchequer was sending to

the king wholly inadequate sums. On 23 April 1328 it despatched 1000 marks, which was deemed quite insufficient by
Robert Wodehouse, the keeper of the wardrobe. Five days
later he complained that this was well below what the wardrobe
required and demanded that the exchequer should send from
time to time such money as came to hand to prevent the
wardrobe from being decried in the country for failing to pay
its way.[54] These experiences may have determined Wodehouse
to regularise the arrangement with the brothers de la Pole.
Under an agreement concluded with them by the wardrobe
on 22 May 1328 they were to provide henceforth £20 a day
for the royal household and were to be repaid out of the
customs.[55]

As their yield could not be foreseen with any great accuracy,
there was a tendency to overcharge the customs with assignments beyond what they could bear. That stage had been
reached by the time of the wardrobe's agreement with the
de la Poles. The exchequer does not seem to have been consulted and its officials made the necessary arrangements only
under protest. They pointed out that, in view of the various
annual fees discharged from the customs payable to notables
like John of Hainault and of the other existing assignments on
them, the customs would hardly suffice to sustain these regular
loans to the household.[56]

Direct taxes on laity and clergy represented the only other
alternative security for the repayment of debts and the con-
traction of new loans. The government was forced to secure
a grant of one twentieth on the movables of laymen, which
began to yield money in March 1328.[57] Its collectors were very
dilatory in sending their rolls of assessment to the exchequer,
whose harassed officials were still very uncertain in late June
how much the tax was likely to yield.[58] By the middle of May
the Bardi were complaining that their assignments on customs
and taxes exceeded the revenues on which they had been
optimistically earmarked.[59] All these signs of growing financial
embarrassment are confirmed by the fresh stocktaking of
treasury reserves on 2 July 1328. On that day, the new treasurer, Bishop Thomas Charlton of Hereford, found in the
treasury no more than £1355 11s. 3½d.[60] The huge reserve

H

inherited from Edward II had been almost entirely dissipated in less than two years and from now on the government would have to live from hand to mouth and to depend for the smooth flow of cash on the goodwill of its financiers.

A large proportion of the lay twentieth and of the clerical tenth was earmarked from the outset for the repayment of debts to John of Hainault. Before 1 March 1328 the Bardi, who acted as his agents, appear to have repaid him a further £7000 and they received assignments for this amount out of these two taxes.[61] Thereafter £14 406 6s. 9d. still remained due to John.[62] A series of letters was exchanged about this between the king and the exchequer in June and July 1328.[63] At first the king insisted that £10 000 should be paid to John at once from assignments or loans. The exchequer protested that it could not raise this sum,[64] nor find another £2000 needed by the constable of Bordeaux. Unlike the peremptory orders of Edward II, his son's letters were persistent in their demands but conciliatory. In the last of these, dated 18 July 1328, the king, after recounting the exchequer's objections, remarked that it was 'nonetheless his duty to excite them to think further how the money might be found'.[65] Ultimately, as a compromise, John's agents, the Bardi, received assignments for £7000 out of the customs and out of lay and clerical taxes. By 20 August John appears to have been satisfied in this way for £6953,[66] but the repayment of the outstanding balance of £7406 6s. 9d. was delayed for nearly a year. Only in June 1329 did the Bardi agree to satisfy this and even then the payments fell short by £2000.[67] There were clearly limits to the resources of the king's principal bankers or at least to the credits that they were prepared to extend to this increasingly embarrassed regime.

It was very fortunate for Mortimer and Isabella that the sickness of Robert Bruce allowed them to make peace on reasonable terms and, when one bears in mind their growing financial distress, the demand for payment of £20 000[68] from Robert Bruce as a provision of the treaty becomes readily comprehensible. Stones' discovery of a set of proposals made by Bruce early in October 1327 reveals his priorities at this stage of the negotiations.[69] They enable us to see why the preliminary negotiations to a treaty were so long drawn out.

The treaty was only ratified at the Northampton parliament in the following May. Among the items on Bruce's list of proposals was the renunciation of all English claims to land in Scotland. This was clearly based on hearty detestation and distrust of the northern English magnates, above all of the lords Percy, Beaumont and Wake, and this was not settled in the treaty. Bruce's title was recognised and the excommunication proceedings in Rome were to be halted with English aid. A marriage alliance was to be made between Bruce's heir, David, and Edward's II's sister, Joanna. This eventually took place at Berwick in August 1328. A year after the campaign Bruce had achieved his life's aim, the recognition of his title and a marriage alliance with England to safeguard his country from future war.

Power was given to Isabella in July 1328 to negotiate an arrangement about the Scottish lands of the northern lords.[70] The delays in securing this agreement probably played their part in determining the alliance between these northern lords and Henry of Lancaster later in 1328. The Scottish war may also have played a part in estranging from the government the two brothers of Edward II, the earls of Norfolk and Kent. It was during the Scottish campaign of July–August 1327 that Norfolk drew up a statement of his rights as Earl Marshal which suggests that he had encountered difficulties or opposition. If the marriage of Mortimer's daughter to Norfolk's son was prompted by Mortimer's desire to regain Norfolk's friendship, it failed to achieve this purpose and later on in 1328 Norfolk and Kent supported Lancaster. Kent, the more forceful of the two brothers, may have been the prime mover here. As his later career shows, he was ambivalent towards Edward II and the news of Edward's death in September 1327 may have made Kent permanently disaffected towards Mortimer.

We do not know how long Lancaster's fury against Mortimer had been simmering. The Scottish peace, made against the wishes of many leading magnates of the realm, seems to have been one of the causes of the final breach. The parliament of Northampton in April–May 1328, which formally ratified that peace, also enacted an important statute for the better maintenance of internal peace in England. This statute was invoked during the hostilities between Mortimer and Lancaster in the winter of 1328–9 as one of the grounds for legal proceedings against Lancaster's followers.[71] It is possible that its enactment could be viewed from the start as an ominous threat against Lancaster and other malcontents against the regime. There were plenty of deeper reasons for Lancaster's hostility. Mortimer had usurped his position as the chief councillor to the king and Lancaster was even allegedly denied ready access to Edward.[72] The beginnings of an open confrontation between Lancaster and Mortimer at the time of the Salisbury parliament in October 1328 may perhaps be best interpreted as an attempt by Lancaster to reassert his personal influence over the king, which completely miscarried.

Lancaster may have played into Mortimer's hands by, at least condoning, if not actually organising himself, the murder of Robert Holland, whose decisive betrayal of Thomas of Lancaster in 1322 had never been forgiven by the more embittered Lancastrian followers. We know from the Leicester chronicle that Lancaster's knight who was chiefly responsible for the murder, Thomas Wyther, was later expressly excepted from the pardon granted to Henry of Lancaster's followers. He had to flee abroad in 1329, where he remained until the overthrow of Mortimer's rule.[73] The murder had certainly to be regarded as a flagrant violation of the newly enacted Statute of Northampton.

Lancaster's open breach with the court seems to have started in the middle of September 1328, when he ceases to attest royal charters.[74] The crisis that followed is made particularly obscure by two sets of circumstances. Neither of the main protagonists seems to have entirely achieved what he set out to do, but this means that their original motives have become concealed by the course of events. If Lancaster aimed above all at regaining control of the king, he certainly failed, but he did not deeply or enduringly alienate Edward. Mortimer was thus unable to remove Lancaster permanently from English politics. To judge by an official government statement of the case against Lancaster,[75] Mortimer would have liked to condemn Lancaster for treason and the official record tortuously construes Lancaster's actions with this in mind. Its failure to do so convincingly suggests that Lancaster was never guilty of starting an overt civil war against the king.

This brings us to our second main reason for our uncertainty about what really happened. We are confronted by two versions of these events: the Leicester chronicle, a pro-Lancastrian narrative of the chronicler Knighton,[76] and the anti-Lancastrian government memorandum.[77] Neither tells the whole story and, at times, they read as if they were discussing quite different happenings. The Leicester chronicler avoided any condemnation of Lancaster. For example, he mentions the murder of Robert Holland immediately before the account of the conflict between Lancaster and Mortimer, but he never admits any connection between these two sets of events. The government memorandum is couched in the form of a speech, intended for some undefined assembly at some date after 7 January 1329 in order to justify the king's actions. Its insistence that the seizure of the estates of Lancaster and his followers represented only a temporary sequestration, as a way of distraining them and not as a permanent forfeiture for treason, perhaps teaches us one important thing about the whole situation. The audience of notables for whom this speech was presumably intended obviously had a horror of anything smacking of charges of undeniable treason and of permanent confiscations reminiscent of the recent terrible happenings between 1321 and 1326. Both Lancaster and Mortimer apparently had to reckon with this mood of the aristocracy and this, better than anything else, may explain why no serious civil war was allowed to occur between October 1328 and January 1329.

The parliament at Salisbury from 16 to 31 October 1328 was to be the scene of the elevation of Mortimer to the earldom of March, though the uniqueness of his title was disguised by conferring at the same time the earldom of Cornwall on the king's younger brother, John, and creating an Irish earldom of Ormond for one of Mortimer's trusted adherents.[78] If Lancaster knew of Mortimer's impending promotion, this would help to explain his refusal to appear at Salisbury. Instead he kept at a safe distance at Winchester, the episcopal city of one of his allies, Bishop John Stratford. According to the official memorandum Lancaster and the magnates with him were at Winchester with a strong force of armed men. This is not borne out by an official inquisition held at Winchester in pursuance of a royal writ of 15 November 1328. The jury may have been influenced by Bishop Stratford's partiality for Lancaster, but it testified unequivocally that Lancaster and his followers had come to Winchester on 30 October unarmed and peacefully stayed there until 3 November 'when they departed and did no harm to anybody'.[79] The Leicester chronicle states that Mortimer assembled a considerable army. That this had already begun to assemble at Salisbury is shown by subsequent payments of £135 to John Mautravers for bringing a force of men-at-arms and infantry to the king at Salisbury and keeping them in his pay until the crisis ended early in 1329.[80]

Stratford's support for Lancaster need occasion no surprise. He had fallen from favour as early as January 1327, when he was dismissed from the office of treasurer. He appears to have been particularly at odds with Henry Burghersh, bishop of Lincoln, one of the regime's staunchest ecclesiastical supporters. Stratford had originally attended the Salisbury parliament, but left without the king's licence before its end to join Lancaster. The government later tried to prosecute Stratford in the King's Bench for thus illegally absenting himself from parliament.[81] A more surprising episcopal recruit to Lancaster's camp was Bishop Adam Orleton of Hereford, the erstwhile 'chaplain' of Mortimer. Orleton had annoyed his former patron by accepting the see of Worcester by papal provision but without the king's permission. He was a courageous and independent man and his adherence to Lancaster in this crisis is possibly an example of Mortimer's arrogant misuse of men who otherwise might have been expected to support him. The same may be true of some of Lancaster's lay followers. We do not know why Hugh Audley should have joined him, but as the only surviving co-heir to the Clare estates, he may have been dissatisfied because he had not been restored in 1327 to a larger portion of the Clare inheritance. The presence of some of the northern lords in Lancaster's camp needs no further explanation. The desertion of Kent to Lancaster's side was probably a last-minute change of allegiance, because he was still at court as late as 20 October.[82] Norfolk changed sides with Kent. Lancaster could also rely upon the new archbishop of Canterbury, Simon Mepeham, for sympathy to his cause, whose later attempts at mediation proved very disappointing to him. The bishop of London was another of Lancaster's open followers[83] and the earl appears to have enjoyed much popularity among the clergy and people of London. This may have been one of the factors which later preserved him from destruction at Mortimer's hands.

According to the royal memorandum, when Lancaster and his followers emerged from Winchester they encountered the king's retinue. Lancaster is alleged to have staged some sort of armed demonstration,[84] but obviously no serious threat of any kind was made to the king. It could have formed an attempt at persuading the king of the serious discontent that Mortimer and his other advisers were arousing. If it was meant to detach the king from his entourage, it failed completely.

According to the royal memorandum, after this incident Lancaster's army proceeded to the centres of Lancastrian power in the Midlands gathering further reinforcements. The Lancastrians were alleged to have destroyed properties of the king and others on their way. Probably we should not treat this statement too seriously as this charge is not substantiated anywhere else, though some plunder and violence did presumably take place. Other charges are more flimsy or strange and suggest that the government was at a loss to build up a serious case against the Lancastrians. The king complained that his marshals and sergeants were refused admittance into Kenilworth, contrary to the king's right to send his servants into every place in the kingdom. The Lancastrians were also accused of disseminating propaganda against the government. In words that could be construed as an accusation of treason, the king charged them with trying to incite his subjects against their lord 'to the destruction of the king and of his people'.[85] Strangest of all was the bizarre complaint that the Lancastrians had been moving about the country disguised as friars 'in despite of the king, condemning and mocking the king and his royal dignity'.[86]

After a council at Worcester, the king issued a proclamation promising a pardon for all those trespasses to all who wanted to surrender to him by the morrow of Epiphany (7 January), except for some named persons who could expect no mercy. According to the Leicester chronicle these exceptions included Henry Beaumont, William Trussell, Thomas Roscelin and Thomas Wyther, the assassin of Robert Holland.[87] This proclamation was read to Lancaster and his followers by Archbishop Mepeham at a meeting in St Paul's cathedral in the City of London. Mepeham seems to have believed that he might achieve a settlement by persuading Lancaster and the other leaders to swear a solemn oath on the Gospels that they had not done anything against the estate of the king or to the dishonour of his royal lordship and the damage of himself, his mother or anyone else.

The king, who by now appears to have become greatly incensed against these 'malcontents', refused to accept this oath as sufficient surrender.[88] As the time limit for their submission had now passed, the government felt justified in taking more drastic measures. Mortimer may have been encouraged by the desertion to his side of Kent and Norfolk, who now accused Lancaster of sedition to the best of their power. The government decreed the sequestration of all the lands and goods of Lancaster, and of all those who remained with him, until they submitted unconditionally. This is presumably the origin of Knighton's statement that a large royal army wasted the country around Leicester for a week in January,[89] though his claim that this began on 4 January cannot in any way be reconciled with the statement in the royal memorandum that sequestration was decreed only after the time limit for submission had elapsed. One suspects that here Knighton is telling the truth. Lancaster, from his camp at Bedford, offered to submit through the further mediation of Mepeham. His followers were obviously abandoning him and it was presumably no part of his purpose to engage in a bitter civil war. The government for its part may have feared that Lancaster might secure wider popular support. Lancaster escaped with a fine of £30000 and his important followers were also heavily amerced,[90] though these fines were later cancelled. The four nobles excepted from the proclamation had to flee abroad, as did also Lancaster's son-in-law, Lord Thomas Wake, who only a year earlier had so eloquently led the agitation for the deposition of Edward II.

The political crisis highlighted the value of the services of the Florentine financiers to the Mortimer regime.[91] The Bardi paid £1260 due to Mortimer for his stay with the king between 28 December 1328 and 17 January 1329, which confirms that he was continually by the king's side during the most dangerous days when England was on the brink of civil war. The sum of £100 of the earl's annual fee was likewise paid by the Bardi. Very appositely, these loans were partly repaid out of a fine imposed on Bishop Stratford for his adherence to Lancaster. The Bardi also repaid a wardrobe debenture of 10 December 1328 for 500 marks due to the Earl Warenne for his stay with the king with an armed retinue, presumably during the Salisbury parliament.

On the eve of that parliament the royal finances were at a fairly low ebb. When on 21 August 1328 Richard Bury succeeded Robert Wodehouse as keeper of the wardrobe, he took over a mere £198 13s. 4d. in cash.[92] During the ensuing year the government's loans from financiers rose to the imposing total of £12512 13s. 2d.[93] The de la Pole brothers fell into arrears with their advances to the household and on 17 August were replaced by the Bardi. During the next fourteen months, down to the overthrow of Mortimer's rule, loans rose to £19453 5s. 6d., the great bulk of the advances coming from the Bardi, though even they were unable or unwilling to discharge all that was demanded of them. Only through loans could the government finance Edward's visit to France in the spring of 1329 and the various embassies to Paris and Avignon.

While Queen Isabella and Mortimer were gorged with grants of land and money, also swallowing up the properties of the king's uncle, the earl of Kent, executed for treason in March 1330, Edward III was personally embarrassed by lack of money. The statements of the chroniclers to this effect find some confirmation in official records. A letter of privy seal of 12 June 1330 addressed by Edward to the treasurer complained that William Zouche, the keeper of the great wardrobe, responsible for purchasing supplies for the household, was threatening to resign unless he was supplied more promptly with money.[94] When on 1 December, slightly over two months after Mortimer's overthrow, the outgoing treasurer, Wodehouse, was handing over the treasury to his successor, he left to him the derisory sum of £41 2s. 11d. out of the enormous treasure left by Edward II.[95] That successor was the same archbishop, William Melton, who on 17 November 1326 had handed over to the first treasurer of Isabella and Mortimer £61 921 4s. 9½d.

The events that led to Mortimer's fall from power still remain very obscure, partly because the chroniclers tell us very little. Secrecy was the vital ingredient in the plot by Montague and Edward III to overthrow Mortimer and very little about it found its way into the chronicles after the event apart from the bald facts. It is possible that Lancaster played a deeper part throughout than we can reconstruct from surviving evidence. Two small incidents suggest this. On one occasion he acted as a surety in the court of King's Bench for a man called Gregory Foriz. Foriz was being prosecuted for murder on this occasion, but was also an associate of William Aylmer who, with the Dunheved brothers, had attempted to free Edward II from Berkeley castle.[96] The second interesting item of evidence concerns Lancaster's itinerary. After brief reappearances at court in February and July 1329, to judge by charter attestations, Lancaster did not again appear there that year nor in the spring of 1330. He returned very briefly to court in June, for a week in July and then, significantly on 16 October, just before Edward and William Montague launched their coup against Mortimer and Isabella at Nottingham.[97]

It was partly the role which Kent had played in Lancaster's rebellion which brought him under close scrutiny by Mortimer. In March 1330 he was arrested after having attempted to find the deposed king in Corfe castle, one of the places which, according to the Fieschi letter, the king had visited secretly after escaping from Berkeley castle. Sealed letters revealing treason were allegedly found on him.[98] A confession was then exacted from him which revealed the collaboration of some very important people including Melton, archbishop of York, who had furnished the plotters with £5000, Stephen Gravesend, bishop of London, Henry de Beaumont and his sister Lady de Vescy and a number of former followers of Despenser including Ingemar Berenger and William Anne.[99] Kent had also received papal absolution for his conspiracy.[100] These people certainly believed that Edward II was alive. Kent was executed on 19 March, two days after his arrest. Apparently he had to wait until the evening because nobody could be found to execute him until a drunken criminal offered to do so.

Kent's death probably served as a warning to the young Edward III that to Mortimer nobody, however near the king, was sacred. Edward, in royal letters, had always addressed Kent most affectionately in contrast to his greetings to Norfolk which were quite neutral. It may be some indication that Edward was resuming some responsibility for Kent's followers and also showing his preparedness to oppose the regime that proceedings in the King's Bench against some of the less important ones were delayed until Mortimer's regime fell. This was done quite simply by the royal attorney announcing that he had not been given his 'brief' for the prosecution so that the case had to be adjourned. This was rather unusual considering the political importance of the trial.[101]

However, a watch was kept on the young king's household and very shortly before the coup many of its members were interrogated. Apparently the bravado of William Montague saved the day. He so forcibly denied knowledge of the plot that Mortimer had to accept his word. On 19 October, with the secret co-operation of the constable of Nottingham, a group of knights who had been hiding in the bushes beneath the castle used a secret underground passage to enter it. Mortimer was surprised in conference with Henry Burghersh, bishop of Lincoln, tried and executed. Queen Isabella was sent to a nunnery.

Edward III's consistent attempts and exceptional success after 1330 at establishing good relations with most of the magnates is one of the outstanding features of the reign.[102] He had obviously learnt many lessons from his father's disastrous period of rule. The continued devotion of many leading magnates to the king all through the lean years of frustrating inactivity and failure in the Netherlands at the beginning of the Hundred Years' War in 1338–40 clearly had deeper roots than their mere pursuit of material advantage. Nor was it a matter of attaching to the king only a few outstanding people, as had characterised Edward II's personal relations. Deliberate attempts were made to conciliate the whole magnate class. At this early stage of his career Edward III appreciated that no important individuals must be left out of royal favour. This was made especially clear in the distribution of grants at the start of the French war. Some men were particularly valued and favoured, but nobody was entirely neglected. Good service was conspicuously rewarded.

This policy was in keeping with Edward's general outlook and character. The positive qualities that stand out are his bravery and knightly prowess which earned the respect of his contemporaries, the magnanimity and lack of enduring vindictiveness in dealing with his subjects, which are entirely in contrast with his father. It is to the personal qualities of Edward, his *excedens virtus*, that Walter Burley, in a commentary on Aristotle's *Politics* begun *c.* 1338–9, attributed the great harmony reigning among the English people in his time.[103]

It was accompanied by skill in choosing collaborators wisely. This was a skill acquired only gradually. It manifested itself at first in the choice of military subordinates. By 1337–8 Edward had assembled around him a team of commanders and aristocratic warriors who continued to serve him with conspicuous success until 1360. The finding of a satisfactory group of leading ministers and officials was not so easy. Initially Edward had to depend on councillors and civil servants inherited from previous regimes. They were highly experienced in the normal routines of peacetime government but did not adjust well to emergencies and some of them may also have been out of sympathy with Edward's wars. Their shortcomings, real or imagined, were a leading issue in the political crisis at the end of 1340. That upheaval also brought to the surface the existence of a deep personal dislike between the king and some of his leading advisers, especially Archbishop John Stratford of Canterbury, who had played such a prominent part in deposing his father.[104] With the dismissal of Stratford and his brother, the chancellor, in November 1340, Edward wiped away some of the last connections with his father's disastrous reign.

Appendix 1

Properties of the Despensers: Main facts and sources

This appendix is not intended as a detailed list of the properties of the two Despensers. Materials for drawing up such a comprehensive list do not exist. Because of gaps in evidence, notably for many of the immense Welsh properties of the younger Despenser, such a list would be of very uneven quality. No cartulary of Despenser properties exists. The evidence about the titles of the Despensers to their various properties and the approximate dates of their acquisition is therefore very uneven, though it can be satisfactorily reconstructed in many cases.

The private archives of the two Despensers, Hugh the Elder, earl of Winchester (Hugh I), and of his son, Hugh II, were seized by the crown in 1326 and remained permanently confiscated so that they still mostly survive. Summaries of their charters and other muniments were drawn up for the use of exchequer officials. Inquiries were held into the value of their English estates and into the goods found on them. The results of these inquiries were conveniently summarised in a single document of ten membranes (Exch.Anc.Extents, E. 142/33). For the vast majority of their English estates we have estimates of their value in 1326 and lists of movable goods kept on each separate estate before these properties were ravaged during the civil war in September–October 1326. It is also often known at what precise date each property has been acquired by the two Despensers and from whom.

A study of the properties of the Despensers must be based on very miscellaneous sources, only some of which can be listed in detail. All the relevant printed records have been used, including the Calendars of Chancery Rolls, of Ancient Deeds, of Inquisitions Post Mortem, of Inquisitions Miscellaneous and of Memoranda Rolls of the Exchequer.

1. Records connected with the confiscation of the estates and the archives of the Despensers in 1326:
    a. Exch.Acts.Var., E. 101/332/27 and E. 101/333/2: lists and partial calendars of the records of the Despensers delivered into the exchequer. Many of the individual deeds are still to be found among the various classes of P.R.O. ancient deeds (cf. *C.Anc.Deeds,* 6 vols.).
    b. Records arising out of the dealings of the Despensers with their bankers,

especially E. 101/127, nos. 5, 17, 22. Cf. E. B. Fryde, 'The deposits of Hugh Despenser the Younger with Italian bankers', *Ec.H.R.*, 2nd ser., 3 (1951), pp. 344–62.

c. A summary, made probably in the exchequer, of the returns of the inquiries into the estates of the Despensers and their associates, Exch. Anc.Extents, E. 142/33. Many of the inquisitions and extents summarised therein survive, including Exch.Extents and Inq., E. 143/10/1 (an original file for Gloucestershire); Exch.Anc.Extents, E. 142/58, nos. 8 and 10 (Thurnhamhall, Yorks., showing how an extent was compiled); E. 142/34; E. 142/files 53–9, 61–2. Other inquisitions held in 1327–30 are in Chanc.Misc.Inq., C. 145/file 13.

d. Proceedings in the exchequer concerning the associates and the victims of the Despensers on K.R.Mem.R. 1–5 Edw. III (including also *Calendar of Memoranda Rolls, 1326–27*, ed. R. C. Latham (1968) and *List.Mem.R.*).

2. The original inheritance of Hugh I can be reconstructed, in addition to sources under 1.a. and 1.c., from Exch.Extents and Inq., E. 143/8/2 (writs of 4 and 8 May 1324) and from Inquisitions Post Mortem on his various relatives. See *C.I.P.M.*, I, no. 807; II, nos. 101, 389; III, no. 425.

3. The division of Clare inheritance 1317. The share of Hugh II set out in Chanc.Misc., C. 47/9/24; the shares of Hugh Audley and Roger D'Amory in C. 47/9/nos. 23 and 25.

4. Properties of the Despensers ravaged by their enemies in the spring of 1321 are listed in *C.Cl.R. 1318–23*, pp. 542–6.

5. Lands of the Contrariants acquired by the Despensers: in addition to sources under 1.a., 1.c. and 1.d., Ministers Accts., S.C. 6/1145 (accounts and files for 1321–2); L.T.R.Misc.Accts., E. 358/14 (enrolled accounts for the estates of the Contrariants); Exch.Anc.Extents, E. 142/31 (roll of leases of confiscated properties by the exchequer, 1322–6).

6. Proceedings against particular Contrariants or personal victims of the Despensers (a selection of the more important cases):

a. Katherine Giffard, widow of William Giffard of Boyton.
Victim of joint proceedings by Hugh II and Bartholomew Badlesmere, who tried from 1317 to acquire her manor of Barewe (Suffolk). Main collection of documents in E. 101/332/27. See also Chanc.Warr., C. 81/98/, nos. 4050, 4051B, 4095 (privy seal letters); L.T.R.Mem.R., E. 368/87, m. 57 (privy seal, 10 April 1317); E. 358/14, m. 4.

b. John de Wilington (1321–2).
W. H. Stevenson, 'A Letter of the Younger Despenser on the eve of the Barons' Rebellion', *E.H.R.*, 12 (1897); Anc.Corr., S.C. 1/44, no. 144.

c. John Latchley, victim of joint proceedings by Hugh II and Bartholomew Badlesmere, which began in 1320.
Main collection of documents in E. 101/332/27. See also J. Conway-Davies, *The Baronial Opposition to Edward II, its character and policy: A Study in Administrative History* (1918), p. 97 and Bertie Wilkinson, 'The

Sherburn Indenture and the attack on the Despensers, 1321', *E.H.R.*, 63 (1948), p. 27.

d. Lordship of Gower (1318–23).

Main collection of documents in E. 101/332/27. See also J. Conway-Davies, 'The Despenser War in Glamorgan', *T.R.H.S.*, 3rd. ser., 9 (1915) and *Sir Christopher Hatton's Book of Seals*, ed. L. C. Loyd and D. M. Stenton (1950), no. 315 pp. 217–18; Anc.Pet., S.C. 8/173/8631 (*C.A.P.*, p. 292).

e. Elizabeth D'Amory, widow of Roger D'Amory and the acquisition by the Despensers of the lordships of Gower and Usk (1322–3).

In addition to sources under 6.d. see B. L., Harleian Ms., 1240 (a Mortimer cartulary), ff. 86–7, including Elizabeth's account, recorded by a notary, of proceedings against her (starting f. 86v); *C.Anc.Deeds*, III, nos. A. 4876, 4885; Anc.Pet. S.C. 8/92/4554 (*C.A.P.*, p. 140).

f. English properties of William de Braose (1322–6).

Main collection of documents in E. 101/332/27. See also E. 142/56, no. 15; Anc.Pet., S.C. 8/157/7805.

g. Elizabeth Comyn (1323–5).

Sir Christopher Hatton's Book of Seals, ed. L. C. Loyd and D. M. Stenton (1950), no. 175, p. 125. Bodleian Library, Dodsworth Ms. 76 (nos. 76, 131, 135, 148, 157); *C.I.M.* II, no. 1024, pp. 254–5; *C.I.P.M.*, VII, no. 391, pp. 287, 292; *Rot.Parl.* II, p. 22, *C.A.P.*, pp. 268, 274.

h. Alice de Lacy, Countess of Lancaster (1322).

Duchy of Lancaster Miscellaneous Books, D.L. 42/11, f. 66v; Chancery Warrants (secret seal), C. 81/1329/42; *Rot.Parl.* II, pp. 57–8. A record of lands that Alice was forced to surrender is summarised in *C.Cl.R.*, *1318–23*, pp. 574–6.

i. John de Sutton (1325).

In addition to sources under 1.a. and 1.c. see *C.I.M.*, II, nos. 965, 1000; E. 142/62, no. 3.

j. Geoffrey D'Abitot and John de Sapy.

In addition to sources under 1.a. and 1.c. see E. 358/14, m.50v. and Bodleian Library, Holkham lat. ms. 29, f. 44r.

k. Hastings wardship (1325–6).

C.I.P.M., VI, no. 385 (on the death of J. Hastings); K.R.Mem.R., 2 Edw. III, E. 159/104, m. 131; E. 142/33 and E. 142/60.

7. Welsh lordships acquired by the Despensers (see also above under 3, 6.d., 6.e., 6.j.). All except 7.d. held by Hugh II.

The acquisition of these lordships is discussed in the text and need not be documented here. The evidence about the value of the lordships listed below is mostly derived from records unconnected with the Despensers. Much of the information about the approximate value of particular lordships was kindly provided by Professor Rees R. Davies and is partly based on sources that are still unpublished.

a. Lordship of Abergavenny (held 1325–6).

Valued at £667 in 1348.

b. Bohun lordships (Brecon, Hay, Huntington).

Average gross receipts, 1337–46, c. £770 a year. These lands together with the Welsh lands of Roger Clifford and a part of the Welsh lands of John Giffard of Brimpsfield (Iscennen) and of Roger Mortimer of Chirk (Blaenllyfni) were granted to Hugh II on 10 July 1322. For Bohun and Mortimer lands he was to render £600 each year.

c. Chepstow (1323–6).

Granted to Hugh II by Thomas, earl of Norfolk, in August 1323 at a yearly rent of £200, which was redeemed on 18 November 1324 for a promise of a single payment of £800, of which £300 was paid at once (cf. E. B. Fryde, 'The desposits of Hugh Despenser the Younger . . .', under 1(b), p. 348 and n. 4).

d. Denbigh (held by Hugh I, 1322–6).

In 1334 the lordship was estimated to be worth £1100 7s. 1¾d. P. Vinogradoff and F. Morgan, eds., *The Survey of the Honour of Denbigh* (1914), p. 323.

e. Gower.

The lordship was valued at £300 in 1316.

f. Pembroke (1325–6).

The lordship was valued at £247 in 1324.

It is possible to ascertain in some cases how the value of the properties of the Despensers was calculated by royal officials in 1327. As was usual in preparing medieval extents, the amounts given represent merely the net value after the deduction of customary expenses. The extents, therefore, almost always understate the real value of each property. The government itself thought so and in several cases we have at least two different sets of figures, derived from two separate inquiries and sometimes as many as three. Whenever this happens I have normally used the highest figures. The resultant valuations can provide only an order of magnitude but can be legitimately used for comparisons between different estates.

This body of statistics can, therefore, also be compared with less uniform figures available for the Welsh properties of Hugh II. Here, information can be assembled from various records dating from the years 1317–26, though some of the figures for the value of certain lordships are only approximate estimates.

Using these figures, derived chiefly from 1326–7, I have tried to estimate what proportion of their wealth was acquired at successive stages in their careers. This included an estimate of the original inheritance of Hugh I, of their 'normal' acquisitions previous to 1321, of their gains from defeated Contrariants in 1321–2 and of their acquisitions by violent or illicit means during their years of supreme power in 1322–6. Each group of figures has also been given as a percentage of their total wealth at the time of their fall in 1326.

Hugh I held in September 1326 estates estimated to be worth at least £3884 10s. 10¼d., with goods on them valued at £4364 19s. 7d. Two-fifths of his properties had been inherited by Hugh I or acquired by him in 'normal' ways before 1321 (valued at £1580 2s. 3¼d., with goods on them worth £2541 4d.). They lay chiefly in Buckinghamshire (with High Wycombe as the chief manor) in the west Midlands (with Loughborough as the chief manor) and Wiltshire (former Basset properties). Fifty-three per cent of Hugh I's properties consisted of grants to him of the confiscated estates of Contrariants (especially in Wiltshire, Hampshire, Gloucestershire and Worcestershire) or were acquired by violent or illegal means (especially in Surrey, Sussex and Kent). Almost all of these were acquired by Hugh I in or after 1322 (estates valued at £1984 7s. 3¾d., with goods on them worth £1356 15s. 8d.).

In 1326 Hugh I owned at least £1600 in cash. A further £1800 in money, with valuables and armour, were plundered in October 1326 from his manor of Loughborough.

Hugh II held in September 1326 English and Welsh lands estimated to be worth at least £7154 14s. 8½d., with goods on them valued at £3136 18s. 7d. (with figures for goods missing for all the Welsh lordships except for Abergavenny). Up to the end of 1317 he inherited or acquired by lawful means estates estimated at £2054 5s. 11¼ (28 per cent of the estimated value of his properties in 1326), including his share of the Clare inheritance (this amounted in 1317 to properties in England and Wales estimated at £1415 7s. 8¾d.). Nearly two-thirds of the Clare lands secured by him in 1317 lay in Wales. Before the end of 1320, by securing a large portion of the dower lands of Matilda de Clare, widow of the last earl, Gilbert of Gloucester, he began to build up a substantial block of properties in Worcestershire and Gloucestershire (including especially the very valuable manor of Tewkesbury in Gloucestershire). Forty-four per cent of Hugh's properties consisted of grants to him of confiscated estates of Contrariants or were acquired by violent or illegal means (estates valued at £3161 1s. 11d., with goods on them worth at least £1819 1s. 5½d.). Unlike his father, Hugh II acquired considerable properties by illicit or at least doubtful means already in the years 1318–21. His most extensive acquisitions in 1322–6 lay, again, in South Wales and the Welsh March. He acquired further properties in Gloucestershire and Worcestershire bordering on his lordship of Glamorgan and Gwent (especially the very valuable manor of Thornbury in Gloucestershire). The other main block of his English acquisitions during these years lay in the south-eastern counties of Kent, Surrey and Sussex, but he picked up some properties in several other southern and eastern counties and in the Midlands.

Early in September 1326 Hugh II held £2545 6s. 9¾d. on deposit with the Bardi and the Peruzzi of Florence. Plate worth £124 2s. 7d. was delivered into the Tower of London after his fall.

Appendix 2

The deposition of Edward II

An account of the deposition of Edward II taken from a chronicle, probably from Canterbury, now Trinity College, Cambridge, Ms., R.5.41 fs. 125r, 125v, 126r.

f. 125r.

Item secundo Nonis Januarii Regina Anglie venit Londonias. Cui processerunt obviam Londonienses in magna solemnitate.

Parliamentum londoniis Rege absente. Eodem tempore VII° Idibus Januarii incepit parliamentum londoniis absente rege in presencia Regine et filii sui ubi londonienses fecerunt sibi iurare Episcopos, Comites et Barones similiter et milites et quotquot ibi erant et Archiepiscopus Cantuariensis, antequam voluerunt ipsum in amicitiam, recipere optulit eis L dolia vini et postea iuramentum fecit. In isto parliamento ex unanimi assensu Episcoporum et procerum et totius populi depositus est dominus Edwardus Rex Anglie secundus a gubernacione terre sue et filius suus primogenitus Edwardus dux Acquitannie subrogatus est ut sequitur.

Forma deposicionis Regis Edwardi Anglie post Conquestum Secundi. Memorandum quod die sancti Hillarii Episcopi et confessoris Anno dominice Incarnacionis MCCCXXVII.° In parliamento apud Westmonasterium prelatorum et procerum fere totius regni mutuo tractatu prehabito in palacio regio in aula magna Westmonasterii acta sunt hec subscripta coram prelatis et magnatibus regni in communi aula convenientibus prelibata. Primo dominus Rogerus Mortimer, cui dictum fuerat ex parte magnatum quod illud quod ordinatum fuerat populo pronunciaret, se excusavit dicendo se non debere culpari de iure super huiusmodi pronunciacione pro eo quod communi omni assensu sibi fuerat hoc iniunctum. Retulit igitur coram populo quod inter magnates ita fuerat unanimiter concordatum quod Rex regni gubernaculum amodo non haberet, quia insufficiens et procerum regni destructor et ecclesie sancte contra iuramentum suum et coronam malo consilio adquiescens fuit. Et ideo primogenitus eius dux acquitannie pro eo regnaret si populus preberet assensum. Et rundit dominus Thomas de Wak' sursum manus extendens: dico pro me numquam regnabit. Et dominus Episcopus herefordie accepit pro themate illud proverbiorum XIII° capitulo: ubi non est gubernator populus corruet. Quo proposito causam destinacionis sue et aliorum magnatum ad Regem apud castrum de

f. 125v.

kenyngworth' et qualiter Regem alloquebatur evidenter exposuit. Premisso enim sue locucionis exordio, videlicet audi preces populi tui, Paralipomenon' II° capitulo VI°, Regi multos et magnos defectus et intollerabiles in suo regimine patefecit, videlicet quod malo consilio et proditorio adhesit, quod etiam proceres regni destruxit et terras corone sue, quas et pater suus Rex Anglie illustris Edwardus integras reliquerat, miserabiliter amiserat. Unde placuit prelatis et proceribus regni filium suum in regni gubernaculo substituere loco sui si ipse suum preberet assensum.

Qui, licet rundebat quod tali consilio quale ei magnates ordinaverant utebatur, tamen factorum suorum penitens hiis que nuncii ipsi postulaverant suum assensum exhibebat et homagia magnatum sibi prius facta et tunc ei reexhabita adnullabantur. Subsequenter dominus Wyntoniensis Episcopus cupiens alloqui populum sic exorsus est. Capud meum doleo, IIII° Regum capitulo IIII°, et protractando per caput ipsum Regem qui est caput regni intelligens pro malo illius capitis gubernaculo se dolere affirmabat et infirmitatem capitis huius in sui dolore retorquebat, iuxta illud poeticum cui capud infirmum cetera membra dolent et alia multa indecencia et mala ecclesie dei et regno illata aperte repetens, filium suum primogenitum unanimi procerum assensu in regni gubernaculo fore substituendum concludebat, si populus huic prelatorum et procerum ordinacioni conniveret. Quo facto, dominus T. de Wak' extensis brachiis et vibratis manibus a populo quesivit si huic ordinacioni consentiret et idem voce clamosa pariter acclamabat. Tandem dominus archiepiscopus Cantuariensis sic incepit alloquendo populum. Vox populi vox dei hec verba in gallico exponendo coram omni populo inquit. Dilectissimi bene nostis quod variis oppressionibus iam per Regem et suos malos consiliarios tempore diuturno afflicti estis. Et idcirco ad deum pro remedio habendo sedulo acclamastis. Unde instanti tempore vox vestra exaudita est ut patet, quia ex omnium magnatum.

f. 126r.

unanimi consensu dominus Rex Edwardus a gubernaculo regni privatus est et filius ipsius in loco eius subrogatus, si unanimiter consentitis. Ita tamen quod sano consilio sapientium virorum regni sui adherat, exposita quoque regis insufficiencia ut prius et gravaminibus ecclesie dei et regni per ipsum illatis. Quod audiens populus universus unanimi consensu rursus manus ut prius extendentes clamabat Fiat, fiat, fiat, Amen.

Homagia Regi Edwardo secundo reexhibita.

Ieo William Trussel procuratour des prelatez countes et barons et des altres nometz en ma procuracie eant assez plein et suffisaunt power les homagez fealtes a vous Edward Roy dengletere cum a Roy qe fuit avaunt cez houres par les ditz persones en ma procuracie nomez en noun de eaux et chescun de eaux pur certeyns causez en la dit procuracie nomez Renge et Robail sus a vous Edward et delivere et face quitez les persones

avauntditz en la meliour manere qe ley et custume donne et face protesta-
cion en noum de eaux et chescun de eaux qil ne voilont deshore estre
en vostre fealte ne en vostre legeaunce ne clayment de vous come de Roy
rien tenir. Et ensy vous teygnent prive persone saunz nulle manere de
Roial dignite. Istud etiam fuit publice proclamatum londoniis. Eodem anno
mense Februarii, videlicet primo die mensis, Edwardus III, primogenitus
Regis Edwardi secundi post conquestum, cinctus est londoniis baltheo
militari a domino Johanne, fratre comitis de henaud'. Similiter et Johannes
de Bohon' comes herefordie et multi alii ibi arma militaria susceperunt
in vigilia Purificacionis beate Marie.

Notes

CHAPTER I PROBLEMS AND SOURCES

1. V. H. Galbraith, *Roger of Wendover and Matthew Paris*, David Murray Lecture, II (1944), p. 20.
2. William Stubbs, *The Constitutional History of England*, vol. II (1875), pp. 304–5.
3. *Ibid.*, p. 309.
4. J. R. S. Phillips, *Aymer de Valence, Earl of Pembroke* (1972); see index under *Indentures*; N. Denholm-Young, *Vita Edwardi Secundi* (1957), pp. 7–8.
5. *Ibid.*, p. 120.
6. K.R.Exch.Acc.Various, E. 101/17/20. The preamble to Howard's account explaining the purpose of his mission is a masterpiece of misrepresentation: 'en eide du Counte Mareschall a desturber les aliens enemis le dit nostre seignur le Roi *en salvacioun* de sa chere compaignye et soun cher fiz e le counte de Kent a le rivaille a Orewelle'.
7 R. E. Latham, ed., *Calendar of Memoranda Rolls (Exchequer) Michaelmas 1326 to Michaelmas 1327* (1968), no. 805, p. 105.
8. *List Mem.R.*, ed. Natalie Fryde, p. XXII and no. 692. This seems to be implied from the fact that he received the massive reward of £300 for holding North Wales 'at the time of the pursuit of Hugh Despenser'. See below, chapter 13.
9. Issue Roll, E. 403/219 under 8 October 1326. Their leader was Badinus de Fourne.
10. M. McKisack, *Medieval History in the Tudor Age* (1971), who prints part of a lively chronicle by William Warner (1558–1609), an acquaintance of Christopher Marlowe, notes on p. 174: 'A disproportionate amount of space seems to be given to Edward II.' His savage denunciation of the Despensers deserves quoting (*ibid.*):
'. . . that misled
the King in Out-rages more great than erst
in England bred,
Prolers, Blood-thirstie, Parasites, Make-shifts and
Bawdes did thrive,

Nor was an ancient English Peere unbanisht or alive:
Yea forraine and domesticke Swords, Plague, Famine
and Exile,
Did more than tythe, yea, tythe of men within this Ile.'

11. T. F. Tout, *The Place of Edward II in English History* (1936), p. 143.

12. See below, chapter 7.

13. His chapter on 'The Neglect of Administrative History' which opens his great series of *Chapters in the Administrative History of Medieval England*, 2nd ed., vol. 1 (Manchester 1937), especially p. 7.

14. K.R.Mem.R., E. 159/100, m. 48, *Br.d.Bar.*, Trinity.

15. *Ibid.*, the same letter, personally addressed to William Melton the treasurer starts with the highly unconventional complaint 'we can scarcely call to mind how many times we have sent letters and ordered . . .' See also below, chapter 7.

16. J. G. Edwards, ed., *Calendar of Ancient Correspondence concerning Wales* (1935), pp. 219–20.

17. Hugh Despenser in a letter to the earl of Kent from Porchester, 28 September 1324. 'Et vraiment sire il ny od autre defaute qe les neifs ne vous eussient venues en temps salve qe le vent lour fust contrere, le quiel nous ne poiens mie tournir a nostre volente' in Pierre Chaplais, *The War of Saint Sardos (1323–1325)*, Camden Soc., 3rd ser., volume 87 (1954), p. 64.

18. Society of Antiquaries Library, Ms. 122 (Chamber account book, 18–20 Edward II), p. 90.

19. Exchequer Miscellanea, E. 163/4/11.

20. Pierre Chaplais, ed., *English Royal Documents, King John–Henry VI (1199–1461)*, (1971), p. 34; Sir F. Palgrave, *The Antient Kalendars and Inventories of the Treasury of His Majesty's Exchequer*, III (1836), p. 104.

21. The exchequer kept such a book for its dealings with Antonio Pessagno and there is a reference to it: E. 159/87, m. 87, *Recorda* (Hilary). For a reference in 1337 to a similar record see *B.I.H.R.*, 22 (1949), p. 135, n. 1.

22. David Douglas, *English Scholars 1660–1730*, revised ed. (1951), p. 268. Some of the records of the medieval keepers of the privy seal were destroyed in a fire under James I.

23. Phillips, *Aymer of Valence* and J. R. Maddicott, *Thomas of Lancaster* (1970) provide the biographies of these two magnates.

24. *Vita*, p. 109.

25. *Henrici Knighton Leycestrensis Chronicon*, ed. J. R. Lumby, vol. 1, *R.S.* (1889).

26. *Vita*, p. 109.

27. *Murimuth*, p. 41., ed. E. M. Thompson, *R.S.*, 93 (1889).

28. See in the bibliography under *French Chronicle of London, Annales Londonienses* and *Annales Paulini*. The best northern chronicles are the *Scalacronica of Thomas Gray of Heton*, the *Annals of Bridlington* and the *Annals of Lanercost*. Further discussion of the sources of this period can

238 OF EDWARD II

be found in the introduction to the *Chronicles of Edward I and Edward II*, ed. W. Stubbs *R.S.* (1883) and T. F. Tout, *Edward II*, pp. 4ff.

29. Trinity College Library, Cambridge, Ms., R. 5. 41.
30. Bodleian Library, Laud Ms. (misc.), 529.
31. See below, chapter 7.

CHAPTER 2 INTRODUCTION: THE KING AND THE MAGNATES BEFORE 1318

1. *Vita*, p. 2. (The tournament took place on 2 December 1307). For the nicknames see T. F. Tout, *The Place of Edward II in English History*, p. 12, n. 2.
2. *Vita*, p. 15.
3. *Scalacronica*, p. 75.
4. Society of Antiquaries Library, Ms. 122, p. 92.
5. Hilda Johnstone, *Edward of Carnarvon 1284–1307*, pp. 122–5, provides most of the known information about the king's youth.
6. An excellent account of the last years of the reign is in Michael Prestwich, *War, Politics and Finance under Edward I* (1972), chapter XII, pp. 262–90.
7. *Vita*, p. 7.
8. It is printed by J. R. S. Phillips, *Aymer de Valence, Earl of Pembroke*, IV, pp. 316–17 and there is considerable dispute amongst the three most recent writers on the first part of the reign as to how far it presages the later troubles between Edward and his magnates. Maddicott, in his biography of Lancaster, *Thomas of Lancaster* (1970), says that in this document 'the magnates are already invoking their own fealty to the King in order to protect him from the consequences of his folly, and even now their watchfulness extends to the rights of the Crown as well as the King's own honour. The letters patent, though couched in most general terms, are surely a covert attack on Gaveston and his wasting of the kingdom.' Michael Prestwich regards the latter as 'the first indication of trouble' (*War, Politics and Finance*, p. 273) and says that 'this is taken by Maddicott as being directed solely against Gaveston, but it seems a curiously oblique way of attacking the royal favourite. Taken in conjunction with the additional clause inserted in the oath sworn by the king at his coronation, in which he promised to observe "the just laws and customs that the community of the realm shall have chosen", it looks as if political arguments were ranging far beyond the immediate issue of the lavish grants that had been made to Gaveston and his objectionable behaviour.' Out on a limb stands Phillips, *Aymer of Valence*, who writes that 'it is implausible that the parties to the agreement would have chosen Boulogne to draw up such a document when the king was present and would know of their actions if they had been his opponents'. In fact Boulogne was an occasion when they happened to be all present together and there seems no

warrant for Dr Phillips' supposition that secrecy could not be preserved.

9. Ernst H. Kantorowicz, 'Inalienability; a note on canonical practice and the English Coronation Oath in the thirteenth century', *Speculum*, 29 (July 1954), p. 489.

10. I am in agreement with Maddicott on the subject of the Coronation Oath (*Thomas of Lancaster*, p. 82). He says, 'There is no ambiguity here about the meaning of *eslira*. The fourth clause of the coronation oath had clearly been intended, not primarily to safeguard Edward I's concession to the baronage but to ensure that in any future struggle the King would be held to observe the magnates' decision. This was the first occasion (when the magnates demanded the exile of Gaveston in the Parliament which met on 28 April 1308 and reminded the King that he was obliged to do what the people had resolved) on which the oath was used against the King and seen thus it appears to be quite as revolutionary as some have judged it.' He follows Bertie Wilkinson in 'The Coronation Oath of Edward II' in *Essays in Honour of James Tait* (1933), p. 407: 'the new form of oath in 1308...was the product not of constitutional growth in the past but of present discontent. The last clause was, it seems probable, a remarkable promise by Edward II to his rebellious barons.' For the view that the oath shows that legislation was being made in response to petition see H. G. Richardson, 'The English Coronation Oath', both in *Speculum*, 24 (October, 1949), pp. 630–44 and *T.R.H.S.*, 4th ser., 23 (1941), pp. 129–55.

11. For thorough treatment of the term 'communitas regni' in the struggles between Henry III and his baronial opponents see R. F. Treharne, *The Baronial Plan of Reform* (1932).

12. Sir J. H. Ramsay, *The Genesis of Lancaster*, vol. 1 (1307–68), (1913), pp. 10–11. This work remains in some ways the most digestible narrative of the reign though his figures for revenue are incomplete and misleading.

13. Maddicott, *Thomas of Lancaster*, pp. 77ff.

14. The coronation order is given in Ramsay, *The Genesis of Lancaster*, pp. 10–11.

15. I am indebted for this fascinating piece of information to Mr P. C. Doherty, who is preparing an Oxford doctoral dissertation on Queen Isabella which should greatly enlarge our understanding of the reign and, particularly, of the years of her personal rule, 1327–30.

16. See note 10, above.

17. *Foedera*, vol. II, part I, p. 50.

18. *Vita*, p. 8.

19. Maddicott, *Thomas of Lancaster*, pp. 92–3.

20. *Leyc.Chron.*; *Brut*, ed. F. W. D. Brie, i, Early English Text Society (1906); J. Taylor, 'The French "Brut" and the Reign of Edward II', *E.H.R.*, 72 (1957), pp. 423–35.

21. *Vita*, p. 8.

22. *Polychronicon Ranulphi Higden,* ed. J. R. Lumby, *R.S.* (1882), p. 315.

23. J. R. Maddicott, 'Thomas of Lancaster and Sir Robert Holland: a study in noble patronage', *E.H.R.,* 86 (1971), pp. 449–72.

24. *Vita,* p. 10. 'The united barons held strongly to their plan, citing many instances, with many threats, and at length almost unanimously took their stand upon them, saying that unless the king granted their demands they would not have him for king, nor keep the fealty that they had sworn to him, especially since he had not kept the oath which he had taken at his coronation.'

25. Maddicott, *Thomas of Lancaster,* p. 319, n. 4.

26. Fryde, 'Pessagno' (1978) and above, chapter 7.

27. Phillips, *Aymer de Valence,* pp. 32ff.

28. Joan Evans, *English Art, 1307–1461* (1949), pp. 23, 177.

29. Well told in Ramsay, *The Genesis of Lancaster,* pp. 64, 68–71.

30. Ian Kershaw, 'The Great Famine and Agrarian Crisis in England 1315–1322', *Past and Present,* no. 59 (May 1973), pp. 3–50.

31. *Vita,* p. 64; G. H. Tupling, *South Lancashire in the Reign of Edward II,* Chetham Soc. (1949), pp. xliiff.; Maddicott, *Thomas of Lancaster,* pp. 174–6.

32. J. B. Smith, 'The Rebellion of Llywelyn Bren' in T. B. Pugh, ed., *Glamorgan County History* (1971), pp. 72ff.

33. E. A. Fuller, 'The Tallage of 6 Edward II and the Bristol Riots', *Transactions Bristol and Gloucester Archaeological Society,* 19 (1894–5), pp. 175ff.

34. Maddicott, *Thomas of Lancaster,* pp. 206–7.

35. J. R. S. Phillips, 'The "Middle Party" and the Negotiating of the Treaty of Leake, August 1318: A Reinterpretation', *B.I.H.R.,* 46 (1973), pp. 11–27.

CHAPTER 3   THE RISE OF THE DESPENSERS

1. Hilda Johnstone, *Edward of Carnarvon, 1284–1307* (1946), p. 102.

2. *Handbook of British Chronology,* 2nd ed., ed. Sir Michael Powicke and E. B. Fryde (1961), p. 71.

3. See appendix 1 above.

4. *Glam.Co.Hist.,* p. 168.

5. *Vita,* p. 44.

6. *Ibid.,* p. 4.

7. For a list of his embassies and offices under Edward I see W. Dugdale, *The Baronage of England,* 2 vols. (1675), I, p. 390; G. O. Sayles, *Select Cases in the Court of King's Bench. Edward II,* vol. IV, *Selden Soc.,* vol. 74 (1955), pp. 32 and 40.

8. *C.Chanc.Warr.,* p. 315.

9. *Vita,* p. 44.

10. *Ibid.,* p. 30.

11. *Baker*, pp. 6–7.
12. *C.I.P.M.*, IV, no. 351, p. 232; K. Fowler, *The King's Lieutenant. Henry of Grosmont, First Duke of Lancaster, 1310–61* (1969), p. 23.
13. For the cases following in this paragraph see appendix 1 above. Some of the transactions figure in the indictment of the Despensers in 1321 (see chapter 4).
14. For this paragraph see similarly appendix 1.
15. G. A. Holmes, *The Estates of the Higher Nobility in Fourteenth Century England* (1957), p. 36.
16. *E.g.* Exchequer of Receipt, Warrants for Issues. E. 404/482/11, no. 15, a debenture in favour of the sheriff of Northamptonshire for payments made by him 'super expensis hospicii domine Alianore le Despenser' while she was in Northampton castle in 1311. In 1309 she used her influence with the king to get justice for her servant, Joan (*C.Chanc. Warr.*, p. 283.). Wardrobe records provide additional and abundant evidence of the king's high regard for Eleanor. In 1311–12 he was even paying her expenses out of court (Bodleian Library, Tanner Ms. 197, m. 12 v.).
17. T. F. Tout, *The Place of Edward II in English History*, p. 15.
18. J. Maddicott, *Thomas of Lancaster* (1970), p. 285.
19. *C.Fine R., 1307–19* (9 January 1310), p. 54.
20. *Ann. Lond.*, p. 200. Maddicott, *Thomas of Lancaster*, p. 87, n. 2, treats it as a certain proof of younger Despenser's friendship with the Ordainers without considering the alternative explanation offered by me.
21. The original grant is *C.Cl.R., 1313–17* (9 October 1313), p. 20. On 18 July 1314, after the battle of Bannockburn, it was withdrawn because of Lancaster's complaint (*C.Fine R., 1307–19*, p. 203). He was granted the Huntingfield wardship and marriage, partly to defray his expenses after Bannockburn, on 12 June 1316 (*ibid.*, p. 278).
22. *Vita*, p. 62.
23. *Glam.Co.Hist.*, p. 61.
24. *C.Fine R., 1307–19*, p. 248 (23 May 1315); *C.Close R., 1313–17* (11 June 1315), p. 306.
25. Charter Roll, C. 53/103 (1316–17).
26. *Rot.Parl.*, I, pp. 352–3.
27. *C.Fine R., 1307–19*, p. 350.
28. See appendix 1.
29. *Ibid.*
30. *C.P.R., 1313–18*, p. 534. By the next April Thomas Blount, the custodian, had still not handed them over to Despenser.
31. L.T.R. Mem. r., E. 368/91, m. 127.
32. *Chronicon Landavensis*, B. L. Cotton Ms., Nero A. IV., f.53v.
33. *C.P.R., 1313–18* (4 March 1318), p. 531.
34. *Glam.Co.Hist.*, p. 169.
35. J. C. Conway-Davies, 'The Despenser War in Glamorgan', *T.R.H.S.*, 3rd ser., 9 (1915), p. 30.

36. See appendix 1.
37. Society of Antiquaries Library, Ms. 121, 'Liber cotidianus de anno XI'.
38. *Bridlington*, p. 55.
39. B.L., Harleian Ms. 6359, f.78.
40. *C.Ch.R., 1300–26*, p. 396.

CHAPTER 4   THE CIVIL WAR, 1321–2

1. *C.Anc.C.*, pp. 259–60. For other detailed narratives of this period see J. Maddicott, *Thomas of Lancaster* (1970); J. R. S. Phillips, *Aymer de Valence, Earl of Pembroke* and T. B. Pugh, *Glamorgan County History*, III, *The Middle Ages* (1971), chapter IV.
2. H. M. Cam, 'Pedigrees of Villeins and Freemen in the Thirteenth Century' in *Liberties and Communities in Medieval England* (1944), p. 130.
3. *List Mem.R.*, p. 45 (no. 373).
4. *Ibid.*, p. 44 (no. 365) for Turberville; *C.Anc.C.*, p. 184.
5. *Vita*, p. 58.
6. *Glam.Co.Hist.*, p. 86.
7. Maddicott, *Thomas of Lancaster*, p. 310. The information about Hereford's intentions is correct, but the writer and recipient of the letter are two of Hereford's sons and it was written in the reign of Edward III.
8. B. P. Evans, *The Family of Mortimer*, Ph.D. thesis, University of Wales (1934), deposited in the National Library of Wales at Aberystwyth, gives a good account of the careers of both Roger Mortimer of Wigmore and Roger Mortimer of Chirk.
9. *The Complete Peerage*, ed. G. H. White, II, 1910–59, pp. 128–9; Phillips, *Aymer de Valence*, pp. 263–4.
10. *Vita*, p. 97; Sir James Ramsay, *The Genesis of Lancaster*, I (1913), pp. 108ff.
11. Maddicott, *Thomas of Lancaster*, p. 249.
12. *Vita*, p. 109.
13. *Ibid.*, pp. 108–9.
14. For the coming of the civil war see the works of Maddicott, Phillips and Pugh cited above and J. Conway-Davies, 'The Despenser War in Glamorgan' in *T.R.H.S.*, 3rd ser., 9 (1915), pp. 20–64.
15. *C.Anc.C.*, pp. 180–1.
16. *Parl.Writs*, II, i, pp. 231–2.
17. See the review by R. R. Davies of J. Maddicott's *Thomas of Lancaster* in *Welsh History Review* 6 (1972), pp. 201–10.
18. Maddicott, *Thomas of Lancaster*, pp. 269ff.
19. W. Dugdale, *The Baronage of England*, I, 1675–6, 144–5.
20. *Annales Paulini*, p. 293; M. V. Clarke, *Medieval Representation and Consent* (1936), p. 242.
21. Maddicott, *Thomas of Lancaster*, p. 285.

22. See above, chapter 3.
23. J. S. Roskell, 'A consideration of certain aspects and problems of the English Modus Tenendi Parliamentum', *Bulletin of the John Rylands Library*, 50 (1968).
24. William A. Morris, 'The Date of the Modus Tenendi Parliamentum', *E.H.R.* 69 (1934), pp. 407–23.
25. Clarke, *Medieval Representation*. A recent hypothetical interpretation of the *Modus* is that it 'had a purely legal and procedural role throughout the later Middle Ages; that it was owned and used only by various branches of the legal profession and in sufficiently large numbers to establish a strong and definitive Ms. tradition. It is also alleged that this Ms. tradition is wholly incompatible with the hypothesis that the *Modus* was a political tract.' Nicholas Pronay and John Taylor, 'The Use of the "Modus Tenendi Parliamentum" in the Middle Ages', *B.I.H.R.*, 47 (1974), pp. 11–23.
26. The text of the English version printed in Clarke, *Medieval Representation*, p. 380.
27. See *C.Cl.R., 1318–23*, pp. 492–4 for the final version of the indictment.
28. For Latchley's case see also appendix 1.
29. *Vita*, p. 113; Phillips, *Aymer de Valence*, p. 210.
30. *Handbook of British Chronology*, 2nd ed., ed. Sir Maurice Powicke and E. B. Fryde, p. 101. *C.P.R., 1321–4*, p. 14 states that he was discharged at his own request.
31. See below, chapter 7.
32. *Vita*, p. 116.
33. Trinity College Library, Cambridge, Ms. R.5.41, pp. 114ff. provides the most detailed narrative.
34. *Scalacronica*, p. 67 and *Murimuth*, p. 54.
35. Issue Roll, E. 403/196 wardrobe charge (Northburgh), 29 October 1321.
36. S.C. 6/1145/8. The issues of Leeds were to be paid into the Chamber by a royal order of 4 November (J. Conway-Davies, 'The first Journal of Edward II's Chamber', *E.H.R.*, 30 (1915) p. 665).
37. *Murimuth*, p. 34.
38. Clarke, *Medieval Representation*, p. 168.
39. *Murimuth*, p. 35.
40. *C.Cl.R., 1318–23*, p. 510.
41. *Register of Walter Stapeldon, bishop of Exeter*, ed. F. C. Hingeston Randolph, pp. 442ff.
42. *Parl.Writs*, II, i, p. 255.
43. For more detailed accounts of the campaign see Maddicott, *Thomas of Lancaster*, pp. 303–11; Phillips, *Aymer de Valence*, pp. 214–39. I have used more fully Bodleian Library, Laud Ms. (misc.), 529, f. 106v; Trinity College Ms. Library, Cambridge, R.5.41, p. 116v.
44. Ministers accounts, S.C. 6/1145/15. The royal custodians started accounting on 28 December 1321.

45. Custodians account for John Mowbray's Isle of Axholm from 10 January 1322, S.C. 6/1145/12; for John Charlton's land of Powys from 19 January, S.C. 6/1146/4; for Hereford's lands on 23 January, S.C. 6/1145/7 and for Wigmore of Roger Mortimer from the same date, Exch.Accts.Various, E. 101/15/39.

46. See below, chapter 7.

47. E. 403/202, wardrobe charge (13 July 1322): payment by the Bardi 'Hugoni de Bungeye armaturario Regis ad armaturas emendas et providendas Londoniis pro Griffith Thloit valletto Regis'.

48. J. G. Edwards, 'Sir Gruffydd Llwyd', *E.H.R.*, 30 (1915), p. 593; *C.P.R.*, *1321–4*, p. 35 (15 November 1321) and p. 122.

49. See below, chapter 7.

50. R. R. Davies, 'The Bohun and Lancaster Lordships in Wales in the 14th and 15th Centuries', Oxford University, Ph.D. thesis (1965). See also J. B. Smith, 'Edward II and the allegiance of Wales', *Welsh Hist.Rev.*, 13 (1976).

51. *List Mem.R.*, p. 56, no. 467. For his career see Ralph A. Griffiths, *The Principality of Wales in the Later Middle Ages* (1972), pp. 99–102.

52. *C.A.P.*, p. 30.

53. *Parl.Writs*, II, ii, pp. 545–54.

54. *C.Cl.R.*, *1318–23*, p. 523.

55. E. A. R. Brown, 'Gascon Subsidies and the Finances of the English Dominions, 1315–1324', *Nebraska Studies in Medieval and Renaissance History*, 8 (1971), p. 132.

56. *C.Fine.R.*, *1319–27*, p. 128.

57. For example on 12 February Edward ordered the selling of wood on Contrariants' lands and the money was to be sent to him. (*C.Cl.R.*, *1318–23*, p. 512). In February he was also using victuals from J. Giffard's lands for the household, E. 404/484/file 30. See also chapter 7.

58. E. 101/15/37. When he reached the king, Edward put him in charge of levying the Yorkshire foot, *C.P.R.*, *1321–4*, p. 76.

59. The sources differ as to how many men he took with him but his defection was probably crucial; cf. J. R. Maddicott, 'Thomas of Lancaster and Sir Robert Holland: a study in noble patronage', *E.H.R.*, 86 (1971), pp. 449–72.

60. *Calendar of Papal Registers* (Great Britain and Ireland), *Letters*, II (1305–42), pp. 447–8.

61. Maddicott, *Thomas of Lancaster*, p. 311. Edward subsequently showed great confidence in Latimer and in October 1322 made him the custodian of the city of York (E. 403/200, wardrobe charge, Waltham, 22 October 1322 and 29 January 1323).

CHAPTER 5   THE AFTERMATH OF CIVIL WAR: IMPRISONMENTS AND
EXECUTIONS

1. *Vita*, pp. 124–5.
2. *Bridlington*, p. 77.
3. *C.Cl.R., 1318–23*, p. 522.
4. *Brut*, p. 222; *Lanercost*, p. 244.
5. *Vita*, p. 126.
6. *Rot.Parl.*, ii, p. 244.
7. *Bridlington*, p. 75.
8. M. Keen, 'Treason Trials under the Law of Arms', *T.R.H.S.*, 5th ser., 12 (1962), p. 102.
9. *Lanercost*, p. 244. See J. Maddicott, *Thomas of Lancaster* (1970), p. 312.
10. *Eulogium Historiarum*, ed. F. Scott Haydon, III, *R.S.* (1863), p. 196.
11. *Bridlington*, p. 77.
12. *Le Livere de Reis de Brittanie*, ed. J. Glover, *R.S.* (1865), p. 343; *C.P.R.*, (*1327–30*), p. 32.
13. *Vita*, p. 117.
14. *Leyc.Chron.*, pp. 426–7.
15. Chronicles give an assorted list of those executed. A complete list of the main combatants appears in *The Complete Peerage*, ed. G. E. Cokayne vol. II, App. C (1910–59), pp. 597–600. There is also a list in the indictment of the Despensers in 1326 (Parliamentary and Council Proceedings, C. 49/roll 11). Cf. also the commissions for the trials, *C.P.R., 1321–4* (March–April 1322), pp. 148–9.
16. Trinity College, Cambridge, Ms. R. 5.41, f. 118. G. O. Sayles, 'The formal judgements on the traitors of 1322', *Speculum*, 16 (1941), p. 60, n. 3 suggests that he was beheaded for flight.
17. R. Butler, 'The last of the Brimpsfield Giffards and the rising of 1321–22', *Transactions of the Bristol and Gloucestershire Archaeological Society*, 76 (1957), pp. 94–5.
18 *Murimuth*, p. 43.
19. See below, chapter 11.
20. *Leyc.Chron.*, p. 427.
21. *Vita*, p. 125.
22. *Eulogium Historiarum*, p. 198.
23. Coram Rege roll., K.B. 27/254, Rex, m. 37.
24. Chancery Warrants, C. 81/340, nos. 7277ff. for instructions to move these prisoners. William Hedersete was to be guarded under pain of 1550 marks.
25. E. 403/207, m. 11.
26. Ancient Correspondence, S.C. 1/37/45.
27. E. 101/380/5; *C.P.R., 1321–4*, p. 405; E. 403/207, m. 12.
28. E. 101/372/16. The three Mortimer boys were moved into the Tower of London on 1 Oct. 1326 (E. 403/219 under 6 Oct. 1326).

29. E. 403/207, mm. 11 and 12.
30. See below, chapter 11.
31. *C.P.R., 1321–4*, p. 84.
32. Conway-Davies, *Baronial Opposition*, pp. 582–3.
33. G. L. Haskins, 'A Chronicle of the Civil Wars of Edward II', *Speculum*, 14 (1939), p. 79.
34. Bodleian Library, Ms. North C. 26, no. 4.
35. E. B. Fryde, 'Parliament and the French War, 1336–40', reprinted in E. B. Fryde and E. Miller, *Historical Studies of the English Parliament*, I (1970), pp. 252–3.
36. *Statutes of the Realm*, I, p. 189. The text was also enrolled on the roll of the King's Bench, K.B. 27/257, m. 24v.
37. A good summary in M. McKisack, *The Fourteenth Century 1307–99* (1959), pp. 72ff. One of the last contributions, which despite its confident title does not represent the last word on the subject, is by D. Clementi, 'That the Statute of York of 1322 is no longer ambiguous', *Album Helen Cam*, II (1961), pp. 95–100.
38. Fryde and Miller, *Historical Studies*, pp. 10–11.
39. J. G. Edwards, 'The personnel of the Commons under Edward I and Edward II', in *Essays in Medieval History presented to Thomas Frederick Tout* (1925), pp. 197–214 and reprinted in Fryde and Miller, *Historical Studies*, pp. 150–67.
40. Conway-Davies, *Baronial Opposition*, p. 583: 'pur plus tost deliverer le people qe veignent au parlement'.
41. *The War of Saint Sardos (1323–25)*, ed. P. Chaplais, *Camden Soc.*, 3rd ser., 87 (1954), p. 134.
42. *Vita*, p. 136.

CHAPTER 6   THE AFTERMATH OF CIVIL WAR: CONFISCATIONS AND THE TERRITORIAL SETTLEMENT

1. A study of Herefordshire and Gloucestershire in 1321–6 is to be found in S. L. Waugh, 'The confiscated lands of the Contrariants in Gloucestershire and Herefordshire in 1322: an economic and social study' University of London, Ph.D. Thesis (1975).
2. *C.P.R., 1321–4* (18 May 1322), p. 151.
3. *Ibid.*, pp. 158–60.
4. K.B. 27/262, Rex, mm. 13–14 and *passim*.
5. For Cornwall see *C.P.R., 1321–4*, p. 9. For Lancashire see G. H. Tupling, *South Lancashire in the Reign of Edward II, Chetham Soc.* 3rd ser., I (1949).
6. The most comprehensive list is in P.R.O. Lists and Indexes, V, *Ministers Accounts*, pt. I, pp. 441–62.
7. *C.Fine R., 1319–27*, pp. 152–3.
8. *Ibid.* Chancery Miscellanea, C.47/34/9, is an original file of such submissions.

9. *C.Fine R., 1319–27* (1 November 1322), p. 168.
10. *Ibid.*, pp. 155, 157.
11. *Ibid.*, pp. 155, 170.
12. Waugh, 'The confiscated lands . . .' pp. 37, 104 and n. 1.
13. *C.P.R., 1321–4*, p. 46; *C.Cl.R., 1318–23*, p. 519.
14. *C.P.R., 1321–4*, p. 103.
15. C. H. Knowles, *The Disinherited, 1265–1280: a political and social study of the supporters of Simon de Montfort and the resettlement after the Barons' War*, Ph.D. dissertation, Wales, part II, pp. 40–41.
16. *C.P.R., 1321–4*, p. 76 (example of King's Lynn).
17. Ancient Petitions, S.C. 8/6/289.
18. *C.A.P.*, p. 282 and *C.I.M.*, II, no. 992; *C.A.P.*, p. 273.
19. S.C. 8/108/nos. 5377–78.
20. K.B. 27/254, Rex m. 60.
21. *C.P.R., 1321–4*, p. 73.
22. *C.Fine R., 1319–27*, p. 100.
23. *Ibid.*, pp. 155, 245; Chancery Miscellanea, C.47/34/9, no. 1; Waugh, 'The confiscated lands . . .', p. 37.
24. *C.Fine R., 1319–27*, p. 145.
25. *C.P.R., 1321–4*, p. 135.
26. E. 403/202.
27. His wife had petitioned at an unspecified date for his release (S.C. 8/59/2731).
28. See below, chapter 13.
29. *C.Fine R., 1319–27*, p. 233.
30. Waugh, 'The confiscated lands . . .', pp. 18–20.
31. Knowles, *The Disinherited*, especially part III.
32. *C.P.R., 1321–4*, p. 275.
33. S.C. 8/7/301.
34. S.C. 8/7/304.
35. The Bractonian text cited in C. D. Ross, 'Forfeiture for treason in the reign of Richard II', *E.H.R.*, 71 (1956), p. 560.
36. C.P. 40/269, m. 29v. and C.P. 40/270, m. 40v.
37. E. 142/31, m. 1. There was, however, considerable confusion and many delays occurred in returning jointures of women and lands belonging to them by virtue of previous marriages. See *C.Cl.R., 1323–7*, pp. 65, 204.
38. *C.P.R., 1321–4*, p. 196.
39. *Ibid.*, pp. 157–8.
40. *Ibid.*, p. 307.
41. See below, chapter 7.
42. *C.P.R., 1321–4*, p. 161
43. *Ibid.*, pp. 108, 144–5, 178
44. *Ibid.*, p. 161.
45. Waugh, 'The confiscated lands . . .', pp. 94–5, 99.
46. See below, chapter 7.

I

47. E. 159/96, mm. 6, 7, 9 (*commissiones*); *ibid.*, mm. 154–6 (*brevia pro rege*).

48. See below, chapter 7.

49. *The Red Book of the Exchequer*, ed. H. Hall, III, *R.S.* (1896), pp. 904–5.

50. L.T.R. Miscellaneous Enrolled Accounts, E. 358/15, m. 45 'sicut-continetur in rotulis memorandorum de terris forisfactis'.

51. E. 159/101, m. 49 (royal mandate of 13 January 1326).

52. K.R.Exchequer Extents, E. 142/31 (compiled after Michaelmas 1325). There is also in D.L. 41/10/15 a record of some of the lands of Thomas, earl of Lancaster and Robert Holland leased for three years from Michaelmas 1323 onwards.

53. Ancient Petitions, S.C. 8/108/5357.

54. E. 142/31.

55. *E.g., ibid.*, m. 1 r., Fulmodeston (Norfolk), extended in 1322 at £34 4¾d., extended by Walter Norwich at £69 9s. 7½d., in the hands of John Frere, 'approuvour' in 1325–6.

56. Waugh, 'The confiscated lands . . .', pp. 66–7, 98.

57. *Ibid.*, p. 66.

58. *Ibid.*, p. 98.

59. *E.g.* Fulmodeston (Norfolk), E. 142/31 m. 1 r. (noted above); Kim-bolton (Hunts.), former property of the earl of Hereford, valued in the second extent at £143 6s. 4¼d. (*ibid.*, m. 1 r.); Disning (Suffolk), former property of Hugh Audley, the younger, valued at £65 3s. 6¼d. (*ibid.*, m. 1 r.).

60. Waugh, 'The confiscated lands . . .', p. 106.

61. See below, chapter 8.

62. Properties in Wiltshire, valued at £54 6s. 0½d. and leased for £60 a year (E. 142/31, m. 2. r.).

63. Enfield (Middlesex), a former property of the earl of Hereford, valued at £37 15s. 8¼d. (*ibid.*, m. 5 v.).

64. In 1326 he held £1000 of the elder Hugh Despenser (E. 142/33, m. 5). He leased properties in Wiltshire valued at £43 8s. 10½d. for annual rents amounting to £47.

65. For his career see below, chapter 8. He leased properties in Suffolk and Essex at an annual rent of £10.

66. For his activities as Despenser's trusted clerk see *Ec.H.R.*, pp. 348, 360. For his service with Prince Edward see N. Denholm-Young, *Collected Papers on Medieval Subjects* (1946), p. 164. He leased Great Riburgh (Norfolk), valued by Walter Norwich at £73 19s. 8½d., for an annual rent of £76.

67. E. 142/31, m. 1 r.

68. *Ibid.*, m. 2 v.

69. Waugh, 'The confiscated lands . . .', p. 29.

70. S.C. 8/7/309.

71. S.C. 8/7/324.

72. S.C. 8/108/5358.
73. E. 142/31, m. 2. r. and 2 v.

CHAPTER 7   ROYAL FINANCE, 1321–6

1. Fryde, 'Pessagno' (1978).
2. What follows is a summary of conclusions which will be documented in greater detail later on in this chapter.
3. 'Issint qe nous ne soioms escriez par pays pur defaute de paiement.' Conway-Davies, *The Baronial Opposition to Edward II, its character and policy: A Study in Administrative History* (1918), p. 556.
4. *Ibid.*, p. 557.
5. This is confirmed by the attitude of exchequer officials in a similar crisis in the spring of 1339. Cf. D. Hughes. *A Study of Social and Constitutional Tendencies in the Early Years of Edward III* (1915), pp. 240–41.
6. Conway-Davies, *Baronial Opposition*, pp. 557–9.
7. Hughes, *A Study of Social and Constitutional Tendencies*, p. 241.
8. Letters of Privy Seal of 21 April 1323 (E. 159/96, m. 25 v.); of 21 September 1323 (E. 159/97, m. 17); of 10 August 1325 (E. 159/100, m. 48).
9. E. 401/325: 'dominus rex exoneravit ab officio Thesaurarii'.
10. E. 403/202, wardrobe charges of Northburgh (13 July 1323) and Waltham.
11. E. 101/27/24.
12. E. 403/196, wardrobe (charge of Northburgh).
13. *Ibid.*
14. *Book of Prests of the King's Wardrobe for 1294–5 Presented to John Gorony Edwards*, ed. E. B. Fryde (1962), p. 226.
15. E. 404/484, nos. 10 and 12.
16. E. 101/127/24 and E. 404/484, no. 11.
17. E. 159/95, m. 32; E. 403/202, wardrobe, Northburgh (under 13 July 1323).
18. E. 372/171, m. 43 v.: (account of James de Ispannia for chamber properties); for other deliveries of smaller amounts see E. 101/15/38 and E. 404/484, file 30.
19. Northburgh on 14 March paid 200 marks to William Roos of Helmsley who had joined the king's army at Burton on Trent on 1 March (E. 101/15/37).
20. Receipt roll, Easter term 1322, E. 401/239.
21. A higher annual average of £2000 is suggested by J. Conway-Davies, 'The first journal of Edward II's Chamber', *E.H.R.*, 30 (1915), p. 668. My lower figure is based on the same sources but excludes extraordinary revenues of 'political' origin.
22. E. 401/239 (under 4 September 1322) and B.L., Stowe Ms. 553, f. 18 v. (wardrobe account book of Roger Waltham).
23. For example it was reported by king's judges in 1323 that treasure and

goods worth £3000 had been carried away from the castle at Skipton and other estates of Roger Clifford (Just.Itin.I/425/, m. 26). For other examples see above, chapters 5 and 6.

24. W. E. Lunt, *Financial Relations of the Papacy with England to 1327* (1939), p. 410 and n. 5.

25. Conway-Davies, *Baronial Opposition*, pp. 582–3.

26. E. 403/198 under 26 July and 12 September 1322, wardrobe (charge of Waltham); E. 401/239 under 23 August 1322.

27. E. 159/95, mm. IV. 32; E. 401/239 under 16 August 1322.

28. E. 403/198, wardrobe (Waltham) under 12 September 1322.

29. B.L., Stowe Ms. 553, f. 18 v.

30. *Ibid.*, f. 27.

31. C. 47/35/17 and C. 49/33/13, cf., G. L. Harriss, *King, Parliament and Public Finance in Medieval England to 1369* (1975), p. 221.

32. J. F. Willard, 'The taxes upon movables of the reign of Edward I', in *E.H.R.*, 28 (1913), p. 521 and *E.H.R.*, 29 (1914), pp. 318–21; *Parliamentary Taxes on Personal Property, 1290 to 1334* (1934), pp. 344–5.

33. E. 159/97, m. 17: 'mettez votre peine qe nous soioms riches'.

34. E. 403/202.

35. Willard, *Parliamentary Taxes* (1934), p. 344.

36. Lunt, *Financial Relations of the Papacy*, p. 411.

37. E. 403/207, m. 13.

38. The main components of this total are: £38 175 of cash handled by Nicholas Huggate, the treasurer in Gascony (B.L., additional Ms. 7967, account from 1 March 1324 to 31 May 1326); £2380 received by William Kirkby, receiver of the fleet of John Sturmy going to Gascony in 1325 (E. 101/16/40); £3471 received by William Otterhampton 1 1325 over and above his deliveries to Huggate (E. 101/17/3); deliveries by Robert Wodehouse, keeper of the wardrobe, of £3500 to the men of Bayonne and of 200 marks to Ralph Basset, seneschal of Gascony (E. 159/102, m. 34); £2000 received in July 1324 by John Travers, constable of Bordeaux from Florentine bankers acting on royal orders (E. 403/207, E. 101/164/18, E. 101/601/7); 1000 marks paid before March 1324 to Arnold Guillaume, lord of Lescun (E. 403/204); £600 on 9 February 1325 to men of Bordeaux for repairing the city walls (E. 403/210, m. 9); at least £540 to Robert Pipishull, for supplying military equipment (E. 403/210, m. 8 and E. 101/17/6).

39. The chief additional item consists of the difference between the total sum charged to Huggate amounting to £49 902 (B.L., additional Ms. 7967, f. 6r.) and the amount certainly received by him in cash £38 175 (cf. additional Ms. 7967). The war necessitated also a multitude of small payments.

40. E. 101/332/20. The silver coins alone amounted to £65 535 15s. 1d.: 'En deniers countees demurrantz en les tresories avantdites au iour

avantdit en la garde des Tresoriers et Chaumberleins, LXV M DXXXV li xvs. 1d.'

41. Lunt, *Financial Relations of the Papacy*, pp. 411–12.

42. C. G. Crump and C. Johnson, 'Tables of bullion coined under Edward I, II and III', *Numismatic Chronicle*, 4th ser., 13 (1913), pp. 232–3.

43. *Ibid.*, pp. 214–15 and Sir John Craig, *The Mint. A History of the London Mint from A.D. 287 to 1948* (1953), pp. 410–12.

44. E. B. Fryde, 'The deposits of Hugh Despenser the Younger with Italian bankers', *Ec.H.R.*, 2nd ser., 3 (1951).

45. *E.g.* E. 403/202, wardrobe (charge of Waltham) under 25 May 1323. Allowance made to the Bardi for a payment of 200 marks to a royal envoy going abroad out of 'illa summa denariorum domini Regis quod iidem mercatores nuper habuerunt apud Londonias in deposito ex deliberacione Walteri Exoniensis Episcopi, Thesaurarii'.

46. E. 159/96, m. 19.

47. This is made clear by a concession requested by the Peruzzi in 1334, which was to confer upon them rights identical with those enjoyed by the Bardi under Edward II, of recovering in the exchequer 'dettes dues a meisme la compaignie ensemblement ove lur damages'. (Ancient Petitions, S.C. 8/no. 11.585.).

48. This total is based chiefly on the receipt and issue rolls for 1323–7 supplemented by the memoranda rolls for the same period.

49. Ancient Deeds, E. 43/607. Cf. also E. 401/258 under 4 Dec. 1325 (purchase by the Peruzzi of wool of the bishopric of Winchester for £240) and E. 159/96, m. 47v. (purchase by brothers Richard and William de la Pole for £227 of wool and lead from Contrariant estates in Derbyshire).

50. E. 403/207, E. 101/164/18, E. 101/601/7.

51. E. 403/220 under 10 January 1327; E. 403/225 under 10 and 12 February 1327. For the financing of Isabella's visit to France see also F. D. Blackley, 'Isabella and the Bishop of Exeter', in *Essays in Medieval History presented to Bertie Wilkinson* (1969), p. 228 and n. 46.

52. E. 101/332/20; E. 403/213, m. 12.

53. E. 101/332/21.

54. T. F. Tout, *Chapters in the Administrative History of Medieval England* 2nd ed., vol. II (1937), p. 275, n. 1 and p. 278, n. 1.

55. *Ibid.*, p. 278.

56. Payments by Wodehouse for the Gascon war are listed in E. 403/207, m. 1. and E. 159/102, m. 34.

57. Tout, *Chapters*, vol. VI (1933), pp. 74–101. Wodehouse's account for 19 Edward II is tabulated on pp. 86–7.

58. Harriss, *King, Parliament and Public Finance*, pp. 146, 523–4. My figures are based on a fresh inspection of this document (Bodleian Library, Ms. North C. 26, no. 4) and differ slightly from the figures cited by Dr Harriss.

I*

59. E. 159/96, m. 26v.
60. J. L. Kirby, 'The Issues of the Lancastrian Exchequer and Lord Cromwell's Estimates of 1433', *B.I.H.R.*, 24 (1951), pp. 132–3.
61. The figure for the Welsh and Irish properties is missing.
62. J. R. Maddicott, *Thomas of Lancaster 1307–22* (1970), pp. 12–13, 22, 27.
63. *Scalacronica*, pp. 69–70.
64. *The Antient Kalendars and Inventories of His Majesty's Exchequer*, ed. Sir F. Palgrave, I (1836), pp. 1–155; *The Gascon Calendar of 1322*, ed. G. P. Cuttino, *Camden Soc.*, 3rd. ser., 70 (1949). See also V. H. Galbraith, 'The Tower as an Exchequer Record Office in the Reign of Edward II' in *Essays in Medieval History presented to Thomas Frederick Tout* (1925), pp. 231–47.
65. The texts are printed in *The Red Book of the Exchequer*, ed. H. Hall, *R.S.*, III (1896), pp. 848–929. A detailed but one-sided discussion of some of the reforms is in T. F. Tout, *The Place of Edward II in English History*, 2nd ed. (1936), pp. 158–83 and *Chapters*, II, pp. 259–67. For the exchequer memoranda rolls see *List Mem.R.*, introduction and the sources there quoted, p. XIV, n. 5. Particularly valuable is J. F. Willard, 'The Memoranda Rolls and the Remembrancers' in *Essays in Medieval History presented to T. F. Tout* (1925), pp. 215–29.
66. The earliest issue roll of the new type is E. 403/218 (Easter term, 1326).
67. E. 159/102, m. 65v. The ordinance is printed in *The Red Book of the Exchequer*, pp. 930–69 and is mentioned in Tout, *Edward II*, pp. 267–8.
68. E. 159/97, m. 42 v. (19 February 1324): 'Et qe vous sachez qe nous avoms ceste busoigne a cuer nous vous escrivoms souz nostre secre seal.'
69. *The Red Book of the Exchequer*, pp. 924–7.
70. *Ibid.*, pp. 882–5, 896–9, 964–7.
71. A mandate of privy seal of 7 March 1326 ordered that the auditors of foreign accounts should reside in a separate building at Westminster and that they should therefore be available to audit accounts 'auxibien apres manger come devant'. Cited in D. M. Broome, 'Auditors of the foreign accounts of the exchequer', *E.H.R.*, 38 (1923), p. 69.
72. E. 159/97, m. 25v. (mandate of 23 November 1323); 16 members of the exchequer staff remained at the exchequer during the vacation in the summer and autumn of 1324 'arrayando diversa officia et faciendo extractas de debitis Regis' (E. 403/207, m. 12).
73. *The Red Book of the Exchequer*, pp. 850–51.
74. *Ibid.*, pp. 894–5.
75. E. 159/95, m. 35 v. and C. 47/35/21 (letter of privy seal of 25 July 1322): 'Nous vous feisoms saver qe nostre entencion est qe les issues de totes les terres et tenementz des forfaitz, auxibien de ceux qe soient lessees come dautres, veignent entierement a nostre Eschekier desore.'
76. D. M. Broome, 'Exchequer migrations to York in the fourteenth and fifteenth centuries', *Essays presented to Tout* (1925), p. 292 and n. 1.

77. Tout in *E.H.R.*, 31 (1916), p. 462, n. 41.
78. He was Lancaster's representative at the York parliament of 1318. Cf. Maddicott, *Thomas of Lancaster*, p. 229.
79. E. 403/200, m. 5 (3 November 1322).
80. Tout, *Edward II*, p. 144, n. 4.
81. Broome in *E.H.R.*, 38 (1923), pp. 63–70.
82. E. 159/96, m. 26 v.
83. E. 159/97, m. 17: 'et mettez votre peine qe nous soioms riches'.
84. *Ibid.*, m. 25 v. 30 v.
85. *Ibid.*, m. 30 v.
86. *Ibid.* The rebuke to Norwich was noted by V. H. Galbraith, 'The Tower as an Exchequer Record Office in the Reign of Edward II'', *Essays presented to Tout*, p. 241.
87. E. 159/97, m. 32.
88. *Ibid.*, m. 42 v.
89. T. F. Tout in *E.H.R.*, 31 (1916), pp. 461–3.
90. E. 159/100, m. 48.
91. Tout, *Edward II*, p. 298.
92. E. 401/261 (3 July 1326) and E. 401/262 (3 and 8 October) recording the receipt of £6083 13s. 4d. of Queen Isabella's revenues; E. 401/262 (3 October), recording the confiscation of £855 belonging to John, earl of Richmond; E. 372/171, m. 42 v. (enrolled chamber account recording receipts of money belonging to various royal enemies, including J. Roos and William Airmyn, bishop of Norwich).
93. E. 403/218 and Latham, *Calendar of Memoranda Rolls, 1326–27*, no. 813; E. 372/171 m. 42 v. (payment into the chamber of £100 by the Bardi).
94. E. B. Fryde in *Ec.H.R.* (1951), p. 362 (appendix, table II).
95. See below, chapter 13.
96. E. 403/218 under 17 September 1326 (£500), 22 September (£400) and 27 September (£100 for Sussex); E. 403/219 under 2 October (£100 for Essex).
97. E. 159/103, m. 115 (payment on 9 October).
98. E. 403/220. Henry Fitz Hugh was to return the prest made to him by the sheriff 'si contingeret prefatum Henricum ad dominum Regem non accessisse'.
99. E. 101/17/18.
100. E. 159/103, m. 24 and Latham, *Calendar of Memoranda Rolls, 1326–27*, no. 212.
101. E. 101/332/21.
102. See below, Epilogue, chapter 15.

CHAPTER 8　THE DESPENSERS' SPOILS OF POWER, 1321–6

1. *Vita*, pp. 135–6.
2. *C.Cl.R., 1323–7*, p. 168; *C.Anc.Deeds*, III, A, 4880; *C.Cl.R., 1323–7*,

p. 327 and *C.P.R., 1324–27*, p. 52; *Ec.H.R.* (1951), p. 348 and mm. 4–6.

3. The sources for the study of the estates of the Despensers are discussed in appendix 1. This lists much of the evidence on which this chapter is based, including especially the valuations of the estates and of the goods on them.

4. *Glam.Co.Hist.*, III, pp. 79, 170–71.

5. *Ec.H.R.* (1951), pp. 347–8.

6. For Lancaster's wealth see above, chapter 7.

7. A former property of Roger D'Amory, mortally wounded at Borough-bridge; granted to Winchester by the king on 4 April 1322 (*C.Ch.R., 1300–26*, p. 442).

8. For the details that follow see above, chapters 3 and 4, and the appendix, above; cf. also *Glam.Co.Hist.*, III, pp. 243–4.

9. While Braose could, and did, invoke the general customs of the March, the weakness of his personal position lay in the fact that Gower had been granted to his ancestor in John's reign by a royal charter and could be legitimately treated by the king as coming under the normal rules of English feudal tenure.

10. The chief source is B.L., Harleian Ms., 1240, fos. 86–7. A version of it is published by G. A. Holmes, 'A Protest against the Despensers, 1326', *Speculum*, 30 (1955), pp. 210–12. For this and other sources about the fate of Usk and Gower in 1322–3 see also appendix 1.

11. B.L., Harleian Ms., 1240, f. 87r: 'Et si a ceo ne voloie assentier ieo ne tiendrois iammes plein pee de terre de mon heritage de dower de mon ioint purchas vivant nostre dit seigneur le Roi.'

12. *Ibid.*, f. 86r. In her protest Elizabeth explained that she gave way for fear of harm to herself and her children imprisoned with her: 'Par queles manaces ieo Elizabeth esmue veiant . . . le peril de mon corps demesne et de mes enfantz ove moi emprisonez . . .' (*Ibid.*, f. 86v.).

13. 'Le roi moi remanda manaceant, qe si ieo ne revenisse et enseallase le dit escript, qil toute la terre qe ieo tint de lui me tondroit, ne iammes plein pie de lui ne tendroie.' (f. 87r.).

14. *Ibid.*, 'et le dit monsieur Hughe par sa seignurie et permy le roial poair a lui accrochez fist lassise passer contre moi et me fist celle terre perdre'.

15. *Ibid.*, ff. 86 v.–87 r.

16. For Braose's poor health in 1322 see Ancient Correspondence, S.C. 1/33/57. For Alina's petition about Wytham see Ancient Petitions, S.C. 8 157/7805. In 1322 Alina was in prison by 26 February (*C.P.R., 1321–4*, p. 75). For her subsequent detention see E. 142/56, no. 15, an inquisition about the Braose lordship of Bramber: 'Et dicunt quod post mortem Johannis de Moubray dicta Alina et Johannes filius eorundem Johannis et Aline incarcerabantur et in carcere detinebantur per procurationem dicti Hugonis comitis Wyntonie, quousque per graves minas ipsius comitis et metu mortis dicta Alina concessit dicto comiti reversionem dicte Baronie.'

17. *Ibid.* The rest of this paragraph is based on this inquisition and on various deeds calendared in E. 101/332/27.

18. *C.P.R., 1321–24* (22 March 1322), p. 84.

19. C. 81/1329, no. 42, a royal letter of secret seal of 7 June 1322, addressed to the earl of Richmond.

20. Miscellaneous Books, duchy of Lancaster, D.L. 42/11, f. 66v.: 'et disoient qele estoit cause de la morte son Baron et qele serroit arz et lavandite Aleyse pur doutee de sa morte se myst haute et bace en lordinance les avant ditz Hugh et Hugh et en la grace le dit Reis'.

21. *Rot.Parl.*, II, pp. 57–8. A record of lands that Alice was forced to surrender is summarised in *C.Cl.R., 1318–23*, pp. 574–6.

22. *Ibid.* (9 July 1322), p. 620. For the grants of Lancaster's other lands to the Despensers see *C.Ch.R., 1300–26*, pp. 449ff.; E. 101/332/2 (calendar of Despenser deeds); *C.Anc.Deeds*, III, A. 4725, A. 4842, A. 4857.

23. J. R. S. Phillips, *Aymer de Valence, Earl of Pembroke*, p. 227 (based chiefly on *C.Cl.R., 1318–23*, pp. 563–4).

24. Phillips, *Aymer de Valence*, p. 235.

25. *Ibid.*, pp. 235–6.

26. *Ibid.*, p. 235.

27. *Ibid.*, p. 237.

28. *Ibid.*, pp. 237–8.

29. *Ibid.*, p. 237.

30. *Ibid.*, p. 238.

31. For the sources see appendix 1.

32. *C.I.P.M.*, VII, no. 391, p. 292.

33. *C.I.M.*, II, 1307–49, no. 1024, p. 255.

34. *C.I.P.M.*, VII, no. 391.

35. *Ibid.*

36. *C.A.P.*, p. 274; *Rot.Parl.*, II, p. 22: 'Et par enprisonement et par duresces et par cohercions tant come ele demurra en dure prisone a Purfrith fust la dist Elisabet costreint a faire le reconissances des Fyns avant nomez . . .'; *C.P.R., 1348–50*, p. 122: 'against her will and by threats of death'.

37. See the sources cited in appendix 1.

38. *Ibid.*, especially *Sir Christopher Hatton's Book of Seals*, no. 175, p. 125.

39. See appendix 1, especially E. 159/104, m. 131.

40. Phillips, *Aymer de Valence*, p. 235 and n. 3; *C.A.P.*, p. 277; E. 142/33 and E. 142/60.

41. E. 159/104, m. 131.

42. *C.Cl.R., 1323–7*, p. 510; *C.Cl.R., 1327–30*, p. 65; *C.I.M.*, II, no. 965, p. 240 and no. 1000, pp. 248–9; E. 142/33, mm. 7, 9 and E. 142/62/3.

43. E. 101/624/24 (17 November 1323).

44. *C.I.M.*, nos. 965 and 1000.

45. *C.P.*, VI, p. 63; S.C. 8/33, no. 2437; E. 142/33, m. 5; E. 142/62/4.

46. *C.I.M.*, II, no. 933.

47. E. 142/33 and C. 145/103/13.

48. *C.Anc.Deeds*, III, A. 3980.

49. E. 101/332/27.

50. *Ibid.*, and *C.Anc.Deeds*, V, A. 13,532.

51. *C.Pap.R.*, II, *1305–42*, p. 477.

52. B.L., Harleian Ms. 1240, f. 87 r.: 'Ore de nouel le dit mons. Hugh le filz...pur envoegler le people et pur moi pluis deceure et a damagier me profre terres en recompensacion de Gower que natteynent poynt a la moite de la value de Gower par an.'

53. *C.Cl.R.*, *1323–7*, p. 532; *C.Anc.Deeds*, I, A. 938; E. 143/10/1.

54. *C.I.M.*, II, nos. 1181 and 1291.

55. B.L., Harleian Ms. 1240, f. 87 r.: 'a quele heure que grace soit pluis overte et ley de terre meulz meintenuz et commune a touz'.

56. The best discussion of the judgement on the younger Despenser and the best version of its text are in G. A. Holmes, 'Judgement on the Younger Despenser, 1326', *E.H.R.*, 70 (1955), pp. 261–7. There is also another text in Bodleian Library, Holkham Misc. Lat. Ms. 29, f. 276 r. John Taylor, *Medievalia et Humanistica*, XII (1958).

CHAPTER 9   THE DEFEAT IN SCOTLAND, 1322–3

1. G. L. Harriss, *King, Parliament and Public Finance in Medieval England to 1369* (1975), pp. 115–16.

2. Ian Kershaw, 'The Great Famine and Agrarian Crisis in England, 1315–22', *Past and Present*, no. 59 (1973), pp. 3–50.

3. Jean Scammell, 'Robert I and the North of England', *E.H.R.*, 73 (1958), pp. 385–404.

4. E. Miller, 'War in the North', *St. John's College, Cambridge, Lecture* (1960), p. 8.

5. For these examples see Scammell, 'Robert I . . .', and *Ancient Petitions relating to Northumberland*, ed. C. M. Fraser, *Surtees Soc.*, vol. 176 (1966), *passim*.

6. *Registrum Johannis de Halton, 1292–1334*, introd., T. F. Tout, Canterbury and York Society (1913), p. xxvi.

7. E. 143/8/4.: '...bona et catalla in predicto comitatu tunc existencia pro maxima parte eorundem depredaverunt (oblit.) et asportaverunt.' No assessment or collection of what remained could be carried out 'eo quod quedam sufferencia que inter predictos Scotos et homines predicti comitatus capta fuit, pro eo quod iidem homines finem per ipsos cum predictis Scotis factam propter eorum impotenciam solvere non potuerunt, fracta fuit ad festum Natalis Domini in predicto anno septimo, propter quod maxima pars hominum predicti comitatus propter metum dictorum Scotorum se cum bonis suis ad diversas partes Regni in fugam posuerunt'.

8. S.C. 1/35, no. 142a (29 December, 1314).

9. E. 143/8/4: 'Et similiter Andreas de Harcla tunc custos et vicecomes

dicti comitatus homines in dicto comitatu tunc remanentes propter defensionem parochie ad se traxit.'

10. Scammell, 'Robert I...', p. 394.
11. *Ibid.*
12. *Ibid.*
13. E. 101/33/25.
14. *Letters from Northern Registers*, ed. J. Raine, *R.S.* (1873), p. 274.
15. Scammell, 'Robert I...', pp. 396–7.
16. J. F. Willard, *Parliamentary Taxes on Personal Property (1290–1334)* (Cambridge, Mass., 1934), pp. 122ff.; 'The Scottish Raids and the fourteenth century taxation of northern England', *University of Colorado Studies*, v (1907–8), pp. 237–42.
17. *The Complete Peerage*, ed. G. H. White, VI, p. 299.
18. *Registrum...Halton*, p. XXVI.
19. *C.Ch.Warr.* (8 November, 1315), p. 443.
20. *C.P.R., 1317–21* (1 November, 1318), p. 228.
21. J. Mason, 'Sir Andrew Harclay, Earl of Carlisle', *Trans.Cumb.West. Arch.Soc.*, XXIX, n.s. (1929), p. 106.
22. C.81/1329 no. 43 (letter of secret seal): 'Car certeinement nous sumes desheitez q' nous ne pooms de nulles busoignes penser.'
23. *Annales* of John Trokelowe, ed. T. H. Riley, *R.S.* (1886), p. 124; B.L. Stowe Ms. 553, ff. 80–4. For details see below.
24. See above, chapter 7.
25. *Ibid.*, pp. 91ff.; J. Maddicott, *The English Peasantry and the Demands of the Crown, 1294–1341*, Past and Present Supplement, 1 (1975), p. 36.
26. Michael R. Powicke, 'The English Commons in Scotland in 1322 and the deposition of Edward II', *Speculum*, 35 (1960), p. 55. A particularly clear account of military service and its political implications is in B. C. Keeney, 'Military Service and the development of nationalism in England, 1272–1327', *Speculum*, 22 (1947), pp. 534–49.
27. Trinity College, Cambridge, Ms. R. 5. 41, f. 118.
28. Powicke, 'The English Commons in Scotland...', p. 55.
29. *Ibid.*
30. *C.Cl.R., 1318–23*, p. 561.
31. For more details see above, pp. 127–8.
32. B.L., Stowe Ms. 553, f. 25.
33. *C.P.R., 1321–4*, p. 84. He also forbade the arrest of foreign merchants except as principals in a debt.
34. Kershaw, 'The Great Famine...', and Maddicott, *The English Peasantry*.
35. Maddicott, *The English Peasantry*, p. 23.
36. B.L., Stowe Ms. 553, f. 18.
37. Bodleian Library, Ms. 956, f. 205.
38. *C.Cl.R., 1318–23*, p. 536–7. He also raised forced loans, *ibid.*, p. 435.
39. *Ibid.*, p. 439.
40. B.L., Stowe Ms. 553, f. 25.

41. See G. W. S. Barrow, *Robert Bruce and the Community of the Realm of Scotland* (1965), p. 344, for the campaign seen from the Scottish side.

42. For the details of his itinerary see B.L., Stowe Ms. 553. This is the main source for the account of the Scottish campaign that follows.

43. *Ibid.* and Natalie Fryde, 'Welsh Troops in the Scottish Campaign of 1322', *B.B.C.S.*, 26 (1974), p. 85. One of Edward's household knights, John Penreth, was actually killed in an affray.

44. B.L., Stowe Ms. 553, f. 56 v.

45. All the information on Edward's army that follows is based on B.L., Stowe Ms. 553, ff. 56–62, 80–84.

46. Harclay's hobelars consisted of one group of 354 paid 6d. a day, who were probably mounted, and of a larger group of 1081 paid only 4d. a day. (*Ibid.*, f. 82 v.).

47. *Ibid.*

48. Natalie Fryde, 'Welsh Troops in the Scottish Campaign of 1322', pp. 82–9.

49. B.L., Stowe Ms. 553, f. 83 r.

50. *Ibid.*, f. 81 r.–81 v.

51. *Ibid.*, f. 82 v.

52. Exchequer Miscellanea, E. 163/4/11, nos. 8, 77.

53. L. Namier, *Vanished Supremacies* (1958), pp. 1–2.

54. B.L., Stowe Ms. 553, f. 67 v.

55. *C.P.R., 1321–4* (20 April 1322), p. 102.

56. *Ibid.*

57. *Ibid.*, p. 26.

58. B.L., Stowe Ms. 553, f. 61.

59. Barrow, *Robert Bruce*, p. 345.

60. E. 163/4/11 nos. 10, 13; *Foedera*, II, part 1, p. 496.

61. B.L., Stowe Ms. 553 is our main source for the details of the Scottish attempt to capture Edward and of his escape.

62. *Foedera*, II, part I, p. 497.

62. Phillips, *Aymer de Valence*, p. 229.

64. B.L., Stowe Ms. 553, f. 68v.

65. *Bridlington*, p. 79.

66. *Ibid.*, p. 80.

67. Barrow, *Robert Bruce*, p. 346.

68. S.C. 1/63/176 (letter of Bishop Hotham to the king).

69. B.L., Stowe Ms. 553, f. 21v.

70. Powicke, 'The English Commons...'.

71. Most of the chronicles mention that the retreating troops were dying of famine. See especially Trinity College Library, Cambridge, R.5. 41, f. 118d; *French Chronicle of London*, ed. G. J. Hungier, *Camden Soc.*, vol. 28 (1844), p. 45.

72. See the example of Henry de Beaumont, below, chapter 11.

73. E. 163/4/11, no. 8.

74. See for example, Ralph Griffiths, 'Local Rivalries and National

Politics,…1452–55', *Speculum* 43 (1968), pp. 601–32, for a revealing picture of how things had developed in parts of the north by the middle of the fifteenth century.

75. Barrow, *Robert Bruce*, p. 355.
76. *Ibid.*, p. 356; Natalie Fryde, 'John Stratford, Bishop of Winchester and the Crown, 1323–30', *B.I.H.R.*, 44 (1971), p. 157; *Select Cases in the Court of King's Bench under Edward II*, vol. IV, *Selden Soc.*, vol. 74 (London, 1957), pp. 122ff.

CHAPTER 10 THE FRENCH WAR

1. Jean Favier, *Un Conseiller de Philippe de Bel, Enguerran de Marigny*, Mémoires et Documents publiés par la Société de l'École des Chartes, XVI (1963), p. 214.
2. *Ibid.*, pp. 220–8.
3. Joseph Petit, *Charles de Valois, 1270–1325* (1900), p. 207.
4. *The Gascon Calendar of 1322*, ed. G. P. Cuttino, *Camden Soc.*, 3rd ser., 70 (1949). It was drawn up between 6 August 1320 and 17 November 1322.
5. The most comprehensive account remains E. Déprez, *Les Préliminaires de la Guerre de Cent Ans. La Papauté, la France et l'Angleterre, 1328–1342*, bibliothèque des Écoles Françaises d'Athènes et de Rome, fasc. 46 (1902), ch. 1.
6. Sir Maurice Powicke, *The Thirteenth Century*, Oxford History of England (1953), p. 654.
7. F. Cheyette, 'The professional papers of an English ambassador on the eve of the Hundred Years' War', in *Économies et Sociétés au Moyen Age. Mélanges offerts à Edouard Perroy*, Publications de la Sorbonne (1973), pp. 400ff.
8. Margery K. James, 'The Fluctuations of the Anglo-Gascon wine trade during the fourteenth century', *Ec.H.R.*, 2nd ser., 4 (1951), p. 175.
9. Y. Renouard, 'Edouard II et Clément V d'après les Rôles Gascons', *Annales du Midi*, 67 (1955), pp. 119–43.
10. J. H. Denton, 'Pope Clement V's early career as a royal clerk', *E.H.R.*, 83 (1968), pp. 303–14.
11. Renouard, 'Edouard II et Clement V…', and my article 'Antonio Pessagno of Genoa, King's Merchant of Edward II of England' (Fryde, 'Pessagno' (1978)).
12. E. Pole-Stuart, 'The Interview between Philip V and Edward II at Amiens in 1320', *E.H.R.*, 41 (1926), p. 412.
13. *Vita*, p. 24.
14. Phillips, *Aymer de Valence*, pp. 205–6.
15. *War of Saint Sardos*, p. IX.
16. *Murimuth*, p. 40.
17. *War of Saint Sardos*, p. 4.
18. *C.P.R., 1324–27*, p. 3.

19. Petit, *Charles de Valois*, p. 211ff.

20. *Ibid.*

21. *War of Saint Sardos*, p. 50.

22. *Ibid.*, pp. 52–3.

23. Jules Viard, 'La Guerre de Flandre', *Bibliothèque de l'École des Chartes*, 83 (1922), p. 362.

24. The account that follows of the English expeditions to Gascony in 1324–5 is based chiefly on *War of Saint Sardos*, and on B.L., additional Ms. 7967 (account of Nicholas Huggate, chief royal receiver at Bordeaux).

25. B.L., additional Ms. 7967, ff. 7 v., 17 v.

26. *Ibid.*, f. 4 r.

27. *War of Saint Sardos*, p. 222.

28. B.L., additional Ms. 7967, f. 4 r.

29. See above, chapter 7.

30. *War of Saint Sardos*, p. 59.

31. *Lit.Cant.*, I, p. 127.

32. *War of Saint Sardos*, pp. 59–61.

33. Charles T. Wood, 'Regnum Francie: A Problem in Capetian administrative usage', *Traditio*, 23 (1967), pp. 121–2.

34. Fryde, 'Pessagno' (1978), p. 175.

35. *War of Saint Sardos*, p. 76. On the negotiations with the Scots see also *Vita*, pp. 132–4.

36. *Vita*, pp. 138–40.

37. *War of Saint Sardos*, p. 142.

38. F. D. Blackley, 'Isabella and the Bishop of Exeter' in *Essays in Medieval History presented to Bertie Wilkinson* (1968), p. 225; *C.P.R., 1324–7*, (30 September, 1324), p. 30.

39. *Bridlington*, p. 32.

40. *War of Saint Sardos*, p. 195. Natalie Fryde, 'John Stratford, Bishop of Winchester and the English Crown', *B.I.H.R.*, 44 (1971), p. 150.

41. *Vita*, p. 135.

42. Blackley, 'Isabella and the Bishop of Exeter', p. 223.

43. *Ibid.*, p. 221.

44. *Lit.Cant.*, I, pp. 137–8.

45. *Ibid.*, pp. 169–70.

46. She stayed with her sister-in-law at Pontoise on 20 March and met her brother briefly in Bois de Vincennes in April, E. 101/380/9.

47. C. 81/1329, no. 164 (letter of secret seal, 2nd April 1325).

48. *Foedera*, II, part I, pp. 599–601.

49. *War of Saint Sardos*, p. 241.

50. *Ibid.*, p. 243.

CHAPTER 11   THE OPPOSITION TO ROYAL TYRANNY, 1322–6

1. Bertha Haven Putnam, *The Place in History of Sir William Shareshull* (1950), p. 20.
2. K.B. 27/257, Rex, m. 20v. J. G. Bellamy, *Crime and Public Order in England in the later Middle Ages* (1973), pp. 79ff.
3. Natalie Fryde, 'A Medieval Robber Baron. Sir John Molyns of Stoke Poges', in *Medieval Legal Records edited in memory of C. A. F. Meekings* (1978), p. 199.
4. *Lit.Cant.*, I, 120.
5. K.B. 27/260, m. 20.
6. Just.Itin. 1/1389, m. 5v.
7. *C.A.P.*, p. 384.
8. Just.Itin. 1/792, m. 1, 1v.
9. *C.P.R., 1321–4* (14 March 1323), p. 309.
10. K.B. 27/264, Rex, m. 10.
11. *Rot.Parl.*, I, p. 422 (no. 22).
12. E. L. G. Stones, 'The Folvilles of Ashby Folville, Leicestershire and their associates in crime', *T.R.H.S.*, 5th ser. 7 (1957), pp. 119, 124ff.
13. *Foedera*, II, part 1, p. 547; Just.Itin. 1/560, m. 29.
14. *Letters from Northern Registers* ed. J. Raine, *R.S.* (1873), p. 324.
15. *Ann.Lond.*, p. 199; *Vita*, p. 117, n. 4.
16. *C.Cl.R., 1319–23*, p. 260.
17. *Vita*, pp. 117–18.
18. *Vita*, p. 127.
19. He had held it since 1311 (*C. Fine R., 1307–19*, p. 103); *C.P.R., 1321–4*, p. 206.
20. *Ibid.*, p. 215.
21. J. Conway-Davies, 'The first journal of Edward's II Chamber', *E.H.R.* (1915), p. 680; E. 372/171, m. 42 (enrolled chamber account).
22. *C.P.R., 1321–24* (28 November 1322), p. 221.
23. B.L., Stowe Ms. 553, f. 68. For a list of his followers see Just.Itin. 1/559.
24. S.C. 1/63/169 (15 November 1322).
25. *Ibid.*
26. B.L., Stowe Ms. 553, f. 68. The king knew of the rising on 20 January 1323. *C.P.R., 1321–4* (5 February 1323), p. 257.
27. B.L., Stowe Ms. 553, f. 27 v.
28. *Ibid.*, f. 68 v.
29. *C.Cl.R., 1318–23*, p. 692. Revocation of commission to him *C.P.R., 1321–4* (12 February 1323), p. 241.
30. *Murimuth*, p. 39.
31. *Lanercost*, p. 235, which gives the most vivid account of Harclay's career.
32. *Melsa*, II, *R.S.* (1867), p. 347.
33. I. J. Sanders, *English Baronies (1086–1327)* (1960), p. 135.
34. Lucy later obtained custody of his lands and a grant of part of them

C.P.R., 1321–4 (19 October 1323), p. 346; *C.Cl.R., 1318–23* (26 March 1322), p. 434.

35. S.C. 1.49/60 nos. 80 and 81; *C.P.R., 1321–4* (14 September 1322), p. 201; Just.Itin. 1/141.

36. Just.Itin., 1/142, m. 1.

37. J. Mason, 'Sir Andrew Harclay, Earl of Carlisle', p. 123; *Scalacronica*, p. 67.

38. B.L., Stowe Ms. 553, f. 69.

39. *Ibid.*, f. 27.

40. *Ibid.*

41. *C.Cl.R., 1323–27*, p. 2.

42. A previously unknown official record of proceedings is in Bodleian Library, Holkham Ms. lat. 29, f. 43.

43. *Foedera*, II, part 1 (10 February 1323), p. 506.

44. *War of Saint Sardos*, p. 192.

45. *Murimuth*, p. 41. The chronicler in fact led this embassy.

46. Natalie Fryde, 'John Stratford, Bishop of Winchester and the Crown 1323–30', *B.I.H.R.*, 44 (1971), pp. 153–61.

47. G. Usher, 'The Career of a Political Bishop: Adam de Orleton', *T.R.H.S.*, 5th ser., 22 (1972), p. 37.

48. E. L. G. Stones, 'The date of Roger Mortimer's escape from the Tower of London', *E.H.R.*, 66 (1951), pp. 97–8.

49. K.B. 27/254, Rex, m. 37.

50. *Leyc.Chron.*, p. 430; *C.Cl.R., 1323–27*, p. 187; K.B. 27/254, Rex, m. 37.

51. M. McKisack, 'London and the succession to the crown during the Middle Ages', in *Studies in Medieval History presented to Frederick Maurice Powicke* (1948), p. 81.

52. *C.P.R., 1321–4* (14 November 1323), p. 349.

53. *Ibid.*, p. 64.

54. *Select Cases in the Court of the King's Bench under Edward II*, vol. IV ed. G. O. Sayles, *Selden Soc.*, vol. 74 (1957), pp. 144ff.

55. K. Hughes, 'Bishops and learning in the reign of Edward II', *Church Quarterly Review*, 138 (1944), p. 70.

56. Natalie Fryde, 'John Stratford...' (1971), pp. 153–61.

57. *War of Saint Sardos* (13 January 1325), p. 195.

58. Sayles, *Select Cases*, p. 155.

59. *C.Pap.R., Letters*, II, *1305–42*, p. 461.

CHAPTER 12   LONDON

1. The best account of London in the thirteenth and earlier fourteenth centuries is in G. A. Williams, *Medieval London. From Commune to Capital* (1963). For London's hostility to Edward II in the last years of his reign see M. McKisack 'London and the succession to the crown during the Middle Ages', *Studies in Medieval History presented to Frederick Maurice Powicke* (1948), pp. 81–2.

2. Williams, *Medieval London*, pp. 109ff.
3. See Fryde, 'Pessagno' (1978), p. 162.
4. Williams, *Medieval London*, p. 272.
5. Phillips, *Aymer de Valence*, pp. 44–5.
6. E. 368/87, m. 34 v., *Attorn.*, Mich.
7. *Select Cases in the Court of the King's Bench under Edward II*,vol. IV, ed. G. O. Sayles, *Selden Soc.*, vol. 74 (1957), pp. 69ff.
8. Williams, *Medieval London*, pp. 265 and 272.
9. E. 368/87, m. 11, *Br.d.Bar.*, Mich., m. 34v.
10. Williams, *Medieval London*, p. 282.
11. *French Chron.Lond.*, p. 41.
12. *The Eyre of London, 1321*, ed. H. Cam, *Selden Soc.*, 85 (1968), *introd.*, vol. 1, p. xx. This is the main source for the account of the eyre that follows.
13. C. 81/1329, no. 26 (letter of secret seal of 14 January 1321).
14. *Ibid.*, p. 10.
15. *Ibid.*, pp. 67ff.
16. *Ibid.*, p. xxxv.
17. J. Maddicott, *Thomas of Lancaster* (1970), pp. 279–80.
18. *Ann.Lond.*, p. 298.
19. *Ibid.*, p. 299.
20. E. 159/95, m. 8, *Br.d.Bar.*, Trin. It may also have been a concession to London that part of the rather paltry proceeds of the eyre went to the London *domus conversorum* (*ibid.*, m. 61).
21. Williams, *Medieval London*, p. 289.
22. See above, chapter 9.
23. *The Eyre of London*, p. xvii.
24. *Ann.Paul.*, pp. 325–6.
25. *Ibid.*, p. 306 giving the precise date of 21 November. On 29 November Edward ordered the reinstatement of Chigwell as mayor (*C.Ch.Warr.*, p. 547).
26. *C.P.R., 1321–4* (6 January 1324), p. 358. Chief of those sheltered were John Dengayne and Thomas Roscelyn. The prior provided mounts and means for them to escape.
27. *Select Cases*, pp. 164–5.
28. E. 403/219 under 7 and 8 October 1326.
29. *C.Cl.R., 1323–7* (28 September 1326), p. 322.
30. *C.Cl.R., 1323–7* (10 March 1326), p. 550.
31. Edward left the Tower of London on 2 October (*Baker*, notes, p. 196). He was at Acton and Ruislip on 3 October, at High Wycombe (a Despenser manor) on 5 and 6 October (Privy Seals, C. 81/133, nos. 7501 and 7503; Society of Antiquaries Library, Ms. 122, a book of the controller of the king's chamber, *passim*.) For Edward's itinerary see above all E. 101/17/18.
32. E. 403/219 under 6 October 1326.

33. M. McKisack, 'London and the succession to the crown...', p. 81, refers to a London tradition preserved by Froissart that a group within London encouraged Isabella to invade England. Froissart adds that without Londoners' 'ayde et puissance', the queen's party 'ne fuissent jamais venus au dessus de leur emprise'.

CHAPTER 13   QUEEN ISABELLA'S INVASION AND THE END OF
THE REGIME

1. *C.P.R., 1324–7*, p. 228.
2. See above, chapter 11.
3. *C.P.R., 1324–7*, p. 145.
4. *Ibid.*, p. 232.
5. *Ibid.*
6. *Ibid.*
7. *Ibid.*, p. 209.
8. *Ibid.*, p. 286.
9. *C.Pap.R.*, II (*1305–42*), p. 479; *French Chron.Lond.*, p. 50; *Ann.Paul.*, p. 312; Cambridge, Trinity College Libary, Ms. *R.S.* 41, f. 120v.
10. *Ann.Paul*, p. 477.
11. Cambridge, Trinity College Library, Ms. R.5.41, m. 121.
12. S.C.1/49, no. 91.
13. At Canterbury itself, in Cambridge University Library (Ee. 5. 31) and in B.L., Cotton Ms. Galba E.IV. The Canterbury collections have been partly printed in *Lit.Cant., R.S.*
14. *C.P.R., 1324–7*, p. 238.
15. Reynolds did, however, have the idea in January 1326 that there were two fleets planning attacks against England, one of which was led by the count of Hainault and by John, King of Bohemia. He believed, however, that it was operating from Normandy (S.C. 1/49/92).
16. *Lit.Cant.* I, 141.
17. *Baker*, p. 19. Bishop Stratford of Winchester was certainly, suggesting this as early as January 1325; *War of Saint Sardos*, p. 195.
18. *Lit.Cant.* I, p. 162.
19. *Ibid.*, p. 172.
20. *Ibid.*, pp. 172–4.
21. *Ibid.*, pp. 168–70.
22. *Ibid.*, pp. 194–5.
23. *Ibid.*, pp. 195–7.
24. *Murimuth*, p. 45.
25. *Ibid.*, p. 46. There is an interesting letter from Stapeldon to the king, explaining his hasty departure, which he claimed was to save his life, and justifying his behaviour (S.C. 1/49/106, 15 January 1326).
26. *Oeuvres de Froissart*, ed. Kervyn de Lettenhove, 18 (1874): *Chroniques, Pièces justificatives* (1319–1399), pp. 9 and 10.

27. B. Jarret, *The Emperor Charles IV* (1935), p. 34.

28. *Les Journeaux du Trésor de Charles le Bel*, ed. J. Viard, (1917), p. 1507 (no. 9419).

29. J. Viard, 'Philippe de Valois avant son avenement au trône', *Bibliothèque de l'École des Chartes*, 91 (1930), p. 324.

30. P. Viollet, 'Comment les femmes ont été exclues en France de la succession á la couronne', *Mémoires de...l'Academie des Inscriptions et Belles Lettres*, 34 (1895), pp. 125–54.

31. H. S. Lucas, *The Low Countries and the Hundred Years' War, 1326–1347* (1929), pp. 53–4.

32. L. G. O. F. de Bréquigny, 'Mémoire sur les différends entre la France et l'Angleterre sous Charles-le-Bel' (1780), reprinted in C. Leber, *Collection des meilleures dissertations relatifs à l'histoire de France*, 18 (1830), pp. 437–8. An account for the seizures of English goods decreed on 16 August 1326 existed in the time of Philip VI. Cf. Ch. V. Langlois (ed.), *Inventaire des Anciens Comptes Royaux dressé par Robert Mignon sous le règne de Philippe de Valois*, (1899) p. 374. For other accounts arising out of the Anglo-French war in 1326 see *ibid.*, pp. 311, 370–71.

33. *Bronnen Tot de Geschiedenis van den Handel met Engeland, Schotland en Ierland, 1150–1485*, ed. H. J. Smit, vol. I, Rijks Geschiedkundige Publicatien 65 (1928), p. 201, no. 339; Lucas, *The Low Countries*, pp. 55–6.

34. Parliamentary and Council Proceedings, C. 49/5/17. See also *Parl.Writs*, II, part II, pp. 754–5.

35. Trinity College Library, Cambridge, Ms. R. 5.41., f. 120 v.; Society of Antiquaries Library, Ms. 122, p. 84 (Chamber account, mentioning payments around 7 September); E. 403/218, m. 18 (including £1542 5s. for wages of infantry and other military expenditure and £335 7s. 9d. for wages of sailors); accounts of the paymaster of this force, John Houton, E. 101/17, nos. 24, 25, 26, 27 (largest payments between 5 and 11 September).

36. *C.P.R., 1327–30* (10 February 1327), p. 10. The original text on the patent roll speaks of a pardon 'terram Normannorum hostiliter ingrediendo et depredaciones, incendia et alia quamplurima facinora ibidem perpetrando dum eramus in partibus illis'. Felton's special attachment to the service of the younger Despenser at this time is mentioned in Society of Antiquaries Library, Ms. 122, p. 79.

37. The best short account of Isabella's invasion and the civil war that followed is in M. McKisack, *The Fourteenth Century 1307–1399* (1959), pp. 83–8.

38. They are listed in *Bronnen Tot de Geschiedenis*, p. 201.

39. Described in Lucas, *The Low Countries*, p. 55.

40. For Wateville's association with Badlesmere see the calendar of Badlesmere records in B.L., Egerton roll 8724. His submission to the king after the civil war is in C. 47/34/9, no. 3. His lands were restored

on 31 October 1322 'at the request' of Hugh Despenser the younger (*C.Cl.R., 1318–23*, p. 602).

41. *War of Saint Sardos*, pp. 218, 222–5, 229.

42. Society of Antiquaries Library, Ms. 122, p. 63. On 16 June the younger Despenser made him a loan of 100 marks, *Ec.H.R.* (1951), p. 362).

43. Wateville's appointment to levy and command troops in six eastern counties, *C.P.R., 1324–27* (27 September 1326), p. 327. Various payments to him or on his authority are recorded on the Issue Roll, E. 403/218 (under 27 September 1326). For other payments for the fleet and army on the east coast that could never be carried out see above, chapter 7. According to the chronicler of Bury St Edmunds, Isabella reached the coast pursued by the fleet of Robert de Wateville (*Mem.St.Edmunds*, p. 328).

44. E. 372/171, m. 43 r. (enrolled Chamber account): 'Et in expensis Roberti de Watevile infirmi existentis ad custus Regis apud Cippenham per XIII dies infra dictum tempus' (the month after Michaelmas 1326), £14 17s.

45. *C.Cl.R., 1323–27*, p. 655.

46. *French Chron.Lond.*, p. 51.

47. See above, chapter 8 and the appendix 1, above.

49. Dugdale, *The Baronage of England*, ii (1675–6), p. 63.

49. *Murimuth*, p. 46. *Mem.St.Edmunds*, p. 328.

50. *Ibid.*

51. Edward, in a letter sent back to Robert Baldock in London on the night after he left the city (Acton, 3 October) instructs him to send out proclamations to counter the letters which the queen had sent to all the towns (C. 81/133/7502).

52. Reynolds reported as far back as January 1326 that Gilbert Talbot 'et touz les aultres sont revenuz en Engleterre et se assemblerount a Londres' (S.C. 1/49/91).

53. See above, chapter 7 and E. 403/219 (under 2 October).

54. *C.Fine. R., 1319–27* (23 February 1324), p. 295.

55. *Calendar of Memoranda Rolls (Exchequer,)* Michaelmas 1326 to Michaelmas 1327, ed. R. E. Latham, no. 2270 (1968), p. 373.

56. *Mem.St.Edmunds*, p. XLVI; *Ann.Paul*, p. XLVI.

57. C. 81/156, nos. 2069–70

58. *Leyc.Chron.*, p. 435.

59. *Ibid.*

60. See above, chapter 12 and Society of Antiquaries Library, Ms. 122, pp. 90ff.

61. *French Chron.Lond.*, p. 51; B.L., Harleian Ms. 6359, f. 81.

62. M. McKisack, 'London and the succession to the crown during the Middle Ages', *Studies in Medieval History presented to Frederick Maurice Powicke* (1948), p. 81.

63. E. 403/219, under 9 October.

64. E. 159/103, m. 115.

65. See above, chapter 7.
66. E. 404/484, no. 776.
67. E. 101/17/18: 'Simoni Frogemor apud Shapstowe 17 die Octobris pro se et sex hominibus suis cariantibus per aquam 10,000 li. de thesauro regis de Glovernia usque Shapstowe et expectantibus dominum Regem ibidem de precepto suo...'
68. *List Mem.R.*, p. xxii.
69. *Ibid.*, p. 81
70. *Murimuth*, p. 47.
71. Society of Antiquaries Library, Ms. 122, p. 90.
72. *Ann.Paul.*, p. 317; *Mem.St.Edmunds*, p. 328.
73. I owe this information to Mr P. C. Doherty.
74. Society of Antiquaries Library, Ms. 122, p. 90.
75. *Ibid.*
76. Pardon to Felton for his resistance at Caerphilly, *C.P.R., 1324–27*, p. 344.
77. Society of Antiquaries Library, Ms. 122, p. 90.
78. *C.P.R. 1324–27*, p. 200.
79. *Ibid.*, p. 333.
80. *Ibid.*, p. 332.
81. *Ibid.*, p. 333.
82. Trinity College, Cambridge, Ms. R.5.41, ff. 123f; *Murimuth*, p. 49.
83. *C.Cl.R. 1323–27*, p. 655.
84. See Trinity College, Cambridge, Ms. R.5.41, f. 124v for the description of Despenser's execution.
85. *Ibid.*, f. 122.
86. John Weston, the constable of the Tower, was ordered by Queen Isabella to surrender the Tower on 6 November, but only complied on 17 November when John Gisors and Richard Betoigne took over its custody (E. 101/531/17).
87. *Ann. Paul.*, p. 315.
88. There is a detailed description of Stapeldon's murder in Canterbury Cathedral Library, Corr., I–IV, no. 47.
89. *Ann.Paul*, p. 321
90. *C.P.R., 1327–30*, p. 230
91. This figure is based on inquisitions summarised in E. 142/33.
92. *Ibid*
93. E. 142/33, m. 10 and E. 142/59, no. 4 (the original inquisition, taken at Loughborough).
94. *C.P.R., 1327–30*, p. 268.
95. N. M. Trenholme, 'The English Monastic Boroughs', *University of Missouri* Studies, 2 (1927), pp. 31–45.

CHAPTER 14   EDWARD II'S DEPOSITION AND ULTIMATE FATE

1. Bertie Wilkinson, *Constitutional History of Medieval England, 1216–1399*, II; *Politics and the Constitution, 1307–1399* (1952), p. 159.

2. The two most detailed discussions of the deposition of Edward II are to be found in Bertie Wilkinson, 'The deposition of Richard II and the accession of Henry IV', *E.H.R.* 54 (1939); M. V. Clarke. *Medieval Representation and Consent*, chapter IX (1936, reprinted 1964).

3. *Ann.Paul.*, p. 324.

4. K.R.Exch.Acc.Var., E.101/18/4.

5. *Infra*, chapter 15 (Epilogue).

6. *Lanercost*, p. 254.

7. The opposition of some of the bishops to Edward's deposition in his absence is mentioned by *Historia Roffensis*. Cf. McKisack, *The Fourteenth Century, 1307–99* (1959), pp. 88–9.

8. *Rotuli Parliamentorum Anglie Hactenus Inediti MCCLXXIX–MCCCLXXIII*, ed. H. G. Richardson and G. O. Sayles, *Camden Soc.*, 3rd ser., 51 (1935), pp. 125–6 (no. 36).

9. Wilkinson, 'The deposition of Richard II...', p. 338.

10. Trinity College, Cambridge, Ms. R.5. 41, f. 125r. This source supplies various details not available elsewhere and helps to clarify the chronology of events in January 1327. For the relevant portion of the text see appendix 2.

11. B.L., Ms. Royal 12, D.XI, f. 30r. For printed texts of the Wallingford proclamation see R. Twysden. *Historiae Anglicanae Scriptores Decem* (1652), vol. 2, coll. 2764–5 and *Foedera* II, part II, p. 169.

12. Twysden, *Historiae Anglicanae Scriptores Decem*, coll. 2765–6, translated in Bertie Wilkinson, *Constitutional History of Medieval England, 1216–1399*, II; *Politics and the Constitution, 1307–1399* (1952), pp. 170–71.

13. Trinity College, Cambridge, Ms. R.5.41, f. 125r.

14. *Ann.Paul.*, p. 324.

15. *Ibid.*, pp. 232–3.

16. *Lanercost*, p. 255.

17. J. G. Edwards, 'Sir Gruffydd Llwyd', *E.H.R.*, 30 (1915), pp. 594–6.

18. *Murimuth*, p. 51, who adds the important information that Edward was threatened with the succession of someone outside the royal line if he did not abdicate.

19. French texts in Trinity College, Cambridge, Ms. R.5. 41, f. 126r. and *Ann.Paul.*, p. 324.

20. Trinity College, Cambridge, Ms. R.5.41, f. 125 v.

21. *Ibid.*, ff. 125 v.–126r.

22. Bodleian Library Ms., 956, f. 205. Wilkinson, 'The deposition of Richard II...', p. 342. Wilkinson's account of the deposition offers the best discussion of these events and nothing in the recently discovered new sources used here modifies it in any matter of substance.

23. Wilkinson, 'The deposition of Richard II...', p. 343.
24. Issue roll, E. 403/228 under 16 July 1327, mentioning a warrant of privy seal of 5 July to pay £200 to Edward's custodians at Berkeley.
25. T. F. Tout, 'The Captivity and Death of Edward of Carnarvon' in *Collected Papers*, III (1934), p. 166.
26. The plots are recounted in detail in Tout, *ibid.*, and F. J. Tanquerey, 'The Conspiracy of Thomas Dunheved, 1327' *E.H.R.*, 31 (1916), pp. 119–24. Coram Rege Roll, K.B. 27/272, m. 2 v. has a trial of some of the conspirators 'for trying to seize the king'. However, this document contributed nothing new to the mystery.
27. *Murimuth*, pp. 53–4.
28. The heart was put into a silver vase, Tout, 'The Captivity and Death of Edward...', p. 169. For the burial of Queen Isabella in her wedding dress see the inventory of her belongings in 1358 in E. 101/393/4. This detail was also noted by H. Johnstone in Tout, *Chapters*, v, p. 249.
29. The order to remove it from Berkeley to Gloucester, E. 368/100, m. 8 (*commissiones*). Expenses of embalming and transport were paid out of the customs (E. 101/383/1) as was the cost of the barricades.
30. Tout, 'The Captivity and Death of Edward...', p. 162, *Polychronicon Ranulphi Higden*, ed. J. R. Lumby, VIII, *R.S.* (1883), p. 325.
31. *Rot.Parl.*, II, 57 'nec unquam scivit de morte sua usque in presenti Parliamento isto'.
32. Stubbs, *Chron. Edward I and Edward II*, II, p. CIV (Cartul. de Mag., Reg. A., fol. 86 v.). Like Tout and Stubbs, I have not myself seen the original document. See also, M. A. Germain, *Publications de la Société Archéologique de Montpellier*, 37 (1877), pp. 118–20; *Proc. Soc. Antiquaries of Newcastle*, vol. IX (1899–1900), p. 49; *ibid.* pp. 171ff. and 173 for the quotation in the text and, most recently, a corrected version edited by G. P. Cuttino in *Speculum*, 53 (1978), pp. 537–8.
33. The letter can be dated before 1345 when Fieschi would have added the title of bishop of Vercelli; Y. Renouard, *Les Relations des Papes d'Avignon et des compagnies commerciales et bancaires de 1316 a 1378* (1941), p. 227. He was a distant cousin of Edward II (Cuttino, *Speculum*, appendix III.)
34. B. Guillaume, *La Cour Pontificale D'Avignon (1309–76) Étude d'une Société* (1962), pp. 308, 314 n. 203, 317.
35. *Infra* chapter 15.
36. Tout, 'The Captivity and Death of Edward...', p. 179.

CHAPTER 15　EPILOGUE: THE REGIME OF MORTIMER AND ISABELLA

1. *Leyc.Chron.*, p. 454.
2. E. 404/2/10.
3. *Leyc.Chron.*, p. 449. There were actually two held. Bedford was the property of the Earl Marshal. The other Round Table took place at Wigmore, Avesbury, p. 284.

4. *Murimuth*, p. 57.
5. *C.P.R., 1327–30*, pp. 299, 327, 328; C. 81/156/2039a.
6. *Melsa*, II, p. 358.
7. T. F. Tout, *Chapters in the Administrative History of Medieval England*, 6 vols. (1920–30; reprinted, revised ed., 1937), p. 232.
8. *Ibid.* and *C.P.R., 1327–30*, pp. 492, 500
9. *C.P.R.*, 1327–30, p. 97.
10. Tout, *Chapters*, III, pp. 5ff.
11. E. 101/383/1.
12. E. 101/332/21.
13. E. 101/383/8, f. 5r. (Wardrobe Book of Robert Wodehouse, *recepta forinseca*).
14. Cf. appendix 1.
15. E. 101/383/8, f. 5v.
16. E. 101/332/26.
17. Issue r., E. 403/220; E. 403/225 under 9 and 23 February 1327.
18. G. W. S. Barrow, *Robert Bruce and the Community of the Realm of Scotland* (1965), pp. 356ff. gives an account of this campaign from the Scottish point of view.
19. Letters of pardon to those still holding it, *C.P.R. 1327–30*, pp. 37–9 (20 March).
20. E. L. G. Stones, 'The Anglo-Scottish Negotiations of 1327', *S.H.R.*, 30 (1951), pp. 54–5.
21. The discussion of debts due to John of Hainault and of their repayment that follows is chiefly based on the account with him in E. 101/18/4.
22. *Leyc.Chron.*, p. 445.
23. E. 101/383/8 f. 6v.
24. *Murimuth*, p. 53.
25. They came from Darlington, *Scalacronica*, p. 81.
26. A. E. Prince, 'The importance of the campaign of 1327', *E.H.R.*, 50 (1935), p. 300.
27. *Bridlington*, p. 96; *Lanercost* p. 256.
28. *Scalacronica*, p. 80.
29. Barrow, *Robert Bruce*, p. 358.
30. Prince, 'The importance of the campaign of 1327', p. 301.
31. For the itinerary of the campaign, see C. 81/146 and 147 where dates can be established from privy seals.
32. *Scalacronica*, pp. 79–80.
33. *Ibid.*
34. Prince, 'The importance of the campaign of 1327', pp. 300ff.
35. *The Buik of the Croniclis of Scotland or a metrical version of the History of Hector Boece by William Stewart*, ed. W. B. Turnbull, vol. III (1858), p. 263.
36. *Scalacronica*, p. 80.
37. *Melsa*, II, p. 356.
38. *Ibid.* and *The Buik*, p. 264.

39. *Scalacronica*, p. 81.
40. *C.P.R., 1327–30*, p. 163.
41. *Leyc.Chron.*, p. 446.
42. *Ibid.*
43. E. 101/332, nos. 26, 28.
44. *C.P.R., 1327–30*, p. 160.
45. E. B. Fryde, 'Loans to the English Crown, 1328–31', *E.H.R.*, 70 (1955), pp. 200–201.
46. Issue Rolls (E. 403) nos. 220 (10 January 1327), 225 (10 and 12 February 1327), 232 (26 October and 19 November 1327).
47. *Ibid.* (10 January, 10 and 12 February 1327), charged to Queen Isabella.
48. There is detailed information about the plunder of the house of the Bardi causing the disappearance of their business records in E. 404/2/10 (a royal mandate of 30 May 1330). A memorandum of the assignment of £700 to the Bardi to pay for their house is on K.R.Mem.r., E. 159/104 m. 125 v. (Hilary term, 1328).
49. *C.P.R., 1327–30*, pp. 140–1 (2000 marks for the Scottish war), £1900 paid to John Hainault (allowed in the Issue r., E. 403/232 under 6 February 1328). For the evidence about the dates of these loans cf. also *Calendar of the Memoranda Rolls, (Exchequer), Michaelmas 1326 to Michaelmas 1327*, ed. R. E. Latham (1968), no. 142, p. 27; Receipt r., E. 401/270 under 29 August 1327; E. 404/507, nos. 267 and 271.
50. E. 159/104, no. 125 (*Recorda*, Hilary term, 1328).
51. E. B. Fryde, 'Loans to the English Crown...' (1955), p. 204 and n.5.
52. E. 101/383/8, f. 16r.
53. Issue r., E. 403/232 under 17 February 1328; E. 101/383/8, fos. 2r., 2v., 3v.
54. E. 101/383/8, f. 2v. and E. 404/2/9.
55. E. B. Fryde, 'Loans to the English Crown...', (1955), p. 201.
56. E. 159/104, m. 153v. (*Recorda*, Trinity term, m. iv.); 'Et memorandum quod cum compoti de exitibus custumarum in portubus predictis de tempore preterito visi fuissent per Barones et similiter assignaciones facte in portubus predictis, de quibus maxime summe adhuc restant solvende, liquet evidenter quod iidem exitus ultra assignaciones predictas per annum proximo futurum vix sufficiunt ad dictas expensas hospicii faciendas.'
57. The earliest surviving receipts of the Bardi to the tax collectors date from March 1328 (E. 404/500, nos. 307, 330; E. 404/502, no. 57).
58. E. 159/104, m. 154r., (*Recorda*, Trinity term, 1328).
59. *Ibid.*, m. 83v.
60. E. 101/332/28.
61. E. 101/18/4; E. 101/383/8, fos. 2v., 3r., 3v.
62. E. 101/18/4.
63. E. 159/104, mm. 97v. (letter of privy seal of 18 July 1328), 153v. and 154r. (replies of the barons of the exchequer to the king in June 1328).

K

64. *Ibid.*, m. 153 v. (the barons of the exchequer to the king, 27 June 1328): 'et si ne trovoms ne trover savoms veie covenable par chevisance ceste parties ne en autre manere coment avenir a la somme contenue en ceste vestre mandement ne a partie de y cele'.

65. *Ibid.*, m. 97v. (letter of privy seal of 18 July 1328): 'il est nepurquant a nous de vous exciter apenser par totes voies possibles coment meismes noz mandementz puissent...estre serviz'.

66. My calculations are based on E. 101/18/4., fos. 3v., 4r. and 16r.

67. E. 101/127/26 (account of the Bardi).

68. Isabella received 1000 m. of the Scottish money on 17 January 1330 (C. 81/168/3211).

69. Stones, 'The Anglo-Scottish Negotiations...', and 'The English Mission to Edinburgh in 1328', *S.H.R.*, 28 (1949), pp. 129–32 and 'An Addition to the "Rotuli Scotiae"', *S.H.R.*, 29 (1950), pp. 23–52 for this important treaty.

70. Stones, 'Anglo-Scottish Negotiations...', p. 53.

71. In Parl. and Council Proc., C. 49/6/13. This document is discussed more fully below. There are lists of those who were present with Lancaster at Salisbury and at Bedford in E. 101/4/27 and 28. See also G. A. Holmes, 'The Rebellion of the Earl of Lancaster, 1328–9', *B.I.H.R.*, 28 (1955), pp. 84–9.

72. *Leyc.Chron.*, p. 447. *Melsa*, p. 358.

73. *Ibid.*, pp. 449, 451.

74. C. 53/117.

75. C. 49/6/13.

76. *Leyc.Chron.*, pp. 449–51.

77. C. 49/6/13.

78. *Leyc.Chron.*, pp. 449–50.

79. *C.Inq.Misc.*, II, no. 1039 (p. 258).

80. E. 404/2/9 (mandates of privy seal of 25 November 1329 and 30 May 1330): 'vynt nadgaires a nous en les parties de Saresbur' molt efforcement ad gentz darmes et apee...en nostre chivauche lors celes parties et nous eantz regard...au grant lieu quil nous tynt en meisme nostre chivauche'.

81. K.B. 27/274–5, Rex m.1.

82. C. 53/115.

83. *Leyc.Chron.*, p. 450.

84. C. 49/6/13: 'a force et armes a graunt nombre de gentz' and encountered the king 'overtement issint armes a vewe de ceux q' adonque estoient en la compaignie nostre dit seignur le Roi'. In Holmes, 'The Rebellion of the Earl of Lancaster, 1328–9' (1955), p. 88.

85. *Ibid.* 'en destruction de lui et des soens'.

86. *Ibid.*, 'et se sont degisez et contrefaitz gentz de religion portantz habit acordant a freres de Pye...en agayt de nostre seignur le Roi et des soens, en despisant et mokant lui et sa roiale dignite'.

87. *Leyc.Chron.*, p. 451.

88. In C. 49/6/13 the oath is denounced as 'nient veritable'.
89. *Leyc.Chron.*, pp. 450.
90. *C.P.R., 1327–30*, pp. 472, 484, 547.
91. The whole of this paragraph is based on E. B. Fryde, 'Loans to the English Crown...' (1955), p. 206.
92. E. 101/384/1, f. 9 (account book of Richard Bury).
93. This and the rest of this paragraph is based on E. B. Fryde, 'Loans to the English Crown...' (1955) *passim*.
94. E. 404/2/10: Zouche had stated 'qil ne purra plus longement ministrer son dit office sil ne soit servi des deniers plus prestement quil nad este piecea'.
95. E. 101/333/3.
96. K.B. 27/274, Rex m. 10.
97. C. 53/117.
98. 81/169/3341.
99. *Murimuth*, appendix, pp. 253–4; Bodleian Library, Ms. 956, f. 208v.
100. *Ibid.*
101. K.B. 27/281, Rex, m.9 and m. 15.
102. The best discussion of Edward's personality and the causes of his success is in M. McKisack, 'Edward III and the Historians', *History*, 45 (1960), pp. 1–15. Some of the general comments that follow are based on detailed unpublished researches on Edward's reign.
103. S. Harrison Thomson, 'Walter Burley's Commentary on the Politics of Aristotle' in *Mélanges Auguste Pelzer, Études d'histoire litteraire et doctrinale de la Scolastique médiévale offertes à Monseigneur Auguste Pelzer* (1947), pp. 577–8.
104. Natalie Fryde, 'Edward III's removal of his ministers and judges, 1340–1', *B.I.H.R.*, 48 (1975), pp. 149–61.

Cited classes of records at the Public Record Office

1. CHANCERY (C.)

C. 47.   Chancery Miscellanea.
C. 49.   Chancery, Parliament and Council Proceedings.
C. 53.   Charter Rolls.
C. 61.   Gascon Rolls.
C. 71.   Scotch Rolls.
C. 81.   Chancery Warrants.
C. 145   Chancery Miscellaneous Inquisitions.

2. EXCHEQUER (E.)

E. 43.   Treasury of Receipt, Ancient Deeds.
E. 101.   K.R.Accounts Various.
E. 142.   K.R.Ancient Extents.
E. 143.   K.R.Extents and Inquisitions.
E. 159.   K.R.Memoranda Rolls.
E. 163.   Exchequer Miscellanea.
E. 175.   Exchequer, Parliamentary and Council Proceedings.
E. 358.   L.T.R.Miscellaneous Enrolled Accounts.
E. 368.   L.T.R.Memoranda Rolls.
E. 372.   Pipe Rolls.
E. 401.   Exchequer of Receipt, Receipt Rolls.
E. 403.   Exchequer of Receipt, Issue Rolls.
E. 404.   Exchequer of Receipt, Writs and Warrants for Issues.

3. JUDICIAL RECORDS

C.P. 40.   Common Pleas, Plea Rolls.
Just.Itin. I. Assize Rolls.
K.B. 27.   Coram Rege, Plea Rolls.

4. MISCELLANEOUS

D.L. 41.   Duchy of Lancaster, Miscellanea.
D.L. 42.   Duchy of Lancaster, Miscellaneous Books.

S.C. 1.   Special Collections, Ancient Correspondence.
S.C. 6.   Special Collections, Ministers' Accounts.
S.C. 8.   Special Collections, Ancient Petitions.

Sources

UNPUBLISHED RECORDS AT THE PUBLIC RECORD OFFICE

1. *Chancery*

The main series of Chancery Rolls are covered for this period by printed calendars. Were searched in additions Gascon Rolls (C. 61), Scotch Rolls (C. 71) and certain Charter Rolls (C. 53), for lists of witnesses to the royal charters at crucial periods in the reign (e.g. 1317–18).

The series of Chancery Warrants (C. 81) was searched for relevant periods as well as appropriate portions of various miscellaneous modern series created chiefly out of Chancery records: Chancery Miscellanea (C. 47), Chancery and Exchequer, Parliamentary and Council Proceedings (C. 49 and E. 175), Ancient Correspondence (S.C. 1) and Ancient Petitions (S.C. 8). The Ancient Petitions proved particularly valuable for the petitions of the Contrariants of 1321–2 and of their relatives and the petitions of the other victims of the Despensers.

2. *Exchequer*

One of the main problems to be solved was the state of Edward's revenue in the years 1321–6. One main source of evidence are the memoranda of transfers of the office of treasurer recorded on the Receipt Rolls of the Exchequer of Receipt (E. 401) and the indentures of transfer (K.R.Exchequer Accounts Various, E. 101/332, nos. 20, 21). Transfers of barrels of silver into the reserve treasury in the Tower recorded on the Issue Rolls of the Exchequer of Receipt (E. 403) provided corroboratory information. All the Receipt and Issue Rolls for the entire period 1320–30 were searched for further details of revenue and expenditure.

One test of the state of the king's finances is provided by his relations with lenders. Receipt and Issue Rolls again constituted the main source, supplemented by the Foreign Merchants' box of the Exchequer Accounts Various (E. 101/127), Writs and Warrants for Issues of the Exchequer of Receipt (E. 404) and Treasury of Receipt, Ancient Deeds (E. 43).

For reconstructing Edward's financial policies the Memoranda Rolls of the Exchequer (E. 159 and E. 368) constitute the most important source. The entire rolls for the years 1307–30 were searched. Of particular importance are royal mandates to the exchequer (in *brevia directa baronibus* section of E. 159). Other similar information was found in E. 404 (mandate files) and in some miscellaneous modern collections (*e.g.* C. 47/35/17 and C. 49/33/13).

The administration of confiscated lands gave rise to voluminous records. Apart from the Memoranda Rolls, the relevant series of Ministers' Accounts were used (S.C. 6) and the various series of Exchequer K.R.Extents (E. 142 and E. 143). The Enrolled Accounts for the estates of the Contrariants are enrolled on L.T.R.Miscellaneous Rolls, E. 358/14–16. The sources used for the study of the estates of the Despensers and of the other properties confiscated in 1326 are described more fully in appendix 1.

The details about the financing of military operations (the Civil War of 1321–2, the Scottish Campaigns, the military preparations and campaigns of 1326) are contained in household records (see below) and in the Exchequer Accounts Various (E. 101), sections on Army and Navy (especially boxes 15–17).

For various other miscellaneous financial transactions search was made through relevant accounts in E. 101, through Exchequer Pipe Rolls (E. 372) and K.R.Exchequer Miscellanea (E. 163).

3. *Household*

The main series of detailed accounts of the king's wardrobe is to be found among K.R.Exchequer Accounts Various (E. 101). In addition to these, use was made of relevant wardrobe books in the Bodleian Library (Oxford) and the British Library (London), listed in detail in the next section of this list.

One of the peculiar features of the later years of the reign of Edward II is the fortunate survival of a fairly complete series of the accounts of the King's Chamber in an enrolled account on a Pipe Roll (E. 372/171, m. 42), among the Exchequer Accounts Various (E. 101) and in the Library of the, Society of Antiquaries (London). These last are listed in detail in the next section of this list.

The secretarial archives of the household have been mostly lost. Their value is shown by a chance survival of a single file of royal letters during the Scottish campaign in the autumn of 1322 (K.R.Exchequer Miscellanea E. 163/4/11.) Other remnants of royal correspondence are to be found among Ancient Correspondence (S.C.1.), which also contains a large proportion of the correspondence of the younger Despenser in the years 1322–6.

4. *Judicial Records*

All the relevant rolls of the King's Bench (K.B. 27, Rex sections) were searched for information about state trials in the years 1322–30. Use was made for the same purpose, and for the study of proceedings against the

Contrariants, of various miscellaneous rolls among the class of Justices
Itinerant (Just.Itin. 1).

Use was also made of relevant files of Chancery Miscellaneous Inquisitions
(C. 145).

Sources for the judicial proceedings of the Despensers against their
various victims are listed in more detail in appendix 1.

UNPUBLISHED SOURCES (NOT IN THE PUBLIC RECORD OFFICE IN LONDON)

1. *Narrative Sources*

  (i) Cambridge:
    Trinity Coll. Library, Ms. R.5.41 (probably from Canterbury).
  (ii) London:
    British Library, Cotton Ms., Faustina B.V. (*Historia Roffensis*).
    Ibid., Cotton. Ms. Nero A. iv (Landaff).
    Ibid., Harleian Ms. 6359.
  (iii) Oxford:
    Bodleian Library, Douce Ms. 128 (French Brut).
    Ibid., Laud Misc. Ms. 529.
    Ibid., Bodleian Ms. 956.

2. *Royal Records*

  (i) London:
    British Library, Egerton Rolls 8723 and 8724 (Calendars of the archives of Contrariants drawn up and in after 1322).
    Ibid., Additional Ms. 17,362, Liber Cotidianus of the Wardrobe 13 Edw. II (Roger Northburgh).
    Ibid., Additional Ms. 9,951, Liber Cotidianus 14 Edw. II (Roger Northburgh).
    Ibid., Stowe Ms. 553, Liber Cotidianus 1 May 1322–19 October 1323 (Roger Waltham).
    Ibid., Additional Ms. 35114, Liber Cotidianus 20 October 1323–7 July 1324 (Robert Wodehouse).
    Ibid., Additional Ms. 7967, account book of the chief receiver for Gascon War, 1 March 1324–31 May 1326 (Nicholas Huggate). Society of Antiquaries Library, Mss. 120 and 121 (Chamber account books 10 and 11 Edward II).
    Ibid., Ms. 122, Chamber account May 1325–October 1326 (Robert Holden).
  (ii) Oxford:
    Bodleian Libr., Tanner Ms. 197, Wardrobe Book 1311–12.
    Ibid., Ms. North, 26. 4. An estimate of the royal revenue in January 1324.
    Ibid., Holkham Ms. Lat. 29, Book of records concerning the jurisdiction of the King's Bench, 1230–1326.

3. *Private Records*

   (i) Episcopal Registers:
   Walter Reynolds, Canterbury (1313–27), at Lambeth Library London.
   John Droxford, Bath and Wells (1309–29), at Somerset Record Office, Taunton.
   Henry Burghersh, Lincoln (1320–40) at Lincolnshire Record Office, Lincoln.
   Adam Orleton, Worcester (1327–30) at Worcestershire Record Office, Worcester.
   William Melton, York (1317–40) at Borthwick Institute Library, York.
   The formulary connected with John Stratford, archbishop of Canterbury and his brother Ralph, bishop of Chichester, at the British Library, London, Ms. Royal 12 D. XI.
   The correspondence of Henry Eastry, prior of Christ Church, Canterbury 1285–1331: Cambridge, University Library, Ms. Ee. 5.31; Canterbury Cathedral Library, Corr. I–IV; London, British Library, Cotton Ms. Galba E. IV.
   (ii) Mortimer Cartularies:
   London, British Library, Harleian Ms. 1240.
      Ibid., Additional Ms. 6041.

Select bibliography

PRINTED SOURCES

Chronicles

Annales Londonienses and *Annales Paulini* in *Chronicles of the Reigns of Edward I and Edward II*, ed. W. Stubbs, vol. I, *R.S.* (1882).

Brut, ed. F. W. Brie, vol. I, *E.E.T.S.*, orig. ser., 131 (1906).

The Buik of the Croniclis of Scotland or a metrical version of the History of Hector Boece by William Stewart, ed. W. B. Turnbull, vol. III (1858).

Chronica Adae Murimuth, et Roberti de Avesbury ed. E. M. Thompson, *R.S.* (1889).

Chronica Monasterii de Melsa, vol. II, ed. E. A. Bond, *R.S.* (1867).

Chronica Monasterii S. Albani, vol. III, *Johannis de Trokelowe et Henrici de Blaneforde Chronica et Annales*, ed. H. T. Riley, *R.S.* (1865).

Chronicon de Lanercost, ed. J. Stevenson, *Bannatyne Club*, vol. 65 (Edinburgh, 1839).

Chronicon Galfridi le Baker of Swynebroke (1303–56), ed. E. M. Thompson (Oxford, 1889).

Chroniques de Sempringham. Le Livere de Reis de Britannie, ed. J. Glover, *R.S.* (1865).

Eulogium Historiarum, ed. F. Scott Haydon, III, *R.S.* (1863).

Flores Historiarum, vol. III, ed. H. R. Luard, *R.S.* (1890).

French Chronicle of London, ed. G. J. Aungier, *Camden Soc.*, vol. 28 (1844).

Gesta Edwardi de Carnarvon Auctore Canonico Bridlingtoniensi in *Chronicles of the Reigns of Edward I and Edward II*, vol. II, ed. W. Stubbs, *R.S.* (1883).

Henrici Knighton, Leycestrensis Chronicon, ed. J. R. Lumby, vol. I, *R.S.* (1889).

Memorials of St. Edmunds Abbey, ed. T. Arnold, vol. II, *R.S.* (1892).

Oeuvres de Froissart, ed. Kervyn de Lettenhove, vol. 18. *Chroniques, Pièces Justificatives (1319–99)*, (Bruxelles, 1874).

Polychronicon Ranulphi Higden, ed. J. R. Lumby, vol. VIII, *R.S.* (1883).

Scalacronica of Thomas Gray of Heton, ed. J. Stevenson, Maitland Club, vol. 40 (Edinburgh, 1836).

Vita Edwardi Secundi, ed. N. Denholm-Young (London, 1957).

Records and Works of Reference

Ancient Petitions relating to Northumberland, ed. C. M. Fraser, *Surtees Soc.*, vol. 176 (London, 1966).

Anglo-Scottish Relations 1174–1328, ed. E. L. G. Stones (London, 1965).

The Antient Kalendars and Inventories of the Treasury of His Majesty's Exchequer, ed. Sir F. Palgrave, vols. I and III (London, 1836).

Book of Prests of the King's Wardrobe for 1294–5 presented to John Goronwy Edwards, ed. E. B. Fryde (Oxford, 1962).

Bronnen Tot de Geschiedenis van den Handel met Engeland, Schotland en Ierland, 1150–1485, vol. I, Rijks Geschiedkundige Publicatien 65 (The Hague, 1928).

Calendar of Ancient Correspondence Concerning Wales, ed. J. G. Edwards (Cardiff, 1935).

Calendar of Ancient Petitions concerning Wales, ed. W. Rees (Cardiff, 1976).

Calendar of Entries in Papal Registers concerning Great Britain and Ireland, Letters, II, *1305–42* (1895).

Calendar of the Memoranda Rolls (Exchequer), Michaelmas 1326 to Michaelmas 1327, ed. R. E. Latham (1968).

Calendars of Ancient Deeds, 6 vols. (1890–1915).

Calendars of Close Rolls, Chancery Warrants, Charter Rolls, Fine Rolls, Inquisitions Post Mortem, Inquisitions Miscellaneous, Patent Rolls for the reigns of Edward II and Edward III.

Calendars of Letter Books of the City of London for the reign of Edward II, ed. R. R. Sharpe (1900–3).

Cartae et alia Munimenta quae ad dominium de Glamorgan pertinent, 2nd ed., ed. G. T. Clark, vols. III and IV (Cardiff, 1910).

The Complete Peerage, ed. G. H. White, 2nd ed., 12 vols. (London, 1910–59).

English Royal Documents, King John–Henry VI, 1199–1461, ed. P. Chaplais (Oxford, 1971).

The Eyre of London, 1321, ed. H. Cam, vol. I, *Selden Soc.*, 85 (1968).

Foedera, ed. T. Rymer, Record Comm. ed., vols. I and II (1816–18).

The Gascon Calendar of 1322, ed. G. P. Cuttino, *Camden Soc.*, 3rd ser., 70 (1949).

Handbook of British Chronology, ed. Sir Maurice Powicke and E. B. Fryde, 2nd ed. (London, 1961).

Household Book of Queen Isabella of England, ed. F. D. Blackley and G. Hermanson, University of Alberta Classical and Historical Studies 1 (Edmonton, 1971).

Inventaire des Anciens Comptes Royaux dressé par Robert Mignon sous le règne de Philippe de Valois, ed. Ch. V. Langlois (Paris, 1899).

Les Journaux du Trésor de Charles IV le Bel, ed. J. Viard (Documents Inédits, Paris, 1917).

Letters from Northern Registers, ed. J. Raine, *R.S.* (1873).

List of Welsh Entries in the Memoranda Rolls, ed. Natalie Fryde (Cardiff, 1974).

Literae Cantuarienses, ed. J. B. Sheppard, vol. III, *R.S.* (1898).

Munimenta Gildhallae Londoniensis, II *Liber Custumarum,* ed. H. R. Riley, *R.S.* (1860).
Parliamentary Writs and Writs of Military Service, two vols. in four, ed. F. Palgrave (London, 1827–34).
Red Book of the Exchequer, ed. H. Hall, vol. III (1897).
Register of Walter Stapeldon, bishop of Exeter (1307–26), ed. F. C. Hingeston Randolph (1892).
Registrum Ade de Orleton, Bishop of Hereford (1317–27), ed. A. J. Bannister, *Canterbury and York Soc.* (1908).
Registrum Hamonis Episcopi Roffensis (1319–52), ed. Ch. Johnson, vol. II, *Canterbury and York Society* (1948).
Rotuli Parliamentorum, vols. I–II (London, 1783).
Rotuli Parliamentorum Anglie Hactenus Inediti MCCLXXIX–MCCCLXXIII ed. H. G. Richardson and G. O. Sayles, *Camden Soc.,* 3rd ser., vol. 51, (1935).
Select Cases in the Court of the King's Bench under Edward II, vol. IV, ed. G. O. Sayles, *Selden Soc.,* vol. 74 (1957).
Sir Christopher Hatton's Book of Seals, ed. L. C. Loyd and D. M. Stenton (Oxford, 1950).
Statutes of the Realms, Record Comm. ed., vol. I (1810).
The War of Saint Sardos (1323–1325), ed. P. Chaplais, *Camden Soc.,* 3rd ser., 87 (1954).

SECONDARY WORKS

Bain, J. *The Edwards in Scotland A.D. 1296–1377* (Edinburgh, 1901).
Balfour-Melville, E. W. M. 'Two John Crabbs', *S.H.R.,* 39 (1960).
Barrow, G. W. S. *Robert Bruce and the Community of the Realm of Scotland* (London, 1965).
Bean, J. M. W. 'The Percies and their Estates in Scotland', *Archaeologia Aeliana,* 4th ser., 35 (1957).
The Decline of English Feudalism, 1215–1540 (Manchester, 1968).
Bellamy, J. G. 'The Coterel Gang: an anatomy of a band of fourteenth century criminals', *E.H.R.,* 79 (1964).
Crime and Public Order in England in the later Middle Ages (Oxford, 1973).
Bernard, J. 'Le népotisme de Clément V, et ses complaisances pour la Gascogne', *Annales du Midi,* 61 (1949).
Blackley, F. D. 'Isabella and the Bishop of Exeter', *Essays in Medieval History presented to Bertie Wilkinson* (Toronto, 1969).
de Bréquigny, L. G. O. F. 'Mémoire sur les différends entre la France et l'Angleterre sous Charles-le-Bel', C. Leber, Collection des meilleures dissertations relatifs à l'histoire de France, 18 (Paris, 1830).
Broome, D. M. 'Auditors of the foreign accounts of the exchequer', *E.H.R.,* 38 (1923).
'Exchequer migrations to York in the thirteenth and fourteenth centuries', *Essays in Medieval History presented to Thomas Frederick Tout* (Manchester, 1925).

Brown, E. A. R. 'Gascon subsidies and the finances of the English Dominions, 1315–24', *Nebraska Studies in Medieval and Renaissance History*, 8 (1971).

Butler, L. H. 'Archbishop Melton, his neighbours and kinsmen 1317–40', *Journal of Ecclesiastical History*, 2 (1951).

Butler, R. 'The last of the Brimpsfield Giffards and the rising of 1321–22', *Transactions of the Bristol and Gloucestershire Archaeological Society*, 76 (1957).

Cazelles, R. *La Société Politique et la Crise de la Royauté sous Philippe de Valois* (Paris, 1958).

Cheyette, P. 'The professional papers of an English ambassador on the eve of the Hundred Years' War', *Économies et Sociétés au Moyen Age. Mélanges offerts à Edouard Perroy*, Publication de la Sorbonne (Paris, 1973).

Clarke, M. V. *Medieval Representation and Consent* (London, 1936).

Fourteenth Century Studies, ed. L. S. Sutherland and M. McKisack (Oxford, 1937).

Colvin, H. M., Brown, R. A. and Taylor, A. J. *A History of the King's Works*, 1 (London, 1963).

Conway-Davies, J. 'The Despenser War in Glamorgan', *T.R.H.S.*, 3rd ser., 9 (London, 1915).

'The first Journal of Edward II's Chamber', *E.H.R.*, 30 (1915).

The Baronial Opposition to Edward II, its character and policy: A Study in Administrative History (Cambridge, 1918).

Craig, Sir John, *The Mint. A History of the London Mint from A.D. 287 to 1948* (Cambridge, 1953).

Crump, C. G. and Johnson, C. 'Tables of bullion coined under Edward I, II and III', *Numismatic Chronicle*, 4th ser., 13 (1913).

Cuttino, G. P. *English Diplomatic Administration, 1259–1339* (Oxford, 1940).

Davies, R. R. 'The Bohun and Lancaster Lordships in Wales in the 14th and 15th Centuries' (Oxford Univ., Ph.D. thesis, 1965).

Review of J. R. Maddicott, *Thomas of Lancaster* (1970) in *Welsh Hist.Rev.*, 6 (1972).

Denholm-Young, N. 'The authorship of the *Vita Edwardi Secundi*', *E.H.R.*, 71 (1956).

History and Heraldry, 1254–1310 (Oxford, 1965).

The Country Gentry in the Fourteenth Century (Oxford, 1969).

Denton, J. H. 'Pope Clement V's early career as a royal clerk', *E.H.R.*, 83 (1968).

Déprez, E. *Les Préliminaires de la Guerre de Cent Ans. La Papauté, la France et l'Angleterre, 1328–1342* (Paris, 1902).

Dugdale, W. *The Baronage of England*, 2 vols. (London, 1675–6).

Duncan, A. A. M. *The Nation of the Scots and the Declaration of Arbroath (1320)* The Historical Association (1970).

Edwards, J. G. 'Sir Gruffydd Llwyd', *E.H.R.*, 30 (1915).
'The personnel of the Commons in Parliament under Edward I and Edward II', *Essays in Medieval History presented to Thomas Frederick Tout* (Manchester, 1925).
Edwards, K. 'The political importance of the English bishops during the reign of Edward II', *E.H.R.*, 59 (1944).
'Bishops and learning in the reign of Edward II', *Church Quarterly Rev.*, 138 (1944).
Evans, B. P. *The Family of Mortimer*, University of Wales, Ph.D. thesis (1934), deposited at the National Library of Wales, Aberystwyth.
Evans, Joan. *English Art, 1307–1461* (Oxford, 1949).

Fairbank, F. R. 'The last earl of Warenne and Surrey', *Yorkshire Archaeological Journal*, 19 (Leeds, 1907).
Favier, Jean. *Un Conseiller de Philippe le Bel, Enguerrand de Marigny*, Mémoires et Documents publiés par la société de l'École des Chartes, xvi (Paris, 1963).
Fowler, K. *The King's Lieutenant. Henry of Grosmont, First Duke of Lancaster, 1310–61* (London, 1969).
Fryde, E. B. 'The deposits of Hugh Despenser the Younger with Italian Bankers', *Ec.H.R.*, 2nd ser., (1951).
'Loans to the English Crown, 1328–31', *E.H.R.*, 70 (1955).
Fryde, E. B. and Miller, Edward, eds. *Historical Studies of the English Parliament*, vol. 1. *Origins to 1399* (Cambridge, 1970).
Fryde, Natalie. 'John Stratford, Bishop of Winchester and the Crown, 1323–30', *B.I.H.R.*, 44 (1971).
'Welsh troops in the Scottish campaign of 1322', *B.B.C.S.*, 26 (1974).
'Edward III's removal of his ministers and judges, 1340–1', *B.I.H.R.*, 48 (1974).
'Antonio Pessagno of Genoa, king's merchant of Edward II of England', *Studi in Memoria di Federigo Melis*, II (1978).
Fuller, E. A. 'The Tallage of 6 Edward II and the Bristol Riots', *Transactions of the Bristol and Gloucester Archaeological Society*, 19 (1894–5).

Galbraith, V. H. 'The Tower as an Exchequer Record Office in the Reign of Edward II', *Essays in Medieval History presented to Thomas Frederick Tout* (Manchester, 1925).
Roger Wendover and Matthew Paris. David Murray Lecture, II, University of Glasgow (1944).
Studies in the Public Records (London, 1948).
'The Modus Tenendi Parliamentum', *Journal of the Warburg and Courtauld Institutes*, 16 (1953).
Grassi, J. L. 'The Clerical Dynasties from Howdenshire, Nottinghamshire and Lindsey in the Royal Administration, 1280–1340' (Ph.D. thesis, Oxford).
'William Airmyn and the bishopric of Norwich', *E.H.R.*, 70 (1955).

Griffiths, Ralph. *The Principality of Wales in the Later Middle Ages, South Wales, 1277–1536* (Cardiff, 1972).

Guérard, L. 'La succession de Clément V et le procès de Bertrand de Got, Vicomte de Lomagne (1318–21)', *Revue de Gascogne*, 32 (1891).

Harding, Alan. 'The origin and early history of the Keeper of the Peace', *T.R.H.S.* 5th ser., 10 (1960).

Harriss, G. L. *King, Parliament and Public Finance in Medieval England to 1369* (Oxford, 1975).

Haskins, G. L. 'A Chronicle of the Civil Wars of Edward II', *Speculum*, 14 (1939).

'The Doncaster Petition of 1321', *E.H.R.*, 53 (1938).

Henneman, J. B. *Royal Taxation in Fourteenth and Fifteenth Century France. The Development of War Financing, 1322–56* (Princeton, 1971).

Highfield, J. R. L. 'The English hierarchy in the reign of Edward III', *T.R.H.S.*, 5th ser., 6 (1956).

Hill, Rosalind, *The Labourer in the Vineyard. The Visitations of Archbishop Melton in the Archdeaconry of Richmond*, University of York, Borthwick Institute of Historical Research, Borthwick Papers, no. 35 (1968).

Holmes, G. A. 'Judgement on the Younger Despenser, 1326', *E.H.R.*, 70 (1955).

'The rebellion of the Earl of Lancaster, 1328–9', *B.I.H.R.*, 28 (1955).

'A Protest against the Despensers, 1326', *Speculum*, 30 (1955).

The Estates of the Higher Nobility in Fourteenth Century England (Cambridge, 1957).

Hughes, D. *A Study of Social and Constitutional Tendencies in the Early Years of Edward III* (London, 1915).

James, Margery K. 'The fluctuations of the Anglo-Gascon wine trade during the fourteenth century', *Ec.H.R.*, 2nd ser., 4 (1951).

Jarret, B. *The Emperor Charles IV* (London, 1935).

Johnson, J. H. 'The system of account in the wardrobe of Edward II', *T.R.H.S.*, 4th ser., 12 (1929).

Johnstone, Hilda. 'The eccentricities of Edward II', *E.H.R.*, 48 (1933).

'Isabella, the She-Wolf of France', *History*, 21 (1936–7).

Edward of Carnarvon, 1284–1307 (Manchester, 1946).

Kaeuper, Richard W. 'The Frescobaldi of Florence and the English Crown', *Nebraska Studies in Medieval and Renaissance History*, 10 (1973).

Kantorowicz, E. H. 'Inalienability; a note on canonical practice and the English Coronation Oath in the thirteenth century', *Speculum*, 29 (1954).

Keen, M. 'Treason trials under the Law of Arms', *T.R.H.S.*, 5th ser., 12 (1962).

Keeney, B. C. 'Military service and the development of nationalism in England, 1272–1327', *Speculum*, 22 (1947).

Kershaw, Ian. 'The Great Famine and Agrarian Crisis in England, 1315–22', *Past and Present*, no. 59 (1973).

Langlois, Ch. V. *St. Louis, Philippe le Bel et lest derniers Capétiens directs (1226–1328)*. E. Lavisse, *Histoire de France*, t. 3, pt. 2 (Paris, 1911).

Lapsley, G. *Crown, Community and Parliament*, ed. H. Cam and G. Barraclough (Oxford, 1951).

Lehugeur, P. *Histoire de Philippe de Long* (Paris, 1897).

Lewis, N. B. 'An early fourteenth century contract for military service', *B.I.H.R.*, 20 (1943–5).

'The Organisation of indentured retinues in fourteenth century England', *T.R.H.S.*, 4th ser., 27 (1945).

Little, A. G. 'The authorship of the Lanercost chronicle', *E.H.R.*, 31–2 (1916–17).

Lodge, E. C. *Gascony under English Rule* (London, 1926).

Lucas, H. S. *The Low Countries and the Hundred Years' War, 1326–1347* (Ann Arbor, 1929).

'The Great European Famine of 1315, 1316 and 1317', *Speculum*, 5 (1930).

Lunt, W. E. *Financial Relations of the Papacy with England to 1327* (Cambridge, Mass., 1939).

McFarlane, K. B. 'Had Edward I a "Policy" towards the Earls?', *History*, 50 (1965).

McKisack, M. 'London and the succession to the crown during the Middle Ages', *Studies in Medieval History presented to Frederick Maurice Powicke* (Oxford, 1948).

The Fourteenth Century, 1307–99 (Oxford, 1959).

'Edward III and the historians', *History*, 45 (1960).

Medieval History in the Tudor Age (Oxford, 1971).

Maddicott, J. *Thomas of Lancaster* (Oxford, 1970).

'Thomas of Lancaster and Sir Robert Holland: a study in noble patronage', *E.H.R.*, 86 (1971).

The English Peasantry and the Demands of the Crown, 1294–1341, Past and Present Supplement, 1 (Oxford, 1975).

Mason, J. 'Sir Andrew Harclay, Earl of Carlisle', *Trans.Cumb.West.Arch. Soc.*, new ser., 29 (1929).

Miller, E. 'War in the North', *St. John's College, Cambridge Lecture* (Hull, 1960).

'War, taxation and the English economy in the late thirteenth and early fourteenth centuries', *War and Economic Development. Essays in Memory of David Joslin* (Cambridge, 1975).

Morris, J. E. 'Cumberland and Westmorland levies at the time of Edward I and Edward II', *Transactions of the Cumberland and Westmorland Archaeological and Antiquarian Society*, new ser., 3 (1903).

Morris, William A. 'The date of the Modus Tenendi Parliamentum', *E.H.R.*, 69 (1934).

Nicholson, Ranald. 'The last campaign of Robert Bruce', *E.H.R.*, 77 (1962).

Edward III and the Scots (Oxford, 1965).

Offler, H. S. 'Empire and Papacy: the last struggle', *T.R.H.S.*, 5th ser., 6 (1956).

Petit, Joseph. *Charles de Valois, 1270–1325* (Paris, 1900).

Phillips, J. R. S. *Aymer de Valence, Earl of Pembroke* (Oxford, 1972).

'The "Middle Party" and the negotiating of the Treaty of Leake, August 1318: A Reinterpretation', *B.I.H.R.*, 46 (1973).

Plucknett, T. F. T. 'The Origins of Impeachment', *T.R.H.S.*, 4th ser., 24 (1942).

Pole-Stewart, E. 'The Interview between Philip V and Edward II at Amiens in 1320', *E.H.R.*, 41 (1926).

Post, Gaines. 'The Two Laws and the Statute of York', *Speculum*, 29 (1954).

Powicke, Michael R. 'The English Commons in Scotland in 1322 and the deposition of Edward II', *Speculum*, 35 (1960).

Military Obligation in Medieval England (Oxford, 1962).

Powicke, Sir Maurice. *The Thirteenth Century Oxford History of England* (Oxford, 1953).

Prestwich, Michael. 'Edward I's monetary policies and their consequences', *Ec.H.R.*, 2nd ser., 22 (1969).

War, Politics and Finance under Edward I (London, 1972).

Prince, A. E. 'The importance of the campaign of 1327', *E.H.R.*, 50 (1935).

Pronay, Nicholas and Taylor, John. 'The Use of the "Modus Tenendi Parliamentum" in the Middle Ages', *B.I.H.R.*, 47 (1974).

Pugh, T. B., ed. *Glamorgan County History*, III, *The Middle Ages* (Cardiff, 1971).

Putnam, Bertha Haven. 'The Transformation of the Keepers of the Peace into the Justices of the Peace, 1327–1380', *T.R.H.S.*, 4th ser., 12 (1929).

Ramsay, Sir J. H. *The Genesis of Lancaster*, vol. 1, *(1307–68)* (Oxford, 1913).

Renouard, Y. 'Édouard II et Clément V d'après les Rôles Gascons', *Annales du Midi*, 67 (1955).

'Les papes et le conflit franco-anglais en Aquitaine de 1259 à 1337', *Études d'Histoire Médiévale* (Paris, 1968).

Richardson, H. G. 'The English Coronation Oath', *T.R.H.S.*, 4th ser., 23 (1941).

'The English Coronation Oath', *Speculum*, 24 (1949).

Richardson, H. G. and Sayles, G. O. 'The early records of the English parliaments', *B.I.H.R.*, 5–6 (1927–9).

'The King's ministers in parliament, 1272–1377', *E.H.R.*, 46–7 (1931–2).

Reid, W. Stanford. 'Seapower in the Anglo-Scottish War, 1296–1328', *The Mariner's Mirror*, 46 (1960).

Roskell, J. S. 'A consideration of certain aspects and problems of the English Modus Tenendi Parliamentum', *Bulletin of the John Rylands Library*, 50 (1968).

Ross, C. D. 'Forfeiture for treason in the reign of Richard II' *E.H.R.*, 71 (1956).

Sanders, I. J. *English Baronies (1087–1327)* (Oxford, 1960).

Sayles, G. O. 'The formal judgements on the traitors of 1322', *Speculum*, 16 (1941).

Scammell, Jean. 'Robert I and the North of England', *E.H.R.*, vol. 73 (1958).

Smith, J. B. 'Edward II and the allegiance of Wales', *Welsh Hist.Rev.*, 8 (1976–7).

Smith, W. J. 'The "Revolt" of William de Somertone', *E.H.R.*, 69 (1954).

Smyth, Sir J. of Nibley. *The Lives of the Berkeleys*, ed. J. Maclean, 3 vols. *Bristol and Gloucestershire Archaeological Society* (Gloucester, 1883–5).

Stevenson, W. H. 'A Letter of the Younger Despenser on the eve of the Barons' Rebellion', *E.H.R.*, 12 (1897).

Stones, E. L. G. 'An addition to the "Rotuli Scotiae"', *S.H.R.*, 29 (1950).

'The Anglo-Scottish Negotiations of 1327', *ibid.*, 30 (1951).

'The date of Roger Mortimer's escape from the Tower of London', *E.H.R.*, 65 (1951).

'Sir Geoffrey le Scrope, Chief Justice of the King's Bench', *E.H.R.*, 69 (1954).

'The Folvilles of Ashby-Folville, Leicestershire and their associates in crime', *T.R.H.S.*, 5th ser., 7 (1957).

Strayer, J. R. 'Statute of York and Community of the Realm', *A.H.R.*, 47 (1941).

Medieval Statecraft and the Perspectives of History (Princeton, 1971).

Stubbs, W. *The Constitutional History of England*, 3 vols. (1875).

Tanquerey, F. J. 'The Conspiracy of Thomas Dunheved, 1327', *E.H.R.*, 31 (1916).

Taylor, John. 'The French "Brut" and the Reign of Edward II', *E.H.R.*, 72 (1957).

The Universal Chronicle of Ranulf Higden (Oxford, 1966).

'The manuscripts of "Modus Tenendi Parliamentum"', *E.H.R.*, 83 (1968).

Tout, T. F. *The Political History of England, 1216–1377* (London, 1905).

Chapters in the Administrative History of Medieval England, 6 vols. (1920–30; reprinted, revised ed., 1937).

'The captivity and death of Edward of Carnarvon' and 'The beginnings of a modern capital: London and Westminster in the fourteenth century' in *Collected Papers*, III (Manchester, 1934).

The Place of Edward II in English History, 2nd ed. (Manchester, 1936).

Tupling, G. H. *South Lancashire in the Reign of Edward II*, Chetham Soc., 3rd ser., vol. 1 (1949).

Turner, T. H. 'The Will of Humphrey de Bohun, Earl of Hereford and Essex', *Archaeological Journal*, 2 (London, 1845).

Usher, G. A. 'The Career of a Political Bishop: Adam de Orleton', *T.R.H.S.*, 5th ser., 22 (1972).

Viard, J. 'La Guerre de Flandre', *Bibliothèque de l'École des Chartes*, 83 (1922).
'Philippe de Valois, avant son avenement au trône', *ibid.*, 91 (1930).

Waugh, S. L. 'The confiscated lands of the Contrariants in Gloucestershire
and Herefordshire in 1322: an economic and social study' (University
of London, Ph.D. thesis, 1975).
Wilkinson, Bertie. 'The Coronation Oath of Edward II' in *Essays in Honour
of James Tait* (Manchester, 1933).
*Studies in the Constitutional History of the Thirteenth and Fourteenth Century
England* (Manchester, 1937).
'The desposition of Richard II and the accession of Henry IV', *E.H.R.*
54 (1939).
'The Coronation Oath of Edward II and the Statute of York', *Speculum*,
19 (1944).
'The Sherburn Indenture and the attack on the Despensers, 1321',
E.H.R., 63 (1948).
Constitutional History of Medieval England, 1216–1399, II: *Politics and the
Constitution, 1307–1399* (London, 1952) and III, *The Development of the
Constitution, 1216–1399* (London, 1958).
'Notes on the Coronation records of the fourteenth century', *E.H.R.*, 70
(1955).
Willard, J. F. 'The Scottish raids and the fourteenth century taxation of
northern England *University of Colorado Studies*, 5 (1907–8).
'The taxes upon movables of the reign of Edward I', *E.H.R.*, 28 (1913).
'The taxes upon movables of the reign of Edward II', *E.H.R.*, 29 (1914).
'The Memoranda rolls and the remembrancers, 1282–1350', *Essays in
Medieval History presented to Thomas Frederick Tout* (Manchester, 1925).
Parliamentary Taxes on Personal Property, 1290–1334 (Cambridge, Mass.,
1934).
Willard, J. F., Morris, W. A. *et al. The English government at Work, 1327–36*,
3 vols. (Cambridge, Mass., 1940–50).
Williams, G. A. *Medieval London. From Commune to Capital* (London, 1963).
Wood, Charles T. 'Regnum Francie: a problem in Capetian administrative
usage', *Traditio*, 23 (1967).

Index

Abel, John, 30
Abergavenny (Welsh March), 115,
  202, 230, 232
accroachment of royal power,
  accusation of, 47, 117, 190
Acton (Middlesex), 188, 263, 266
Adam, son of King Edward II, 131
administrative reforms, 7, 8, 89,
  98–100, 252
Agenais (France), 55, 136, 137, 141,
  148
Alcrum Moor (Roxburgh), 129
Aldham, Francis, 61
Alnwick (Northumberland), 213
Angus, Robert de Umfraville, earl of
  (d. 1325), 60
Annales Londonienses, 237
Annales Paulini, 101, 237
Anne, William, 76, 209
Aquinas, Thomas, 162
Aristotle, 226
arraying of shire levies, 124–5, 184, 211
Artois, Robert of, 136
Arundel, Thomas Fitzalan, earl of
  (d. 1326), 18, 48, 52, 53, 58, 60,
  77, 109, 183, 194, 208, 209, 210
Ash, Gilbert, 75
Ashburn, Henry, 63, 160
Ashburn (Derbyshire), 85
Ashburnham, Bartholomew, 61
Aston, Robert, 81
Atholl, David, earl of (d. 1335), 59, 60
Audley, Hugh, the Elder (justice of
  North Wales), 41, 55, 63
Audley, Hugh, the Younger (earl of
  Gloucester 1337), 26, 34, 41, 43,
  44, 48, 55, 62, 220, 229, 248
Avenel, Gervase, 34
Avignon (France), 96, 108, 204, 223
Aylmer, William, 224

Badlesmere, Bartholomew, 20, 32, 36,
  46, 50–51, 52, 61, 79, 92, 108,
  185, 186, 229, 265
Badlesmere, Giles, 160
Badlesmere, Guncelin, 50
Baker, Geoffrey, chronicler, 29, 140
Baldock, Richard, 209
Baldock, Robert (chancellor 1323–6),
  52, 59, 114, 140, 160, 191, 192,
  193, 204, 266
Ballardi (of Lucca), bankers, 91
Balliol, Edward, 132
Balliol, John, King of Scotland,
  133
Banaster, Adam, revolt of, 24
bankers, Florentine, 250; Italian, 6,
  53, 87, *see also* Bardi; Ballardi;
  Frescobaldi; Peruzzi; Pessagno,
  Antonio; Pole, William de la;
  Scala; Spini
Bannockburn, battle of (1314), 23, 31,
  32, 38, 87, 119, 122, 124, 132,
  241
Bardi (of Florence), bankers, 53, 56,
  91, 92, 93, 95, 96, 104, 108, 174,
  193, 194, 214, 215, 216, 223,
  232, 244, 251, 271
Baret, Stephen, 61, 117; widow of
  (Lady Baret), 117
Barewe (Suffolk), 229
Barking Abbey (Essex), 110
Basset, Alina, 31
Basset family, properties of, 232
Basset, Philip, 28
Basset, Ralph, seneschal of Gascony,
  48, 141–2, 183, 250
Bath and Wells, John Droxford, bishop
  of, 160
Bavaria, Lewis of, 182
Bayonne (Gascony), 136, 143, 250
Beauchamp, Giles, 55